JERRY HERRING'S

GUIDE TO
UNDERSTANDING AND ENJOYING
HOUSTON

EDITED AND DESIGNED BY
JERRY HERRING

A BRIEF HISTORY BY
GEORGE FUERMANN

RESTAURANT REVIEWS BY
TERESA BYRNE-DODGE

THE ARTS BY
JIM SANDERS

CONTRIBUTIONS BY
FRED COLLINS, JAN GRAFTON,
ROBERT MACIAS, WALKER STEWART

ART AND MAPS BY
TOM McNEFF, WILLIAM SOO,
STEVE FREEMAN AND
ELLEN McCORMICK MARTENS

PUBLISHED BY
HERRING PRESS
HOUSTON, TEXAS
1992

Guide to Understanding and Enjoying Houston

Design, edited and major photography by Jerry Herring

Text by Jerry Herring, George Fuermann, Teresa Byrne-Dodge, Jim Sanders, Walker Stewart, Jan Grafton, Fred Collins, Robert Macias, Ellen McCormick Martens and Rita Burton

NOTE: *Most, but not all, restaurant reviews are by Teresa Byrne-Dodge.*

Maps by Tom McNeff, Ellen McCormick Martens, William Soo

Illustrations by Tom McNeff and William Soo

Research by Steve Freeman, Ellen McCormick Martens, Rita Burton and Debbie Moss

Cover illustration by Tom McNeff

Additional photography by:
Paul Hester, page 40
F. Carter Smith, page 110
Steve Brady, pages 148,160

Additional photography courtesy of:
Houston Metropolitan Research Center, Houston Public Library, pages 10,14; The Lancaster, page 45; The Menil Collection (Hickey & Robertson), 57; Museum of Fine Arts, Houston, pages 67,143; Museum of Natural Science, page 73; Tony's (Janice Rubin), page 156; Brennan's, page 184; San Jacinto Museum of History, page 206; Dancie Perugini Ware Public Relations, page 238; Leo Touchet, page 249.

Maps by Herring Press redrawn from existing maps courtesy of:
Pierson Graphics, pages 22-23; University of St. Thomas, page 58; Rice University (by Maurice Lewis), pages 88-89; University of Houston, pages 192-193; Texas Southern University, page 194; Houston Baptist University, page 229.

Printed in Canada

ISBN 0-917001-09-5

Published and distributed by

Herring Press
1216 Hawthorne
Houston, Texas 77006
(713) 526-6084

For multiple, non-bookstore orders, contact the publisher direct.

Special Thanks

Sandy, Stephen and Matthew Herring; Lynn, Kelly and Colleen McNeff; Sandy Wilson and Kelsey Freeman; Sue Soo; and David Moss.

Acknowledgments

Mark C. Wells, Bill Noblitt, RICE UNIVERSITY; C. Vivien Arnold, HOUSTON BALLET; Kimberly Goldberg, THE HOUSTON SYMPHONY; Tammie Kahn, Shirley Hines, Karen Galetka, Greg Most, Ken Soh, MUSEUM OF FINE ARTS; Mary Marshall Rives, Ruthie Rodriguez, ALLEY THEATER; Dolores Johnson, Rodi Franco, Greg Holland, HOUSTON GRAND OPERA; Judy Rainey, Larry Spasik, SAN JACINTO MUSEUM OF HISTORY; Ross Underhill, HOBBY AIRPORT; Dan Olive, SKYTRACKERS; Fran Berg, THE PAVILLION; Sharon Saunders, HOUSTON BAPTIST UNIVERSITY; Chuck Smith, Alvia Wardlaw, Dr. Ronald Hull, Joshua Hill, TEXAS SOUTHERN UNIVERSITY; Stacy Akerholm, Ed Sanfield, UNIVERSITY OF ST. THOMAS; Michelle Williams, Tom Brents, CHILDREN'S MUSEUM; Gwen Griffin, Robert Lueck, SPACE CENTER HOUSTON; Randy Drake, DRAKE PRINTING; Chris Cornell, WETMORE PRINTING; Jim Walker, EMMOTT WALKER PRINTING; Charlie Brookshire, Teresa Williams, HOOVER AND FURR; Kim Nugent, Henry Pyle, Susan Elmore, THE LANCASTER; Allison Eckman, BAYOU BEND; Judith Livingston, HOUSTON ACADEMY OF MEDICINE; Barbara Wolfe, JOHN BURGEE ARCHITECTS; Larry Plotsky, THE PLOTSKY GROUP; Connie Lewis, CUSHMAN WAKEFIELD; Jim Frantz, TEXAS PARKS AND WILDLIFE; Kathleen Williamson, JoAnn Boot, HOUSTON HEIGHTS ASSOCIATION; William Kirkendall, JESSE JONES LIBRARY; Bill Handle, RICHARD FITZGERALD AND PARTNERS; Richard Chambers, MORRIS ARCHITECTS; Susan King, Ethan Cartwright, Logan Goodson, HOUSTON SPORTS ASSOCIATION; Jim Gatton, Lee Fontaineau, CRSS; Gary Keller, HOUSTON ASTRODOME; John Kaiser, MENIL COLLECTION; Terrell Falk, MUSEUM OF NATURAL SCIENCE; Bill Ghant, STATE HIGHWAY DEPARTMENT; Paula Ramsey, HOUSTON BUSINESS JOURNAL; Lauren Pollard, THE SUMMIT; Nellene Harvey, MERCER ARBORETUM AND BOTANIC GARDENS; Mary Schiflett, TEXAS MEDICAL CENTER; Diane E. McLaurin, BATTLESHIP TEXAS HISTORIC SITE; Debra Ford, ASTROWORLD; Randi Barrett, LYONDELL PETROCHEMICAL COMPANY; Becky Barefoot, Eric W. Miller, UNIVERSITY OF HOUSTON; Christopher Fisher, Jack Mayer, Glen Rawlinson, Stan Watson, Joe Chow, CITY OF HOUSTON; Paul G. Gibbs, PIERSON GRAPHICS CORP; Courtnay Tartt, BRENNANS; Rick Dewees, HOUSTON PARKS AND RECREATION DEPARTMENT; Kim Kirkpatrick, HINES INTERESTS; John Heck, JOHN HECK DESIGN; Laura Lee, Dancie Ware, DANCIE PERUGINI WARE PUBLIC RELATIONS; Jolynn Rogers; Linda Herring, SWIFT ENERGY; Nancy Hadley, HOUSTON MEROPOLITAN RESEARCH CENTER, HOUSTON PUBLIC LIBRARY; Stephen Stuyck, UNIVERSITY OF TEXAS M.D. ANDERSON CANCER CENTER; Dan Bowen, UNIVERSITY OF HOUSTON CLEAR LAKE; Tim Salaika, SALAIKA AVIATION.

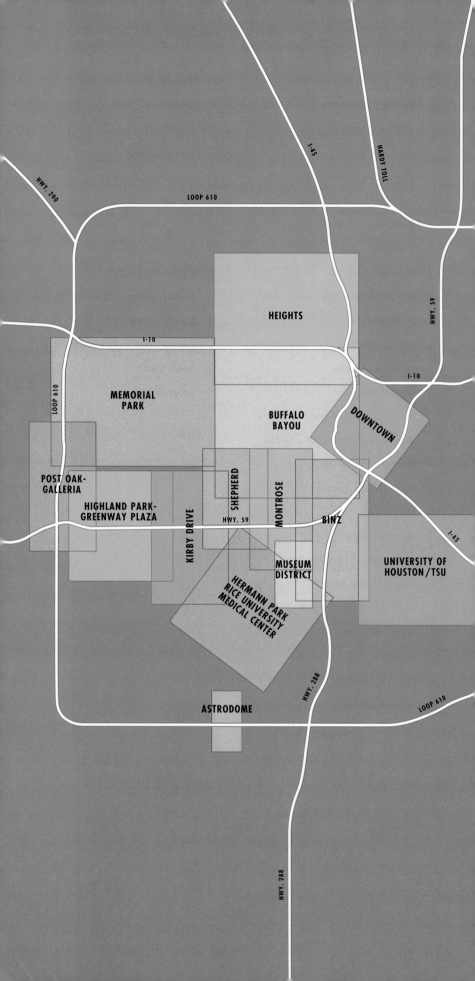

The *Guide* is divided by neighborhoods, the locations of which are indicated on the opposite and following two pages. Each neighborhood section has a general area map highlighted with numbered red dots to indicate points of interest (restaurants are indicated by numbered blue dots). The text for each section is numbered correspondingly. Areas with multiple points of interest are indicated by a large numbered red dot, with a corresponding detail map (with text that is letter coded to match the small detail map).

General Area Map

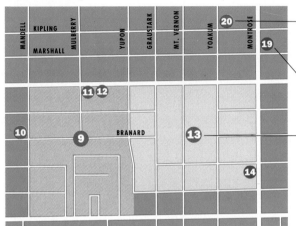

Red dots:
Points of interest, numbered to match text.

Blue dots:
Restaurants, numbered to match text.

Large red dots:
Areas with multiple points of interest that have a corrsponding, more detailed map provided.

Detail Map

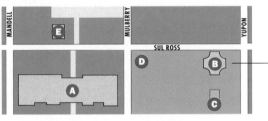

(On Detail Map)
Red or blue dots:
Points of interest, with letters to match corresponding text.

Text Page

Montrose   **1** — **Page number.**

Refer to map on page 54

— **Neighborhood or topic.**
— **Page with corresponding map.**

9   The Menil Area
John and Dominique de Menil have been, in the classic sense, civic patrons. So many major works in Houston—from the Philip Johnson structures at the University of St. Thomas to the Rothko Chapel to the impressive Menil Collection—are products of the de Menils' collective vision.

— **Points of interest, numbered to match corresponding map.**

A   Menil Collection
1515 Sul Ross (525-9400) (Renzo Piano, 1987) A simple cypress exterior belies the cultural riches within. This state-of-the-art structure by Renzo Piano holds the remarkable private acquisitions of John and Dominique de Menil. The eclectic, some might say eccentric, collection ranges from Byzantine and tribal art to the twentieth-century schools of Cubism, Minimalism and Pop. Few museums can hold a track light to the Menil's Surrealist works, i.e., Ernst and Magritte. Houston philanthropy at its finest. Wed-Sun, 11am-7pm. Free admission.

— **Points of interest, with letter to match corresponding detail map.**
— **Architect and year built, if important.**
— **Address and phone number.**
— **Hours and cost of admission.**

14   The Black Labrador
4100 Montrose (529-1199) The cozy English-pub setting in what was at one time a church is perfect for enjoying a pint of ale, a game of darts, perhaps a bite to eat. The kitchen is not strictly English (burgers and Tex-Mex dishes turn up among the shepherd's pie and bangers and mash), but it's probably much better than its equivalent in Merry Old England. Mon-Thu 11am-11:30pm (kitchen closes at 11pm), Fri-Sat 11am-12:30am, Brunch Sun noon-3pm, Sun noon-10:30pm, (kitchen closes 10pm). Reservations. Credit Cards, Inexpensive.

— **For restaurants: reservations, credit card acceptance and relative cost of average meal.**

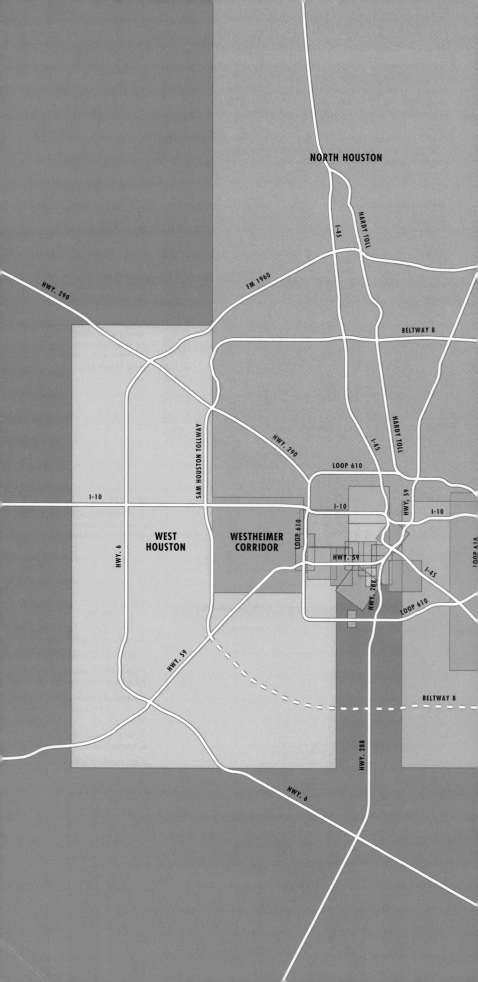

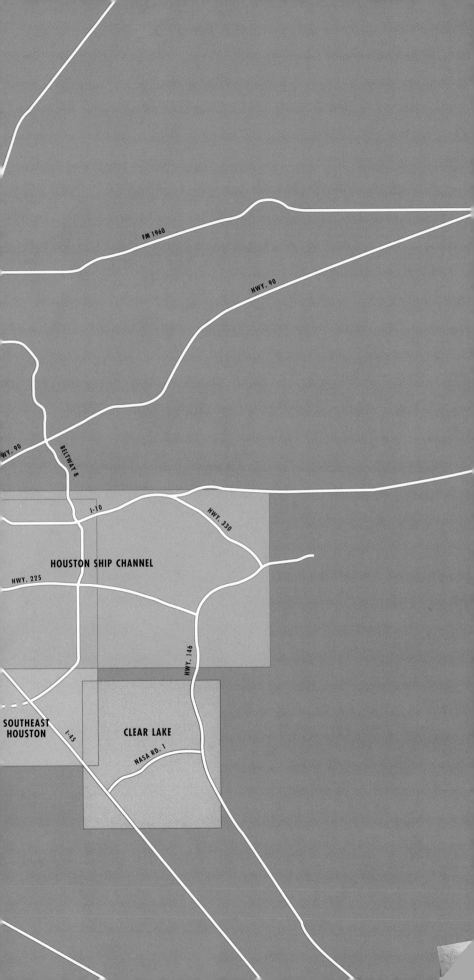

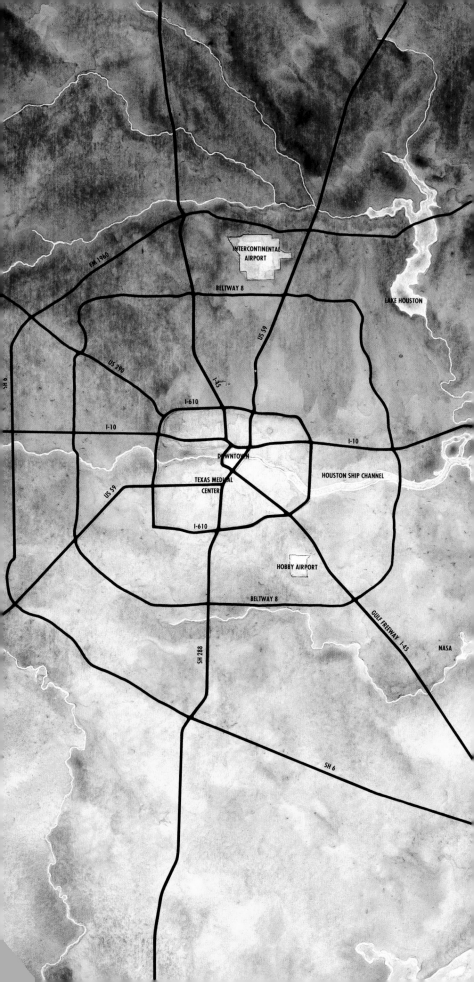

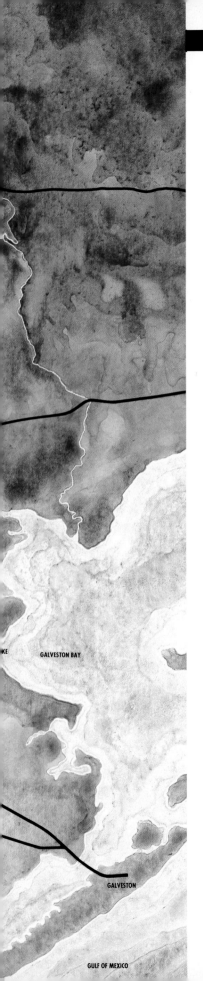

GALVESTON BAY

GALVESTON

GULF OF MEXICO

Founded
Founded in 1836 by land speculators Augustus and John Allen. The brothers placed an advertisement in newspapers around the country soliciting settlers and investors for their new town.

Namesake
General Sam Houston, leader of the Texas Army that defeated General Santa Anna and the Mexican forces at San Jacinto, securing independence for Texas.

Population
1,630,533 people live in Houston, give or take a few, based on the 1990 census. The Houston metropolitan area has 2.5 million residents.

Geography
Houston covers 450 square miles of flat land 50 miles inland from the Gulf of Mexico, approximately 100 feet above sea level.

Weather

Average Temperatures

	High	Low
Summer	93°	72°
Fall	82°	59°
Winter	65°	43°
Spring	72°	51°

Houston is reportedly the most air-conditioned place on the earth. The climate is classified as marine or semi-tropical. There are about 80-85 days during the summer when the temperature tops 90°, but the humidity can be near the same level. The trade-off is that Houston has relatively mild winters. Houston has some precipitation during approximately 100 days a year.

Ethnic mix
More than 90 languages are spoken in Houston.

Ethnic Mix

Houston Ship Channel
The 52-mile, man-made waterway connects Houston to the Gulf of Mexico, allowing Houston to be an inland city and a seaport at the same time.

Port of Houston
The Port of Houston ranks third amoung U.S. ports in total tonnage handled.

Major Industries
Where cotton was once king, now Houston relies on the energy and petrochemical, medicine and space industries.

The Arts
Houston is one of only four cities in the country that maintains permanent ballet, opera, symphony and repertory theater companies. The Museum of Fine Arts, Contemporary Arts Museum, Menil Collection and Bayou Bend Collection are Houston's major art museums.

Colleges and Universities
Approximately 135,000 students are enrolled in seven two-year and 11 four-year institutions.

Professional Sports
Houston fields professional teams in baseball (Astros), football (Oilers) and basketball (Rockets).

Freeway Miles inside the City
675 miles

Main Street, in 1934,
with Jesse H. Jones'
Gulf Building towering
in the background.

A BRIEF HISTORY

They say it got its name from Scotland. We know it was named for Samuel Houston, that vain and touchy God's assistant, that Indian-flavored, whisky-seasoned saga seeker, that friend of Andrew Jackson who was U.S. congressman and governor of Tennessee before he became the first president of the Republic of Texas.

Centuries before Samuel, one Sir Hugh of Padivan, a Norman knight, helped William the Conquerer rape England. His reward was a strip of land lying along the Scottish border. The Scots, perhaps unable to pronounce "Padivan," called him Sir Hugh and his castle Hugh's town, or Hughstown. The descendants of this progenitor of the Texas hero came to call themselves Houston.

The brothers Augustus C. and John K. Allen, the founders of Houston, were New Yorkers who moved to Texas in 1832, settling in Nacogdoches, speculators dealing in Mexican land titles. Augustus talked of building a city on Galveston Island, but the land title was not cleared, and the brothers looked inland to Harrisburg.

The area now covered by Houston was first settled by Anglo-Americans in 1822, four years before a townsite was surveyed for John Richardson Harris, who named the place Harrisburg. An upstate New Yorker who was a member of Stephen F. Austin's first Texas colony, Harris was granted a league of land (4428 acres) at the junction of Buffalo and Brays Bayous.

Harrisburg (annexed by Houston in 1926) might
have succeeded, for its townsite was superior to that
which would become Houston's, but for two events
other than Harris' death in 1829. On April 16, 1836,
Antonio Lopez de Santa Anna, the Mexican dictator, in
pursuit of Sam Houston and the Texan Army, rode into
the almost deserted village and destroyed it by fire.
The second event was the decision of those other New
Yorkers, the Allens, to start a town at the most interior
point of year-round navigation in Texas.

The Texans lost every battle of the war with
Mexico except the last one, when they overwhelmed
Santa Anna and his larger force. The battle was over in
18 minutes. Before sundown, 600 Mexicans lay dead
and more than 200 others were wounded; by the next
day, the Texans had secured more than 700 prisoners,
including Santa Anna. On the Texas side, nine were
killed or mortally wounded and 30 were less seriously
wounded. Among the latter was Gen. Houston, who
had been shot in the ankle.

The Allens, foreseeing that Buffalo Bayou would be
important as an exit route for cotton and other crops
grown along the Brazos River, tried to buy Harrisburg.
But its title was involved in fraudulent claims made
against the Harris estate, and in August 1836, they
bought a site a few miles farther up the bayou.

The Allens were neither heroes of the Texas revolution—they did not fight in the Battle of San Jacinto or
in any other—nor were they otherwise distinguished.
Today we would call them real estate promoters.
Augustus had just turned 30 and John was 26 when
they bought the land for Houston. On August 24 and 26,
1836, they bought the bulk of the John Austin Survey.
The original townsite—6642 acres south of Buffalo
Bayou—cost the Allens $9,428, about $1.42 an acre.

They hired Gail and Thomas Borden, publishers of
the *Telegraph and Texas Register* and also surveyors, to
stake out the town. But the Bordens were busy in
Columbia, where their newspaper was then published,
and most of the surveying was done by Moses Lapham,
a young Ohioan who worked for the Bordens.

He began staking out the town in October 1836.
When he finished seven weeks later, the Bordens
announced in the *Telegraph,* "We have at length, and
almost without the use of mechanical instruments,
completed a plan for the City of Houston..." Two years
later, while surveying near San Antonio for Samuel
Maverick, Lapham was scalped by Indians. Like one
of Houston's founders, the man who laid out the city
is buried elsewhere, in San Antonio.

On August 30, four days after the Allens acquired
the land, they advertised their nonexistent town, saying
it would become "beyond all doubt, the great interior
commercial emporium of Texas." In October John Allen
proposed that the congress, then meeting at Columbia,
move the government to Houston; if so, the Allens
would build a capitol for it. The congress approved
(in an action later denounced as one of the three most
corrupt acts of the first congress), and the Allens began
to build in fact what had succeeded in fancy.

They sold the first lots in January 1837; the government moved to Houston in May, before the capitol had a roof; and the city was incorporated in June. The historian Andrew Forest Muir has shown that January 19, 1837, when the Allens sold the first lots (with the exception of one lot sold January 1) marks Houston's beginning. Most of the first lots sold for $500, a big price for a small piece of forlorn, unimproved prairie in 1837. Sam Houston first saw his namesake three months later, when he estimated the population at 1500, almost certainly an inflated figure for the infant hamlet.

The city was lucky. The first movers and shakers saw at once that the key to success was access to the sea. Improvement of the bayou was begun in 1839 with funds raised by public subscription and lotteries. The Port of Houston was established by city ordinance in 1841. Widening and deepening of the channel began in 1869 and continued for more than a century. ("Probably the greatest, most farseeing project ever consummated in Texas," the *Dallas Morning News* said of the ship channel in an editorial in 1955.)

Though their town would become one of the leading cities of North America, though it would one day be abashed by a legend of riches—the Promised Land, the New Golconda—neither founder profited from the venture. John died in Houston two years after buying the land. Augustus lived until 1864, but he left Houston in 1850 after signing over to his wife, Charlotte, most of his remaining interest.

Only Charlotte, whose inheritance had bankrolled the city's birth, was to profit from the Texas city conceived by New Yorkers. Living to a great age, she still owned Houston land when she died at her home, now the site of the Gulf Building, in 1895.

Houston was the capital of the republic until September 1839 and briefly again in 1842. Muddy and beset by yellow fever epidemics, the common curse of the age, the town grew slowly until after the Civil War. When the war began, Houstonians voted overwhelmingly for Texas to secede from the United States. Gov. Sam Houston tried unsuccessfully to prevent the state's secession, and upon his refusal to swear allegiance to the Confederacy in March 1861, he was deposed; he died two years later.

The city, a lair for Union blockade runners, was briefly threatened late in 1862 when Union forces captured Galveston Island. On January 1, 1863, using two small vessels fortified with bales of cotton, a sea attack was mounted from Houston down Buffalo Bayou to help recapture the island in a fierce battle with Union forces. In 1863 Houston became the headquarters for the Confederacy's Trans-Mississippi Department (Texas, New Mexico and Arizona). With the fall of the Confederacy, Houston was occupied by Union troops on June 20, 1865; Reconstruction ended in January 1874.

Two critical periods in Houston's growth were the half-decade from 1857 to 1861, when it became the rail center of Texas, and the decade beginning with the

The busy Buffalo Bayou wharfs at Allen's Landing, photographed from the Main Street Viaduct around 1890.

Spindletop gusher in 1901. Two others are the decade after the deepwater Houston Ship Channel was opened in 1914, a period further stimulated by World War I, and the inception of the federal space laboratory, now the Johnson Spacecraft Center, in 1961.

Houston's quick growth between 1940 and 1960, when its population rose from twenty-seventh to sixth place among U.S. cities, was owed to the linking of three things: the ship channel; immense resources of oil, natural gas, sulphur, lime, salt and water; and the fact that the product of one chemical plant is often the raw material of another. This combination created on the banks of the ship channel one of the world's greatest concentrations of petrochemical industries.

Like all cities, Houston has always been full of itself. Alexander Sweet and J. Armoy Knox, in their book *On A Mexican Mustang Through Texas* (1883), struck just the right note: "After you have listened to the talk of one of these pioneer [Houston] veterans for some time, you begin to feel that the creation of the world, the arrangement of the solar system, and all subsequent events, including the discovery of America, were provisions of an all-wise Providence, arranged with a direct view to the advancement of the commercial interests of Houston."

Houston has never been so much a maker as a beneficiary of history, and disaster has often served it well. Each of four wars, from the Battle of San Jacinto to World War II, and the great Galveston flood of 1900, in which 6000 perished, had important roles in the city's success.

Beginning life 3000 years after Athens and 2000 after London, beginning two centuries after Boston and New York, 50 years after Los Angeles and at nearly the same time as Chicago, Houston suddenly joined the family of metropolises midway in the twentieth century. The great cities of Europe (and those of the eastern U.S. seaboard) grew gradually over centuries, but Houston and other American Sunbelt cities moved from wilderness to what may fairly be called bewilderness in little more than a century.

The Houston metropolitan area is considerably larger than the state of Rhode Island, and the same area is larger in population than each of 15 states.

Indeed, the four states of Vermont, Delaware, Wyoming and Nevada have a combined population smaller than Houston's (though *they* are represented by eight U.S. senators). That statistical hocus-pocus is offered to suggest the dimension of the municipal heebie-jeebies occasioned by sudden urban growth.

Houston lies astride the thirtieth Parallel—as does Cairo. Houston is farther south than Algiers, than Baghdad. In fact, Houston lies partly in the same latitude as the Sahara Desert. Those notes answer any questions a visitor might have about climate. Our weather, now, is something else—the sort of weather Noel Coward described in *Mad Dogs and Englishmen*, a forget-it kind of weather, Maalox weather. Eccentrics love it.

Some will tell you we are not a Christian city, but don't believe it. The evangelist Billy Graham, with a preacher's license to scare hell out of the flock, exhorted a crowd of 40,000 in Rice Stadium in 1952, describing Houston as "a more wicked city than Hollywood." He had said earlier "that less [sic] people probably go to church in Houston than in any other city in Texas." He had come to change all that, though Houston then had more than 1200 churches.

The Rev. Mr. Graham was by no means the first to decry our wicked ways. In January 1838, the diarist John Hunter Herndon called Houston "the greatest sink of disipation [sic] and vice that modern times have known."

Francis C. Sheridan, a young Irishman in the British diplomatic service, foretold the Rev. Mr. Graham's doom-saying in earnest. "The most uncivilized place in Texas," he wrote, "is I believe Houston the former Capital — I heard and read of more outrage and blackguardism in that town... than throughout the whole of Texas." Yet Houston's in the Bible Belt — and don't forget it.

The city has astonished, not to say bemused, writers through all its history. "Air conditioned Tower of Babel, anchored on gold, gall and guts," the author James Street wrote of Houston in the Land-of-the-Big-Rich era following World War II. Houston, the reporter for the *London Daily Mail* wrote in 1955, "has caused me to lift my ban on the word fabulous." A year later the *London Times* speculated that America might "eventually be based on a quadrilateral of great cities—New York, Chicago, Los Angeles and Houston."

The *Times* had it right, exactly so, for more than three decades later those four were indeed the four largest, most influential American cities. The first three were already perceived as the First Three in 1956.

Houston had to move up—a *long* way up from its place in 1956—to become the fourth in the prophesied quadrilateral. So, some call it the Horatio Alger of U.S. Cities, fair enough as to luck and pluck yet missing the point. For Houston is the Johnny-on-the-Spot of urban America. Above all else, it is the clone of its namesake, the indomitable, resourceful, yea-saying general, statesman and nation-maker, Sam Houston.

View of the Downtown Business District from the 60th floor observation deck of the Texas Commerce Tower.

DOWNTOWN BUSINESS DISTRICT

The Houston skyline is known the world over for its signature architecture, the showplace of major international architects during the boom years of the '70s and early '80s. The central business district hums throughout the day in the millions of square feet of office space and in the miles of underground tunnels that connect these spaces. At night, the city is turned over to the performing arts complex made up of an opera house, symphony hall and theater. And on the weekends, people come down to visit the historic homes in Sam Houston Park or attend one of the many celebrations that are scheduled here during the year. With the addition of the George R. Brown Convention Center in 1989, the city now attracts major conventions and exhibitions downtown, such as the meeting of world leaders at The 1990 Economic Summit, the international attraction that is FotoFest and the 1992 Republican National Convention.

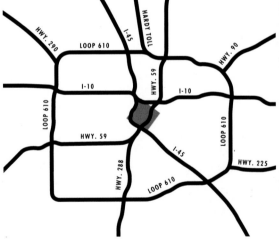

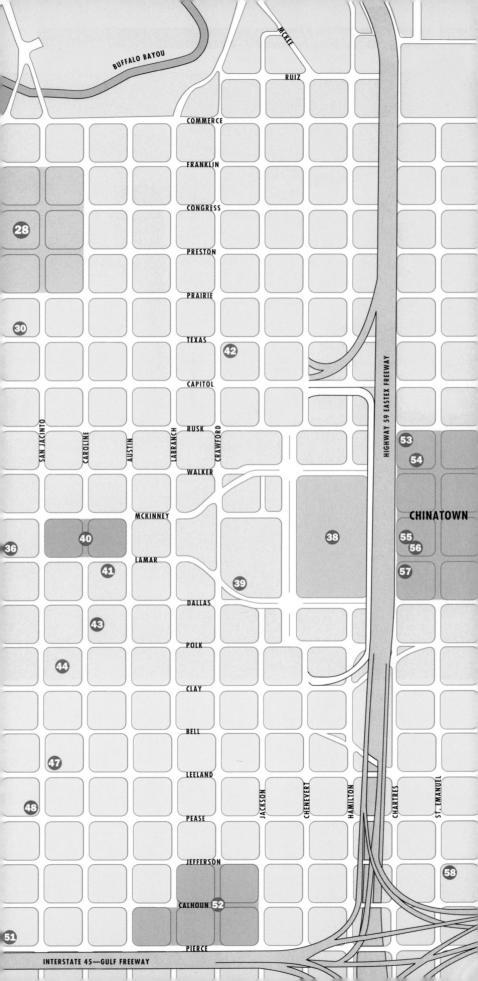

BUFFALO BAYOU

McKEE

RUIZ

COMMERCE

FRANKLIN

CONGRESS

28

PRESTON

PRAIRIE

30

TEXAS

42

CAPITOL

SAN JACINTO
CAROLINE
AUSTIN
LABRANCH
CRAWFORD

RUSK

WALKER

53

54

MCKINNEY

CHINATOWN

36

40

55

56

LAMAR

41

57

39

DALLAS

43

POLK

44

CLAY

BELL

47

LEELAND

JACKSON
CHENEVERT
HAMILTON
CHARTRES
ST. EMANUEL

48

PEASE

JEFFERSON

58

CALHOUN **52**

51

PIERCE

38

HIGHWAY 59 EASTEX FREEWAY

INTERSTATE 45—GULF FREEWAY

Downtown Skyline

During Houston's latest boom years—from the mid seventies into the early eighties—the city became an architectural laboratory where some of the greatest architects of our time tried out new ideas in a wide open setting. Philip Johnson, I.M. Pei, Skidmore, Owings & Merrill and Cesar Pelli built here. By the time the frenzied building began to subside, the Houston skyline (shown above from the west) had become recognizable around the world, symbolizing the "new" city. The beginning of this movement may have been One Shell Plaza, a 50-story tower that was built as a home for the energy giant in 1971 by developer Gerald Hines. It strengthened Houston's status as the U.S. energy capital and catapulted Hines into the upper echelon of real estate developers. The tallest building in Houston, for that matter in Texas, was also developed by Gerald Hines. In 1981 Hines commissioned I.M. Pei to design the 75-story Texas Commerce Tower, a 1002-foot granite and glass skyscraper that sits on the north edge of downtown.

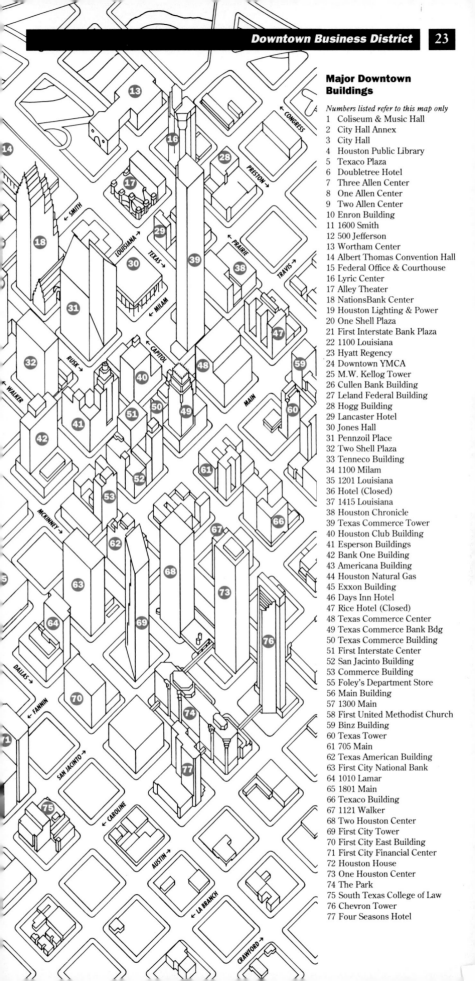

Major Downtown Buildings

Numbers listed refer to this map only

1 Coliseum & Music Hall
2 City Hall Annex
3 City Hall
4 Houston Public Library
5 Texaco Plaza
6 Doubletree Hotel
7 Three Allen Center
8 One Allen Center
9 Two Allen Center
10 Enron Building
11 1600 Smith
12 500 Jefferson
13 Wortham Center
14 Albert Thomas Convention Hall
15 Federal Office & Courthouse
16 Lyric Center
17 Alley Theater
18 NationsBank Center
19 Houston Lighting & Power
20 One Shell Plaza
21 First Interstate Bank Plaza
22 1100 Louisiana
23 Hyatt Regency
24 Downtown YMCA
25 M.W. Kellog Tower
26 Cullen Bank Building
27 Leland Federal Building
28 Hogg Building
29 Lancaster Hotel
30 Jones Hall
31 Pennzoil Place
32 Two Shell Plaza
33 Tenneco Building
34 1100 Milam
35 1201 Louisiana
36 Hotel (Closed)
37 1415 Louisiana
38 Houston Chronicle
39 Texas Commerce Tower
40 Houston Club Building
41 Esperson Buildings
42 Bank One Building
43 Americana Building
44 Houston Natural Gas
45 Exxon Building
46 Days Inn Hotel
47 Rice Hotel (Closed)
48 Texas Commerce Center
49 Texas Commerce Bank Bdg
50 Texas Commerce Building
51 First Interstate Center
52 San Jacinto Building
53 Commerce Building
55 Foley's Department Store
56 Main Building
57 1300 Main
58 First United Methodist Church
59 Binz Building
60 Texas Tower
61 705 Main
62 Texas American Building
63 First City National Bank
64 1010 Lamar
65 1801 Main
66 Texaco Building
67 1121 Walker
68 Two Houston Center
69 First City Tower
70 First City East Building
71 First City Financial Center
72 Houston House
73 One Houston Center
74 The Park
75 South Texas College of Law
76 Chevron Tower
77 Four Seasons Hotel

Refer to map on page 18-19

**Central Library
Floor Plan**

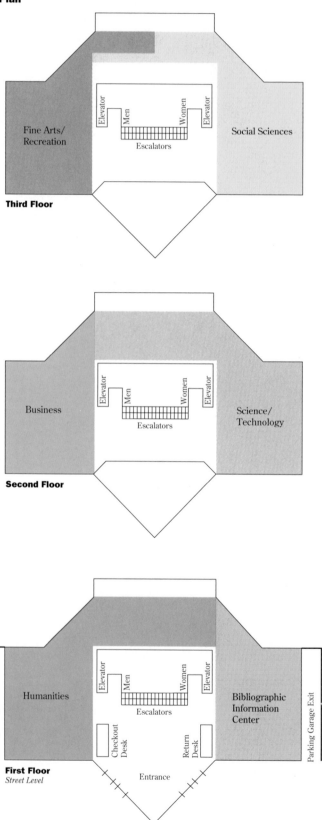

Third Floor

Fine Arts/
Recreation

Social Sciences

Elevator | Men | Escalators | Women | Elevator

Second Floor

Business

Science/
Technology

Elevator | Men | Escalators | Women | Elevator

First Floor
Street Level

Humanities

Bibliographic
Information
Center

Elevator | Men | Escalators | Women | Elevator

Checkout Desk

Return Desk

Entrance

Parking Garage Entrance

Parking Garage Exit

Refer to map on pages 18-19

1 Sam Houston Park
See section starting on page 46.

2 Theater District
See section starting on page 36.

3 City Hall
901 Bagby (247-2200) (Joseph Finger, 1939) This limestone
"tower" has long since been overshadowed by the skyscrapers
of downtown Houston. But it has kept its dignity, thanks in
part to the park and reflecting pool that lie in front of the
building. This public space is used during many of the
downtown celebrations, such as the International Festival.

4 Central Library
600 McKinney (236-1313) (S.I. Morris Associates, 1975)
The downtown library's familiar pink granite facade hides
four floors' worth of books as well as newspapers, magazines,
annual reports, art reproductions, cookbooks, tax information,
stock quotations, CD collections, etc. The list goes on. The
first floor's humanities collection, in addition to the usual
complement of philosophy, language and literary criticism,
stocks local, national and foreign newspapers with back issues
held on microfilm. The business section staff on the second
floor can help you find annual reports, 10Ks and proxies for
the asking. All the fine arts, photography collections, music
and design-oriented texts are located on the third floor. The
social sciences are shelved here as well: law texts, sociology,
political science and education volumes. A film library is
located on the fourth floor, which loans 16mm films and
videotapes. A Children's Room is located in the basement.
You may park in the building, entering the underground
garage from Lamar. Mon-Fri 9am-9pm, Sat 9am-6pm, Sun 2pm-
6pm. (Children's Room Mon 9am-9pm, Tue-Sat 9am-6pm,
Sun 2pm-6pm.)

City Hall.

5 Julia Ideson Building and Texas Room
500 McKinney (247-1664) (Cram & Ferguson, 1926) The
Texas Room, as it's known to writers and local history buffs,
is housed in the Julia Ideson Building next door to the Central
Library. The Ideson Building was the second permanent home
for Houston's library, built in 1926 to house a 56,000-volume
collection. Visiting the Texas Room is like stepping back in
time. To this day it remains in magnificent condition, a fitting
home for academic research. Among the old wood paneling,
high ceilings and giant windows of the second floor Texas
Room, you'll find over 28,000 books, early Texas imprints,
some 27,000 scholarly (and popular) periodicals, an important
map collection (with some "landmark" maps) and newspapers
from early Texas days. Also worthy of note in the Texas Room
is the "Texana" collection of sheet music, antique prints and
time-worn photographs, as well as census
rolls, a sampling of early county
records and legislative archives. An
added bonus: the staff bends over
backward as a matter of routine
for users of the collection. Mon-
Sat 9am-6pm.

**6 Geometric
Mouse X**
501 McKinney
(Claes Oldenburg,
1971) Red painted
steel sculpture. Sits
on the plaza between
the Central Library
and Julia Ideson
Building.

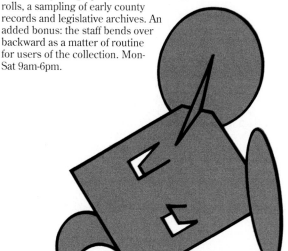

Refer to map on pages 18-19

7 Monument au Phantome

Corner of Louisiana and Lamar (Jean Dubuffet, 1977) Seven-part poly-chrome, polyester, resin and fiberglass sculpture.

8 Luther's

1100 Smith (759-0018) and other locations. Although it has detractors who begrudge its popularity, Luther's is many Texans' favorite barbecue joint. Most locations are barn-sized, and you walk through cafeteria-style. (Here it's tucked into the corner of a parking garage.) Brisket, sausage, ribs and all the side dishes (including fantastic skinny onion rings) are here. Mon-Wed 10:30am-6:30pm, Thu-Fri 10:30am-7pm. Credit Cards, Inexpensive.

9 Harry's Kenya Continental Restaurant

1160 Smith (650-1980) Animal trophies line the walls, pro-viding the perfect backdrop for power lunching. After all, what could better enhance an executive's image than dining in the company of Africa's great (and vanquished) prey? Ambitious Continental menu is served in a striking dining room that turns romantic by night. Convenient to the theater district. Lunch Mon-Fri 11am-2pm, Dinner Mon-Thu 5:30pm-10pm, Fri-Sat 5:30pm-11pm. Reservations. Credit Cards, Expensive.

10 Doubletree at Allen Center

400 Dallas (759-0202) 20 stories, 341 rooms. Double $108-$118, Suite $175-$300.

11 High Plains Drifter

500 Dallas (Peter Reginato, 1973) Cor-Ten steel sculpture.

12 Bob Smith Fountain

Louisiana at Clay. R.E. "Bob" Smith ranked among the greatest of the great Texas oilmen; this fountain was constructed in dedication to him and wife, Vivian, both eminent Houston philanthropists and civic builders during the '40s and '50s.

13 Hyatt Regency

1200 Louisiana (654-1234) 30 stories, 942 rooms. Double $155-$180, Luxury Level $155-$850, Suite $250-$850. The largest downtown hotel and host to many conventions, meetings and balls. The hotel has the Hyatt trademark, a towering atrium lobby.

Spindletop, a revolving restaurant, sits atop the hotel and offers a panoramic view of downtown architecture. Lunch Mon-Fri 11am-1:30pm, Cocktails 4:30pm-6pm, Dinner Mon-Sat 6pm-10:30pm. Credit Cards, Moderate-Expensive.

The Hyatt Regency (right) as a backdrop to the Bob Smith Fountain.

14 Antioch Baptist Church

500 Clay (Richard Allen, 1879) What began as a church for emancipated slaves thrived in one of Houston's more established black neighborhoods. But as the downtown grew, the neighborhood gave way to tall buildings until all that was left is the church, which still houses Houston's oldest black Baptist congregation.

15 Frozen Laces-One

1400 Smith (Louise Nevelson, 1980) Black painted steel sculpture sits in front of the Enron Tower.

16 Downtown YMCA

1600 Louisiana (659-8501) (Kenneth Franzheim, 1941) The Downtown Y occupies an attractive, 10-story "Tuscan Renaissance" building completed in 1941 on land that was then on the far Southwest edge of downtown. During the early days the YMCA was a place to live for a while, take classes or meet people when moving to the big city. While it is still a residence for some, the main use of the building is now as a health club for busy downtown executives. Two gymnasiums, three squash courts, seventeen handball and racketball courts and one volleyball court are packed during the noon hours. The Y is also the headquarters for a myriad of joggers who start here and wind their way along Buffalo Bayou. Mon-Fri 5am-10pm, Sat 8am-6pm, Sun 10am-6pm.

Refer to map on pages 18-19

17 Texas Limited

Amtrak Station, 902 Washington Avenue (522-9090) The
Texas Limited, a throwback to the era of luxurious Pullman
lines, operates seven refurbished cars exclusively on a
Houston-Galveston route. Each car dates back to the height of
the rail era, the '30s, '40s and '50s. A thirty-five mile-per-hour
pace and attentive service make for a leisurely two hour and
fifteen minute journey. Cellular-equipped bellmen will snatch
up reservations at the restaurant or hotel of your choice.
There is a cash bar and complimentary hors d'oeuvres; first
class passengers can pick up a light snack and enjoy a bit
more space. Upon arrival at Galveston's Railroad Museum
(25th and The Strand) passengers can stroll along The Strand
(the one-time "Wall Street of the South"), catch a trolley or
take advantage of discounted admission to the Tall Ship *Elissa*.
Fri-Sat depart Houston 9:30am, arrive Galveston 11:45am;
Fri-Sat depart Galveston 3pm, arrive Houston 5:15pm;
Sun depart Houston 11am, arrive Galveston 1:15pm;
Sun depart Galveston 5pm, arrive Houston 7:15pm.
Call for fares, schedule variations and special excursions.

18 Central Post Office

401 Franklin (227-1474) Very busy spot the night of April 15.
Mon-Fri 7am-7pm. The lobby is open 24 hours for automated
services.

19 University of Houston-Downtown

One Main Street (221-8000) The University of Houston-
Downtown was founded in 1974 and offers open admission to
its Bachelor's programs. U of H-Downtown enrolls about 8700
students, concentrating on providing opportunities for first
generation college students and "non-traditional" students
looking for career and educational enhancement. It is a
favorite refuge of professionals working for major corporations
who wish to shape up their careers.

20 Allen's Landing

The spot on which the Allen Brothers established the city of
Houston. It's historical, but no place for a picnic.

21 Bayou Belle

Allen's Landing (661-9811) Climb aboard the *Bayou Belle*
on weekdays and weekends alike for narrated tours of
Buffalo Bayou and the Houston Ship Channel. The old-
time paddler launches from Allen's Landing or Shanghai
Red's restaurant (near Loop 610 East). Private charters
are available. Call for the many options.

Bayou Belle.

22 Spaghetti Warehouse

901 Commerce at Travis (229-0009) Convenient to the
courthouses, the antique-filled dining room sends pasta-
packed, energized office workers and families out to face the
world. It's a colorful, stained-glass wonderland. Mon-Thu
11am-10pm, Fri 11am-11pm, Sat noon-11pm, Sun noon-10pm.
Credit Cards, Inexpensive.

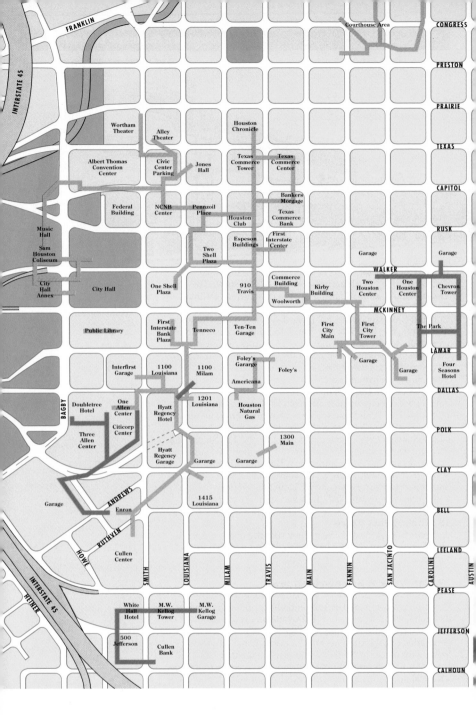

The Downtown Tunnel System

In the 1930s, entrepreneur Will Horwitz yearned to connect his businesses together underground. One of his theaters, the Isis, was on Travis; the Texan and the Uptown theaters sat on Capitol. Horwitz built his tunnel and later put a restaurant and a shop or two in it. He even included a penny arcade. In 1947 Foley's dug a tunnel to connect its new 19-story building to the garage. Tenneco followed suit in 1963. The tunnel adjacent to Woolworth's took the baton in the 1970s, when thousands of feet in retail space were added. That was the beginning of the 6.3-mile, 200,000-square-foot maze known today as the Houston tunnel system. Over 100,000 people whiz along the system, in and out of over 100 restaurants and shops, five days a week. Though similar systems exist in other cities, the Houston tunnel system is unique in that it is intended to keep downtowners out of the heat and rain, as opposed to the cold and snow.

Refer to map on pages 18-19

23 The Magnolia Ballroom
715 Franklin (223-8508) A turn-of-the-century ballroom and bar that caters to private parties and banquets.

24 La Carafe
813 Congress (229-9399) This warm and friendly pub is housed in a building built in 1845, the oldest Houston commercial building still on its original site (and not significantly altered). Draws an eclectic crowd of artists and business types. Mon-Fri 12pm-2am, Sat-Sun 1pm-2am. Credit Cards, Inexpensive.

25 Treebeard's
315 Travis on Market Square (225-2160) and other locations. Treebeard's reputation grows as Houstonians discover the red beans and rice, boudin, shrimp etouffee and rotating menu of lusty dark gumbos. Walk through, cafeteria-style, for a quick, stick-with-you lunch. Mon-Fri 11am-2pm. Credit Cards, Inexpensive.

26 Majestic
911 Preston (224-7226) (William Ward Watkin, 1926) What remains of the great downtown theaters of the '20s was refurbished in 1990 and is now used for parties and concerts.

27 Pillot Cafe
1012 Congress (222-9090) Located in an historical (circa 1858) cast-iron-fronted building near the courthouse, this newcomer attracts a downtown business clientele for continental breakfasts and easy lunches of burgers, sandwiches and salads. Occasional entertainment. Mon-Fri Breakfast 8-10am, Lunch 11am-2pm. Credit Cards, Moderate.

28 Court House Area
A small complex of government buildings has built up around the Harris County Civil Courts Building, which was originally the Harris County Court House (Lang & Witchell, 1910). The tunnel system is shown in red.

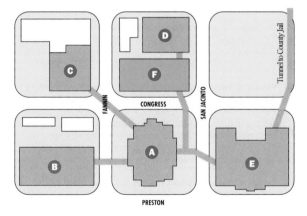

A Civil Courts Building
301 Franklin

B Harris County Administration Building
1001 Preston

C One Congress Plaza (Jury Assembly)
1019 Congress

D Family Law Center
1115 Congress

E Criminal Courts Building
301 San Jacinto

F Quebedeaux Park

La Carafe.

29 Rice Hotel
Main Street and Texas Avenue (Mauran, Russell & Crowell, 1913) Now standing closed and vacant, this was once the center of the downtown power brokers. This hotel built by one of Houston's great builders, Jesse H. Jones, sits on the spot where the capitol of Texas once stood. Jones built his hotel in 1913 and it immediately became the social hub of Houston. Personages from President Franklin D. Roosevelt to the prince of Saudi Arabia stayed here, as did President John F. Kennedy the night before he headed to Dallas, November 21, 1963.

Refer to map on pages 18-19

30 Christ Church
1107 Chartres (224-8091) Stately Christ Church Cathedral has mothered many of Houston's Episcopal institutions. Founded in 1845—shortly before the Republic of Texas joined the Union—it is the oldest congregation in Houston and the sole institution occupying its original site. Services in the present church began on Christmas Eve 1893 and have continued without interruption through the present day, saving only a brief 1938 pause caused by fire. An intricate dark wood gothic-style carving called the Rood Screen (above) was singed in that fire. This elegant work of religious art survives, today watched over by some 20 opalescent stained-glass windows of a quality seldom seen in Texas. One of the most beautiful of the windows is the Tiffany creation entitled Caritas (love) in which an allegorical matron holds her arms about her huddled children. Special tours of this majestic cathedral can be arranged by appointment.
Cloister Restaurant serves lunch in the church's hall and courtyard, Mon-Fri 11am-1:30pm.

The Esperson (left) and Gulf Buildings' classic tops.

32 Personage and Birds
(Joan Miró, 1979) Polychrome bronze sculpture.

31 Texas Commerce Tower 60th Floor Sky Lobby
600 Travis. A spectacular view of downtown Houston (see page 16) can be seen from the 60th floor observation area in Texas Commerce Tower. The elevator goes directly from the main lobby to the sky lobby. No admission. Mon-Fri 9am-5pm.

33 Esperson Building
808 Travis (John Eberson, 1927) The 32-story tower built by Mellie Esperson as a memorial to her husband still adds a touch of character to a downtown dominated by modern buildings. The architectural monument's classic top is lit at night, making it easy to find among the surrounding skyscrapers.

34 Texas Commerce Bank Building (The Gulf Building)
712 Main (Alfred C. Finn, Kenneth Franzheim and J.E.R. Carpenter, 1929) Built by Jesse H. Jones in 1929, this 36-story tower was the tallest building in Houston for over 30 years. The banking hall designed into the building was for National Bank of Commerce, TCB's predecessor, and is loaded with art deco grilles, railings, elevator doors and trim.

35 Original James Coney Island
1011 Walker (227-2669) and other locations. In 1923, at this location, Jimmy Papadakis brought the Coney Island chili dog to Houston. From this chili-stained start a string of 18 restaurants has sprung up around Houston. Mon-Sat 10am-9pm, Sun 10:30am-4pm. Inexpensive.

36 Family of Man
Fannin and Lamar (Barbara Hepworth, 1970) Nine abstract bronze figures spaced out in the courtyard in front of First City Tower.

37 Foley's
1110 Main (651-7038) Built in 1947, the original Foley's was the largest store in the thriving Main Street area, the heart of Houston. The shopping in Houston has spread to the far corners, but people who find themselves downtown still make this a busy place. Mon-Fri 9:30am-6pm, Sat 9:30am-5:30pm.

Refer to map on pages 18-19

38 George R. Brown Convention Center

1001 Convention Center Blvd. (853-8000) (Golemon & Rolfe Associates, John S. Chase, Molina & Associates, Haywood Jordan McCowan and Moseley Associates with Bernard Johnson and 3D/International, 1987) The George R. Brown Convention Center is a successful building, from both design and economic perspectives. It was completed in 1987 by a consortium of architectural firms who cooperated in bringing this bold and dominating 1.6 million-square-foot building to life. Inside, three cavernous two-story exhibition halls (approximately 125,000 square feet) have been placed in abutting fashion, then capped by a third floor of meeting, exhibition, reception and ballroom areas. The Civic Center Office will arrange group tours. Open for events only.

39 George R. Brown Statue

(Wili Wang, 1988) Bronze sculpture honoring longtime civic booster and the convention center's namesake.

40 The Park

McKinney at San Jacinto (654-3000) Connecting with Houston Center via skywalks, the Park is Houston's nearest approximation to a thriving downtown shopping center. The 80-store, 180,000-square-foot mall, well within range of the George R. Brown Convention Center, hums with life beginning at about 11am every weekday, when hordes of business suits pour through its doors from the tunnel system and skywalks. The Park has an array of clothing and specialty stores, including Brooks Brothers, but the largest attraction during the noon hour is the food court area. Mon-Fri 10am-7pm, Sat 10am-5pm.

40 Four Seasons Hotel

1300 Lamar (650-1300) 30 stories, 399 rooms. Double $185-$220, Suite $325-$825. This luxurious hotel is a favorite for convention goers and power lunchers.

Deville in the Four Seasons

1300 Lamar (650-1300) Savvy downtowners flock to this dining room for some of the most sensational (if pricey) Southwestern food in the city. Try the lamb nachos, smoked tenderloin, onion-crusted softshell crawfish and other innovations. As with any Four Seasons property, the support staff is topnotch. Lunch Mon-Fri 11am-2pm, Dinner Mon-Sun 6pm-11pm, Brunch Sun 11am-2pm. Reservations. Credit Cards, Expensive.

41 Annunciation Catholic Church

1618 Texas Avenues (222-2289) (Nicholas Clayton, 1871) Home of the oldest Roman Catholic parish in Houston, this church is noteworthy for its magnificent architecture. The church is a total reconstruction project by nineteenth-century Galveston architect Nicholas Clayton, renown for his many famous buildings on the Island, including The Bishop's Palace, Old Red and the Sacred Heart Church. Open only for services.

Refer to map on pages 18-19

43 Josephine's Ristorante

1209 Caroline at Dallas (759-9323) Near the convention center, this family-operated blue-jeans luncheonette is cafeteria-style at lunch, and full-service Italian at dinner. The lasagne primavera and ravioli are both terrific, and the double-chocolate marshmallow cake is wicked and wonderful. Mon-Fri Lunch 11am-4pm, Dinner Mon-Thu 4pm-9:30pm, Fri-Sat 4pm-10pm. Credit Cards, Moderate.

44 South Texas College of Law

1303 San Jacinto (659-8040) From it's humble beginnings in 1923 with only 34 students in the basement of the YMCA building, South Texas College of Law has not only survived but has prospered. Now, South Texas' 11-story tower holds 1400 full and part-time students and has become the eighth largest law school in the nation, one of the top four law schools in the state. Traditionally, the College's strengths have been in the "nuts and bolts" of law practice, such as litigation and advocacy training. South Texas' Jesse H. Jones Legal Center was the site of the fiery final arguments in the famous 1986 Texaco vs. Pennzoil case.

45 Souper Salad

*1001 Fannin in the First City Tower (651-9895) and other.
locations.* A great concept and usually well carried out, this chain of salad bars also features a changing selection of soups and homemade breads every day. It's the dieter's friend—but jammed at high noon. Mon-Fri 11am-2pm. Credit Cards, Moderate.

46 First United Methodist Church

1320 Main (652-2999) Built in 1910 in what was once a neighborhood of large Victorian homes.

47 Brown Book Shop

1517 San Jacinto (652-3937) Brown Book Shop is reputed to be the Mecca for engineers and Houston's still-burgeoning population of petroleum finders and seekers. You'll also find an excellent medical section stocked with the latest texts. Brown is a major source for just about any trade publication as well. Mon-Thu 8:30am-8pm, Fri 8:30am-6pm, Sat 9am-6pm.

48 Zydeco Louisiana Diner

1119 Pease (759-2001) A Treebeard's knock-off, this Cajun lunch spot is noisy, friendly and serves up a good jambalaya. Mon-Fri 11am-2pm. Catering. Credit Cards, Moderate.

49 Adrian's

1919 Louisiana at Pierce (951-9651) Popular and easy lunch spot for mainstream Tex-Mex becomes a raucous party during happy hour and dinner. Noisy as a bowling alley, there is usually a marimba player whose music lends the goofy feel of a 1930s cartoon. Fajitas, quesos and ceviche are dependable. Mon-Thu 11am-10pm, Fri-Sat 11am-11pm, Sun 11am-9pm. Credit Cards, Inexpensive.

50 World Newsstand

809 Pierce (650-6397) Daily papers from around the state and country. Wide selection of magazines. Daily 7am-11pm.

51 Sacred Heart Co-Cathedral

1111 Pierce (659-1561) The Co-Cathedral (with St. Mary's Cathedral in Galveston) of the Roman Catholic Diocese of Galveston-Houston.

52 St. Joseph Hospital
1919 La Branch (757-1000) St. Joseph's Hospital, owned
by the Sisters of Charity of the Incarnate Word, has been a
Houston institution for over 105 years; this huge complex
occupying seven buildings and 12 city blocks specializes in
women's and children's medicine and runs an extensive ortho-
pedics and a nationally respected sports medicine center.

53 Hunan Palace
801 Chartres at Rusk (225-5661) A dependable Chinatown
favorite convenient to the Brown Convention Center, the
Hunan menu offers nearly 100 selections with nary a weak
spot. Fried dumplings, General Tso's chicken and whole fish
in garlic sauce are all recommended. Mon-Fri 10am-10pm,
Sat-Sun 11am-10pm. Credit Cards, Moderate.

54 Long Sing Supermarket
2017 Walker (228-2017) Wander the aisles at this Chinatown
supermarket, and you'll forget you're in America. The seafood
counter offers shellfish and finfish not usually found in
Houston (the shrimp prices are excellent), and you'll find a
vast array of inscrutable condiments, dried goods, noodles and
wrappers. Up front, at the hot deli, don't be surprised to find a
whole, crisply roasted pig hanging, waiting to be cut into
chunks as customers order. Happily, the staff speaks English.
Open daily 9am-7pm.

55 Actors Workshop
1009 Chartres (236-1844) A semi-professional theater
company that offers training in theater arts plus an ongoing
season of five mainstream theater productions a year. Call for
current information.

56 Chin's Restaurant Equipment Co.
2011 Lamar (224-2822) Asian food-lovers could easily make a
day of strolling and shopping Chinatown's many emporia, finishing up at this purveyor of kitchen gadgets. Here you'll discover stacks of Chinese cookware, bushels of cleavers and
knives, towering bamboo steamers, handsome tableware and
mysterious widgets, all at small prices. Stop also at the Long
Sing Supermarket (see above) and one of the several medic-
inal herb traders (such as Van Tin Long Trading Company at
819 Chartres, 757-7974) before heading home to cook your
own Chinese banquet. Mon-Sat 10am-6pm, Sun noon-6pm.

57 Silver House
1107 Chartres (224-8091) Good, cheap Chinese food is abun-
dant in Chinatown. Of the eateries scattered behind the Brown
Convention Center, the bustling, barn-sized Silver House is
among the best, especially in the evening when the menu lists
pages and pages of meals, covering the gamut of Chinese deli-
cacies. Mon-Thu 11am-10pm, Fri 11am-11pm, Sat noon-11pm,
Sun 4pm-10pm. Inexpensive.

58 Kim Son
1801 St. Emmanual (222-2461) The garlicky crabs
can't be beat and the shatteringly brittle cha gio are
delicious dunked in salty-sweet nuoc cham at this
funky cultural crossroads on the fringes of
Chinatown. It's Houston's favorite Vietnamese
restaurant. Sun-Thu 9am-midnight, Fri-Sat 9am-
3am. Inexpensive.

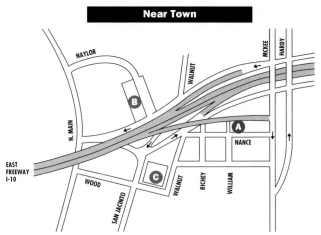

Near Town

A   Last Concert

1403 Nance (226-8563) There is no sign out-side and you still have to knock on the red door to get in. Dancing on the tables, free-flowing sangria and beer and a diverse crowd are the attractions at this world-famous Houston secret. The Tex-Mex food is not always great, but the scene—especially out on the patio—is so strange and wonderful, you can have a terrific time anyway. Lunch Mon-Fri 11am-2pm, Dinner Mon-Wed 5pm-11pm, Thu-Sat 5pm-2am. Credit Cards, Moderate.

B   DiverseWorks

1117 East Freeway (223-8346) DiverseWorks, hidden among warehouses in a part of town defined more by industry than by art, is Houston's answer to cutting edge, avant garde art programming. A 4000-square-foot gallery space supports visual artists whose work finds little space in profit-based commercial galleries. DiverseBooks boasts a wide array of lit-erary and art publications, and there's even a (free) phone-in reading service, PhoneWorks (228-2882). Most art exhibits and readings are free. Performance pieces and film screen-ings require admission fees. DiverseWorks/DiverseBooks : Tue-Fri 10am-5pm, Sat-Sun 12noon-5pm.

C   Downtown Grounds

908 Wood Street, Suite 130 (225-3203) This downtown ware-house offers musical acts ranging from acoustic to World Beat. It's also an art gallery that gives exposure to young hopefuls. Though coffee is the drink generally preferred by the young, artsy crowd, beer and wine are also served. For great people-watching, catch open-mike poetry night on Wednesdays and open mike acoustics on Sunday. Sun-Thu 8pm-2am, Fri-Sat 8pm-4am.

F   Vaquero

3725 Fulton in Moody Park (Luis Jimenez, 1978) The brightly colored, molded fiber-glass sculpture of a cowboy mounted on a bucking horse is one of the more popular public works in the city.

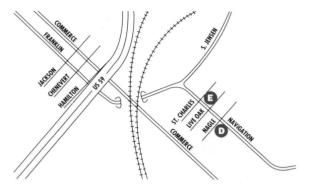

D   Original Ninfa's

2704 Navigation (228-1175) Many have
tried but none have equaled Mama
Ninfa's original green sauce. Loaded on
chips or dribbled over the combination
platter, it manages to be both cool and
incendiary at the same time. Most
Houstonians think the original Navigation
location is clearly the best. Mon-Thu
11am-10pm, Fri-Sat 11am-11pm, Sun
11am-10pm. Credit Cards, Inexpensive.

E   Meridas

2509 Navigation (227-0260) In the
shadow of the more famous Ninfa's down the street, this
pleasant restaurant boasts a wonderful mural by Mexican
artist Eduardo Jaramillo, depicting his conception of the
sacred Mayan city. Daily 7am-10pm. Credit Cards,
Inexpensive.

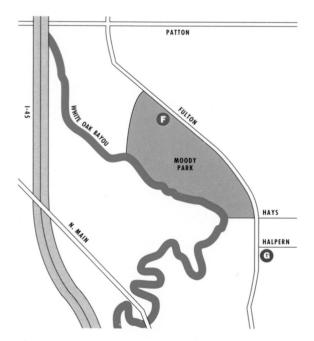

G   Original Doneraki

2836 Fulton near Quitman (224-2509) The original Fulton
location is the real thing—a good Mexican restaurant in the
heart of a Hispanic neighborhood. The interior is just tacky
enough, with beer signs tacked about, mariachis and good
margaritas, too. Open very late on the weekends. Noisy.
Sun-Thu 11am-midnight, Fri-Sat 11am-3am. Credit Cards,
Inexpensive.

Wortham Theater
Center

THEATER DISTRICT

The performing arts are alive and well in city center. Houstonians are loudly proud that theirs is one of the few U.S. cities able to sustain permanent ballet, opera, symphony and repertory theater companies. Find them all in the Theater District, not far from where Texas Avenue meets Louisiana. As you face the Alley Theatre's fortress-like facade, Jones Hall, home of the Houston Symphony and Society for the Performing Arts, is to your right, while on your left is Wortham Center, the magnificent venue for Houston Grand Opera and Houston Ballet. A bit upstream on the banks of Buffalo Bayou is the Music Hall, host to Theatre Under the Stars' Broadway-lavish musicals and national touring companies. On a high-season Saturday night, the District offers a heady mix of world-class culture and home-grown street theater.

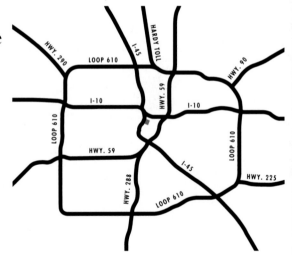

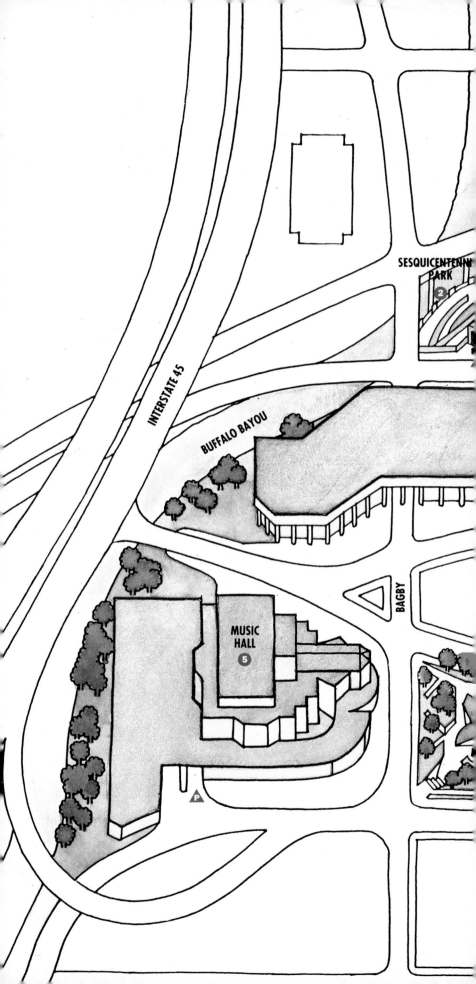

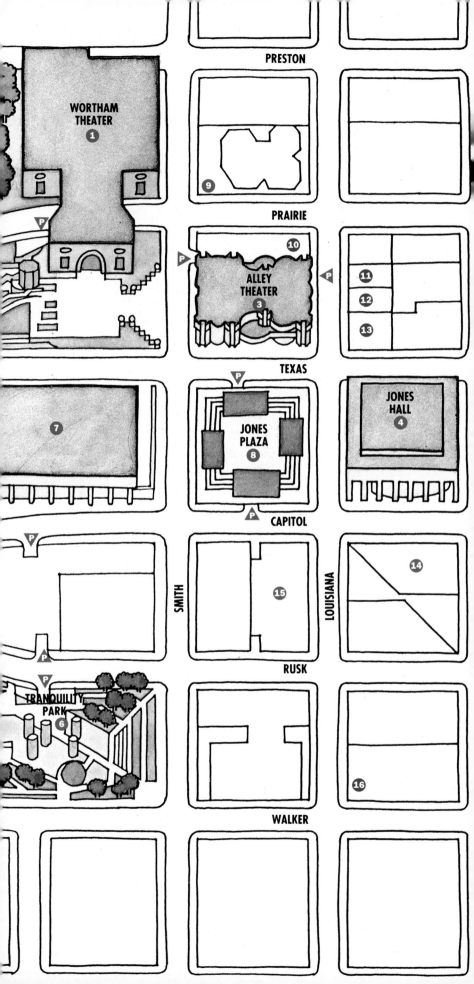

PRESTON

WORTHAM
THEATER
1

9

PRAIRIE

10

ALLEY
THEATER
3

11
12
13

TEXAS

7

JONES
PLAZA
8

JONES
HALL
4

CAPITOL

SMITH

15

LOUISIANA

14

RUSK

TRANQUILITY
PARK
6

16

WALKER

Refer to map on pages 38-39

The soaring, whimsical sculptures of Albert Paley line the escalators leading up to the Grand Foyer of the Wortham Center.

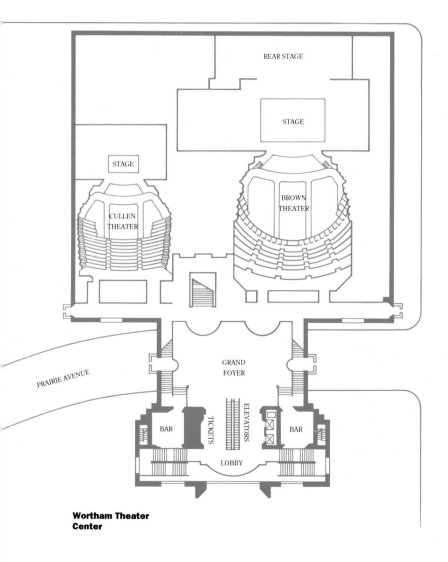

REAR STAGE

STAGE

STAGE

BROWN
THEATER

CULLEN
THEATER

PRAIRIE AVENUE

GRAND
FOYER

TICKETS

ELEVATORS

BAR

BAR

LOBBY

**Wortham Theater
Center**

Refer to map on pages 38-39

1 The Wortham Center

500 Texas (Morris-Aubry Architects, 1987) Houston has a proud tradition of acting out its civic pride. The Gus S. Wortham Theater Center is a great example of one of these exercises, as it was built with private funds while the city was still going through the rough days of recovering from "the oil bust." The interesting two-theater design was built specifically to house the Houston Grand Opera and Houston Ballet, with either company performing in the grand 2225-seat theater or in the more intimate Cullen Theater (1102 seats). Patrons can enter The Wortham from the plaza on Texas Avenue or from Prairie, which cuts through the center of the building. The ride up the sculpture-lined escalator to the magnificent Grand Foyer is one of the more spectacular entrances one could experience.

Houston Ballet

The Wortham Center, 500 Texas (523-6300) With Artistic Director Ben Stevenson at the helm, this professional company has made giant leaps forward in polish and international prestige, presenting "ballet a big public wants to see," according to the *London Times*. Its September-June season totals over 100 performances ranging from classical to contemporary. This is the only U.S. company invited to participate in an exchange with the Peking Ballet. A tough ticket, so call 227-ARTS early.

Houston Grand Opera

The Wortham Center, 500 Texas (546-0200) Fifth-largest opera company in the country and justly proud of its worldwide reputation for premiering new works by contemporary composers. During a typical October-July run, HGO General Director David Gockley has staged as many as a dozen operas, at times running lavish productions of ever-popular "warhorses" like *La Bohéme* back to back with an avant-garde *Nixon in China*, lighting up both Wortham Center stages. Call 227-ARTS for current offerings and reservations.

2 Sesquicentennial Park

Between Buffalo Bayou and The Wortham Center (TeamHou, 1989) This small park is the first step in a program to beautify Buffalo Bayou's downtown shoreline and commemorates the city's 150th birthday.

Wortham Center's Brown Theater Seating

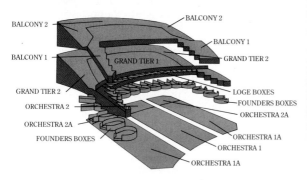

Wortham Center's Cullen Theater Seating

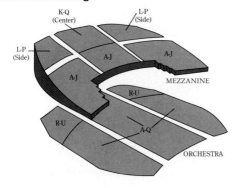

The Houston Grand Opera championed the use of computer-generated surtitle captions, helping to make foreign language opera more understandable.

Refer to map on pages 38-39

3   The Alley Theatre

615 Texas (Ulrich Franzen & Associates with MacKie & Kamrath, 1969) This poured-concrete bunker of a building houses Houston's best theater company, aptly named Alley Theatre. The building itself has two theaters: the main theater with 800 seats horseshoed around the thrust stage, while the 300-seat Arena Theater is similar in design but on a smaller scale.

Alley Theatre

The Alley Theatre, 615 Texas (228-8421) Yes, it literally began in an alley but has since moved uptown. Now it is Houston's only resident professional repertory theater company and the Southwest's largest Equity house. The Alley's two stages offer a diverse nine-month season of new plays, drama classics and the occasional musical. Edward Albee, arguably America's leading playwright, has recently been much in residence. Ring the box office number above for a pair on the aisle.

4   Jones Hall

615 Louisiana (Caudill Rowlett Scott, 1966) The 3000-seat Jesse H. Jones Hall for the Performing Arts is home to the Houston Symphony and the Society for the Performing Arts. Built in 1966 with private funds provided by the Houston Endowment, the theater building has withstood the tests of time. Originally the home of the Opera and Ballet as well as the Symphony and single performances, the building was designed with a movable ceiling allowing the hall to be configured for different types and sizes of performances. Today the structure is still respected for its acoustics.

The Houston Symphony

Jones Hall, 615 Louisiana (224-4240) Mozart-Wagner specialist Christoph Eschenbach is the latest in a distinguished lineage of HSO maestros: Stokowski, Barberolli, Previn, Comissiona. Dating from 1913, the orchestra is one of America's oldest performing arts groups. Ninety-eight musicians strong, it now performs some 200 classical, pops and children's concerts during a year-round season. Touring often and recording frequently, the Symphony has recently reasserted itself as one of the brighter jewels in Houston's cultural crown. Once again, 227-ARTS for times and tickets.

**Jones Hall
Seating**

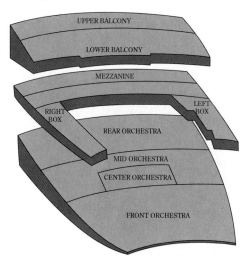

Society for the Performing Arts

Jones Hall, 615 Louisiana (227-1910) Betwixt and between the Ballet/Opera/Symphony trinity, SPA hosts Houston appearances of outstanding international dance groups, orchestras and solo artists. Everything from the Kronos Quartet to Mexico's Ballet Folklorico. Call 227-ARTS to see if SPA is on stage at present. Its season is a bit catch-as-catch-can.

NationsBank Broadway Series

Jones Hall, 615 Louisiana (629-3700) A "division" of the Society for the Performing Arts, this subscription series hosts national and road-company tours of recent hits from the Great White Way. Original stars and name talent head most casts. Single tickets and group rates are available.

5   Sam Houston Coliseum and Music Hall

810 Bagby at Walker (Alfred C. Finn, 1937) Jesse H. Jones spearheaded the construction of Houston's first large Public Works Administration project, a symphony hall attached to a rodeo and convention area. Over the years it has hosted the Fat Stock Show to a hockey team to Saturday night wrestling.

Theatre Under the Stars

Music Hall, 810 Bagby at Walker (622-TUTS) "Under the stars" has become something of a misnomer since TUTS first trod the boards in Hermann Park's outdoor theater. Today, this purveyor of Broadway musicals offers five to six shows per year in its Theater District home to the delight of hundreds of thousands of patrons. Now a full-fledged Equity showcase, TUTS imports name talent to headline evergreen hits by Lerner & Lowe, Rogers & Hammerstein and the ubiquitous Andrew Lloyd Webber. Recent seasons have shown more daring, but TUTS still believes you should walk out humming the score. Curtain up fall to spring. Call for current bookings.

Music Hall Seating

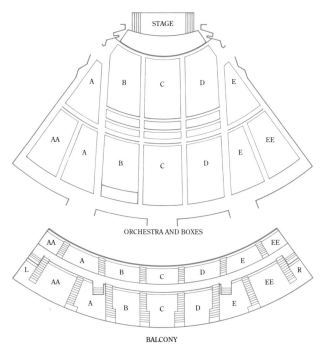

Refer to map on pages 38-39

6   Tranquility Park
Between Smith, Walker, Bagby and Rusk (Charles Tapley Associates, 1979) A tribute to Houston's space heritage, this park is named after the Sea of Tranquility where astronaut Neil Armstrong uttered the first words from the moon: "Houston, Tranquility base here. The Eagle has landed."

7   Albert Thomas Convention Center
612 Smith (Caudill Rowlett Scott, 1967) Once the city's mainstay convention center, now used sporadically.

8   Jones Plaza
Between Texas, Louisiana, Capitol and Smith. An elevated square that serves as a cover over the entrances to the Civic Center Underground Parking Garage.
Party on the Plaza
Jones Plaza, Downtown. Party on the Plaza is a series of festive outdoor concerts at Jones Plaza, running from March to November. The five-year-old Houston tradition showers jazz, blues, rock & roll and zydeco music upon more than 5000 nacho-eating, beer-drinking nine-to-fivers every Thursday night till 10, weather permitting. Past performers have been local favorites like jazzman Kirk Whalum and folk songwriter Shake Russell. The revelry has become one of Houston's more popular public events. Free.

10   Birraporetti's
500 Louisiana (224-9494) and other locations. Good pizza and a lively Irish bar atmosphere, with a clientele that varies by location, characterize this local chain of American-Italian restaurants. Downtown location on Louisiana is a good pre-theater bet. Sun-Sat 11am-2am. Inexpensive to Moderate.

Executive Carriages
Downtown Theater District (522-5665) Carriage rides of approximately 30 minutes are available in the Theater District evenings starting at 6pm. Reservations can be made by calling ahead. $25 per couple.

11 Longhorn Cafe and Saloon

509 Louisiana (225-1015) Great spot to unwind with a beer after work, the Longhorn is also known for its topnotch chicken-fried steaks and delicious (if sloppy) chiliburgers. Mon-Fri 11am-9pm, Sat 11am-3pm. Credit Cards, Inexpensive.

12 Charley's 517

517 Louisiana (224-4438) Manager/co-owner Clive Berkman is in the kitchen, and Charley's has never been better, offering an American take on Continental cuisine. It's nestled in the heart of the Theater District, and the staff caters to theater-goers, even fetching tickets. There's an award-winning wine list, too. Lunch Mon-Fri 11:30am-2pm, Dinner Mon-Sat 5:30pm-11pm. Reservations. Credit Cards, Expensive.

13 Lancaster Hotel

701 Texas (228-4016 or 228-9500) (Joseph Finger, 1926) 12 stories, 93 rooms. Double $145-$185, Suite $280-$780. Revived as a small, deluxe hotel in the early eighties. While the rooms are nice and the service superb, it is probably best known among Houstonians for its grille, a before and after stop for theater-goers.

Lancaster Grille

701 Texas (228-9502) The kitchen's revolving door has made it hard in recent years to get a fix on the direction of this hotel dining room with the English-manor decor. It's usually at its best serving simple Anglo-American grill items, such as chops, steaks, crabcakes and its famous onion soup. Great spot for before or after the theater. Mon-Fri 6am-11pm, Sat-Sun 7am-11pm. Credit Cards, Moderate.

9 Virtuoso

(David Addicks, 1982) Steel structure with cement. Controversial sculpture in front of the Lyric Center Building.

14 Pennzoil Place

711 Louisiana (Johnson/Burgee Architects, 1976) Local developer Gerald Hines put Houston on the architectural map for good when he brought Philip Johnson and his partner John Burgee to town to build the twin towers of Pennzoil Place. This building "broke the box," the rectangular shape of most buildings being built at the time. Its revolutionary shape caused a great deal of attention and controversy and led to an opening up of what corporate America came to expect from a headquarters building. Pennzoil Place was the ultimate "modern" building, comprising two sleek, geometric shapes separated by a mere ten feet.

15 NationsBank Center (RepublicBank Center)

700 Louisiana (Johnson/Burgee Architects, 1983) Seven years after building Pennzoil Place, the same team of Hines, Johnson and Burgee would contrast this "modern" structure with the ultimate "post-modern" building, the RepublicBank Center (now called NationsBank Center). Compared to this building, the controversy around Pennzoil Place seems pale. RepublicBank was laughed at, praised, condemned and wondered about, all at the same time. (To enjoy the contrasting styles, try standing in the towering lobby of NationsBank Center, next to the large free-standing clock, and look to the east, where the gap of the twin towers of Pennzoil Place lines up perfectly through the high, arching windows.

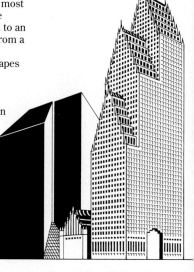

Pennzoil Place (left) and the NationsBank Center

16 XIT Restaurant & A-OK Bar

815 Louisiana at Walker (228-4400) Popular after-work meeting spot where the Tex-Mex, Southwestern food is not the main attraction. Mon-Thu 11am-8pm, Fri 11am-10pm. Reservations. Credit Cards, Moderate.

St. John Church in
downtown Houston's
Sam Houston Park

SAM HOUSTON PARK

The restored houses in Sam Houston Park offer a stark contrast between the buzz of modern life and the quiet of the eighteenth century, when it all began for Houston. This quaint park can seem unreal, for it testifies to how much Texas—and the world—has changed over the 150 years since these homes were built. It may be the Bayou City's best reminder of its past. Modern-day Houstonians, whizzing across the Pierce Elevated, pass rooftops below them that shelter the oldest buildings in Houston, and structures that reflect how Houstonians lived before the first freeway appeared here.

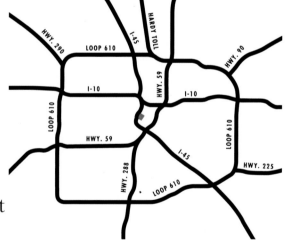

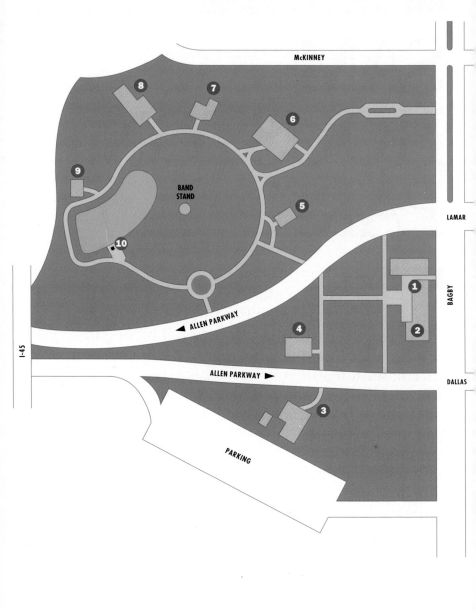

McKINNEY

LAMAR

BAGBY

DALLAS

I-45

BAND
STAND

ALLEN PARKWAY ◄

ALLEN PARKWAY ►

PARKING

1 "The Long Row"

1100 Bagby. This structure replicates Houston's original business building, a continuous storefront of a few hundred feet in length erected by Houston's founders, the Allen brothers. The original row was built in 1837 and burned down on the eve of the Civil War. The present reconstruction was finished in 1967 and houses the Harris County Heritage Society and the related Museum of Texas History, Yesteryear Shop and Tea Room.

Harris County Heritage Society

1100 Bagby (655-1912) The Heritage Society, founded in 1954, has restored six historical Texas homes and a tiny nineteenth-century church in downtown's Sam Houston Park. Preservationist groups have praised the Society's work with awards, including a special citation for its "well organized docent program to interpret structures to visitors." Four homes can be experienced firsthand in Heritage Society daily tours. During the Christmas season Christmas Candlelight Tours brighten the six Heritage Society homes with nineteenth-century reminiscent decorations, Dickensian carolers singing from porches and a boys' choir warming the cozy wooden church. There are also old-fashioned Fourth of July celebrations held here. Daily tours $4. Hourly Mon-Sat 10am-4pm, Sun 1pm-5pm.

The Museum of Texas History

1100 Bagby (655-1912) Within the museum's four walls is a 6000-square-foot exhibit space full of memorabilia and sundry artifacts from Texas' past, dating back to the days when Spanish navigators set their sights on Texas. There are three galleries in the museum, one a permanent collection with items from 1519 to 1961. This collection numbers over 100,000 items, so displays do rotate. A second gallery emulates the Duncan Family General Store, a turn-of-the-century emporium, moved from Egypt, Texas, to Sam Houston Park. The third gallery hosts changing exhibits on subjects from Texas' history. There is a brief introductory film. Admission is free. Mon-Sat 10am-4pm, Sun 1pm-5pm.

The Yesteryear Shop

1100 Bagby (655-9114) The Yesteryear Shop, the Tea Room's next-door neighbor in The Long Row, offers a selection of gifts and Texana in an atmosphere patterned after early Texas boutiques. Items crafted by local artisans enhance the small town theme. Handmade quilts—imported from the country's oldest maker in Virginia—and pottery from Marshall, Texas, are examples of wares brought in from what, in the early days, was "far afield." Mon-Sat 10am-4pm, Sun 1pm-5pm.

2 The Tea Room

1100 Bagby in the Long Row (655-8514) The Tea Room maintains the old Texas theme of Sam Houston Park with a menu mirroring our "culinary heritage": bread pudding, honey-wheat bread, iced tea, soup, sandwiches, etc. Mon-Sat 10am-4pm, Sun 1pm-5pm. Credit Cards, Inexpensive.

10 Spirit of the Confederacy (Louis Amateis, 1900) Bronze statue of a mournful winged youth, placed in the park in 1908.

Refer to map on page 48

3   Kellum-Noble House

(1847) One of the oldest surviving buildings in Houston and the impetus to form the Harris County Heritage Society, which was organized to save the house from destruction in 1954. The

home was originally built in 1847 by Nathaniel Kellum along the banks of Buffalo Bayou on the outskirts of Houston. He also built a sawmill, brickyard, tannery and blacksmith shop on the site. In 1850, the house was sold to Houston's first banker, B.A. Shepherd, who turned around and sold it a year later to Ms. Zerviah Noble, who established a school in it. In 1899 the City of Houston bought the house and surrounding property, establishing the city's first public park. The building fell into disrepair before a group of citizens banded to form the Heritage Society and restore the house.

4   Nichols-Rice-Cherry House

(c. 1850) This is the first building to be moved into Sam Houston Park by the Heritage Society. Ebeneezer B. Nichols, a New Yorker, built the Greek Revival house about 1850. William Marsh Rice, a noted financier whose will established Rice University, lived in the house between 1856 and 1873. In 1897 the house was moved from its original site on Congress Avenue across from Courthouse Square to a different location by Mrs. Emma Richardson Cherry, Houston's first resident artist. She used it as a studio. After her death it was acquired by the Heritage Society in 1959 and moved into the park.

5   St. John Church

(1891) This wood-sided church is the favorite photographic subject in the park, often being photographed with the city's shining glass buildings behind it for contrast. German Evangelical Lutherans built the church in 1891 among the farms near Mangum Road and the White Oak Bayou in northwest Harris County. Its original altar-pulpit and cypress plank pews are still in the church. The building was moved into the park in 1968.

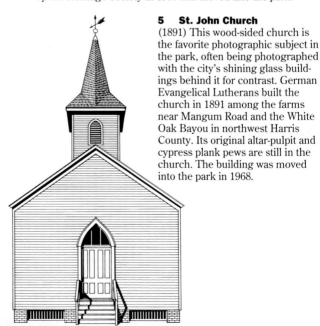

6   Staiti House

(1905) Oilman Henry T. Staiti bought this house in 1905, after it had been built on a speculative basis in Houston's upscale Westmoreland Addition. The large, 17-room house featured electricity, which was a novelty at the time, as well as professional landscaping. Noted architect Alfred Finn designed an addition to the house, which was moved into the park in 1986.

7   San Felipe Cottage

(1868) This simple, six-room structure is typical of the "Gulf Coast cottage" style of house built in Houston in the middle 1800s. First owned by the Ruppersbergs, a German family, the house was located on old San Felipe Road, which is now called Dallas Street. The house was restored in 1963 and moved into the park in 1972.

8   Pillot House

(1868) Eugene Pillot built this house in 1868 on McKinney Street where the George R. Brown Convention Center now stands. According to the Harris County Heritage Society, "the mid-Victorian structure features significant innovations, including gaslights. Its kitchen is believed to have been the first attached kitchen in Houston." The house was occupied by Pillot family members for 97 years before it was moved into the park in 1965.

9   Old Place

(c. 1825) Thought to have been built by colonist John R. Williams about 1823 to 1825, this style of structure is typical of the earliest houses built in the Houston area. The home was originally located on Clear Creek in southwest Houston. According to historian Stephen Fox, it is made with rough-hewn cedar logs for framing and features a "mudcat" chimney. It may be the county's oldest remaining structure.

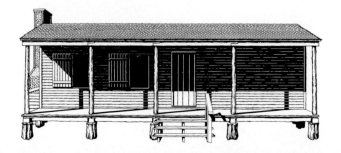

Dining outside at The Black Labrador on Montrose Boulevard.

MONTROSE

Montrose Boulevard connects the Museum District to the south with the lower Westheimer area to the north. Between these two extremes is Houston's most eclectic, most diverse neighborhood. World renown museums and seedy rock 'n' roll bars, rare antiques and everyday junk coexist here. It is a place where new restaurants seem to open every month, while others have survived here for years, becoming venerable institutions. It is fashionable yet a little dangerous. Chic and seedy. It is a neighborhood of shady treelined streets and friendly neighbors during the day and bustling restaurants and loud clubs at night. But mostly it is known as the "art community," where the artists live and work, and where many are shown.

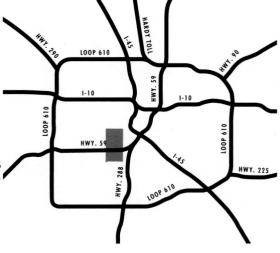

Refer to map on page 54

1 North and South Boulevards
Between Graustark and Mandell Streets. Two of the most beautiful streets in Houston, with the branches of grand oaks weaving canopies over the boulevards. Great place to jog.

2 Butera's
4621 Montrose in Chelsea Market and 2946 W. Alabama at Shepherd (520-8426) What began as a deli counter in John Butera's grocery on Bissonnet has become two trendy meeting places for yuppies and intellectuals dining on salads, pastas and imported waters. Mon-Fri 7am-10pm, Sat 9am-10pm, Sun 9am-8pm. Credit Cards, Inexpensive.

3 Anthony's
4611 Montrose in Chelsea Market (524-1922) Restaurateur Tony Vallone developed the less-tony Anthony's to be a more casual version of his flagship restaurant Tony's, long considered Houston's finest restaurant. There's nothing cut-rate, however, about the exquisite sauces, succoring hearth cooking or fine wine list. The classic dining room is all rosy tones, the service taut. Lunch Mon- Fri 11:30am-2pm. Dinner Mon-Thu 5:30pm-11pm, Fri-Sat 5:30pm-11:30pm, Sun 5:30pm-9:30pm. Reservations recommended. Credit Cards, Expensive.

North Boulevard.

4 Spellbinder's Comedy Club
4617 Montrose in Chelsea Market (520-9595) HBO, Showtime and Comic Strip Live alumni put on a show at Spellbinder's; the club features professional, nationally recognized acts, mostly from Hollywood, L.A., or San Francisco. Lounge opens at 6:30pm. Shows Tue-Thu and Sun 8pm, Fri-Sat 7:45pm and 10:15pm.

5 Earth Star
4503 Montrose (523-3614) Cactus and herbs are the stars here, although there is a strange collection of assorted T-shirts and curios as well. Mon-Wed 10am-6pm, Thur-Sat 10am-9pm, Sun 11am-6pm.

6 Kam's
4500 C Montrose (529-5057) Jeffrey Cheung's New Age Chinese restaurant caters to the area's health-conscious diners, offering a generous slate of pasta and vegetarian specialties. Spare, chic decor and a tiny dining room. Mon-Thu 11am-10pm, Fri 11am-11pm, Sat noon-11pm, Sun 5pm-10pm. Credit Cards, Inexpensive.

7 Kathy's
4319 Montrose (529-4600) Shoulder-pad types like this classy-low-key bistro. Owner/namesake Kathy Ruiz has been fine-tuning the menu, but you can expect seafood, yummy salads, Sunday brunch and little snacks to nibble with drinks. Brunch Sun 11:30am-2:30pm, Lunch Tue-Fri 11am-2pm, Dinner Tue-Thu 5:30pm-10pm, Fri-Sat 5:30-midnight. Credit Cards, Moderate.

8 Chapultepec
813 Richmond (522-2365) College students pack this funky third-world Mexican joint, lured by the free soup that comes with most meals. The neighborhood and the hygiene are not for the faint-hearted. Sun-Thu 9am-1:30am, Fri-Sat 9am-3:30am. Inexpensive.

Refer to map on page 54

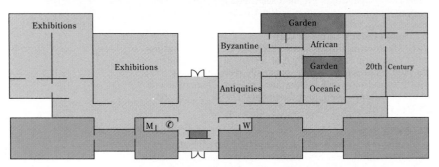

**The Menil
Floor Plan**

Exhibitions

Exhibitions

Byzantine

Antiquities

Garden

African

Garden

Oceanic

20th Century

M   W

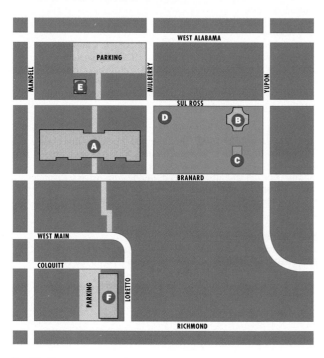

**The Menil
Area**

Refer to map on page 54

9   The Menil Area

John and Dominique de Menil have been, in the classic sense, civic patrons. So many major works in Houston—from the Philip Johnson structures at the University of St. Thomas to the Rothko Chapel to the impressive Menil Collection—are products of the de Menils' collective vision.

A   Menil Collection

1515 Sul Ross (525-9400) (Renzo Piano, 1987) A simple cypress exterior belies the cultural riches within. This state-of-the-art structure by Renzo Piano holds the remarkable private acquisitions of John and Dominique de Menil. The eclectic, some might say eccentric, collection ranges from Byzantine and tribal art to the twentieth-century schools of Cubism, Minimalism and Pop. Few museums can hold a track light to the Menil's Surrealist works, i.e., Ernst and Magritte. Houston philanthropy at its finest. Wed-Sun, 11am-7pm. Free admission.

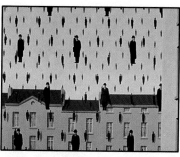

Golconde
(René Magritte, 1953)
Oil on canvas
31 1/2 x 39 1/2 in.

B   The Rothko Chapel

3900 Yupon at Sul Ross (524-9839) Yet another example of the de Menils' benevolence, this all-faiths sanctuary holds 14 specially commissioned paintings by the American abstract expressionist Mark Rothko. It is a frequent site of ecumenical and ethnic celebrations. Barnett Newman's sculptural memorial to Martin Luther King, *Broken Obelisk*, graces the reflecting pool at the chapel's entry. Free admission. Daily 10am-6pm.

D   Bygones

Sul Ross at Mulberry (Mark di Suvero, 1976) Corten steel beams and milled steel plate sculpture.

E   Brazos Bookstore at the Menil Collection

1520 Sul Ross (521-9148) This small bookstore serves as the museum's bookstore and is a treasure trove of art books and periodicals. Wed-Fri 11am-5:30pm, Sat-Sun 11am-6:45pm.

F   Richmond Hall

1416 Richmond Avenue (520-8512) Associated with the Menil Collection, this gallery features single installations such as its initial show, 42 large canvases by Andy Warhol. Wed-Sun 11am-7pm.

10   Da Camera Society

Office 3912 Mandell (524-7601) and Ticket Services Center 3920 Mandell (524-5250) Where to go for chamber music and small-ensemble programs? Wherever Da Camera is at the moment. Founder Sergiu Luca is professor of violin at Rice University, so expect the Society to opt for more programs in the Shepherd School concert hall. Box office hours Mon-Fri 11am-6pm.

11   Houston Center for Photography

1441 W. Alabama (529-4755) A small but active exhibition space offering contemporary photographic shows, publications and workshops. The lens cap is on during August. Free admission. Tue-Fri 11am-5pm, Sat-Sun noon-5pm.

12   Graham Gallery

1431 W. Alabama (528-4957) Founded in 1981 by Bill Graham, the gallery is best known for mounting exhibitions of emerging and mid-career Texas artists including painters, photographers and sculptors. Tue-Sat 10am-5:30pm.

C Broken Obelisk
(Barnett Newman, 1967) Cor-Ten steel sculpture set in a reflecting pool in front of the Rothko Chapel.

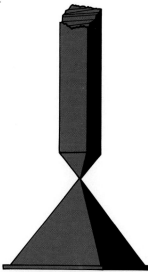

Refer to map on page 54

University of St. Thomas Campus

A	Anderson Hall	R	Meteorology, Computer Science
B	Chapel	S	Modern Foreign Language Annex
C	Chapel Garden	T	Mt. Vernon House
D	Chemistry-Physics Building	U	Murphy Hall
E	Communications	V	Psychology House
F	Counseling and Testing Center, Job Placement	W	Religious Education
G	Crooker Center	X	Shadwell Hall
H	Cullen Hall	Y	Strake Hall
I	Doherty Library	Z	Sullivan Hall
J	Donoghue Hall	AA	Tennis Courts, Swimming Pool
K	General Office	BB	Tiller Hall
L	Guinan Residence Hall	CC	UST Apartments
M	History House	DD	Welder Hall
N	Hughes House		
O	Jerabeck Activity and Athletic Center		
P	Jones Hall		
Q	Link-Lee Mansion		

Refer to map on page 54

13 University of St. Thomas

3812 Montrose (522-7911) The University of St. Thomas
began in the Link-Lee Mansion at 3812 Montrose in 1947 under
the direction of the then-Bishop of Galveston. (J.W. Link, the
builder of the famous present-day home of the university, was
head of The Houston Land Corporation, the primary developer
for the Montrose area.) St. Thomas is largely a Roman Catholic
college with a liberal arts bent, though some 40% of the student
body is non-Catholic. The school is small, with fewer than
2500 students. Admission is not open; a usual guideline is
that applicants fall in their classes' top half. Highlighting the
11-block campus is the academic mall, designed by architect
Philip Johnson.

Link-Lee Mansion on the campus of the University of St. Thomas.

The Crooker Center Gallery
Jones Gallery
Little Gallery of Archaeology

University of St. Thomas, Main Entrance, 3812 Montrose. All
three spaces may be offering student work or special-interest
exhibits at the moment. Call 522-7911 for specifics.

14 The Black Labrador

4100 Montrose (529-1199) The cozy English-pub setting in
what was at one time a church is perfect for enjoying a pint of
ale, a game of darts, perhaps a bite to eat. The kitchen is not
strictly English (burgers and Tex-Mex dishes turn up among
the shepherd's pie and bangers and mash), but it's probably
much better than its equivalent in Merry Old England. Mon-
Thu 11am-11:30pm (kitchen closes at 11pm), Fri-Sat 11am-
12:30am, Brunch Sun noon-3pm, Sun noon-10:30pm, (kitchen
closes 10pm). Reservations. Credit Cards, Inexpensive.

15 Bistro Vino

819 W. Alabama (526-5500) Deep in the heart of Montrose,
this restored old home offers romantic Continental dining with
a fireplace and pianist. Alternatively, al fresco dining on the
private, tucked-away deck is among the most pleasant in the
city. Mon-Sat 11:30am-midnight. Reservations. Credit Cards,
Moderate.

16 High School for the Performing and Visual Arts

4001 Stanford (522-7811) HSPVA is a nucleus of Houston's
young artistic talent; accordingly, several concerts and performances can be expected here throughout the year. On the list
is an all-school musical, chamber recitals, orchestral performances, wind, jazz, and vocal events, plus dance shows. Five
or six theater productions fill out each arts season as well.

Refer to map on page 54

17 Blue Bird Circle Resale Shop

615 W. Alabama (528-0470) Surely the largest resale shop in Houston, selling furniture and clothing on consignment and from donations. The Blue Bird Circle Resale Shop is a non-profit, all-volunteer organization that supports pediatric neurological research at Baylor's Blue Bird Circle Clinic. Mon-Fri 10am-4pm, Sat 10am-1pm.

18 Access Houston

3900 Milam (524-7700) Non-profit corporation that supplies public programming for airing over cable TV in Houston. They can arrange for previously filmed work to appear on the public access airways or aid in the production of programming. There is some fine print, of course. Office hours: Mon-Fri 8am-5pm, Operating hours: Sat-Sun 1pm-10pm.

19 The River Cafe

3615 Montrose (529-0088) Located on the left bank of the Rio Montrose, the River Cafe is a favorite watering hole of the area's hippest arts crowd. Good jazz, nice patio. Lunch Mon-Fri 11:30am-2:30pm, Brunch Sat-Sun 11:30am-4pm, Dinner Sun-Thu 6pm-11pm (bar open Fri-Sat until 2am). Credit Cards, Moderate.

20 Greek Orthodox Cathedral Annunciation

3511 Yoakum (526-5377) The Greek Orthodox Cathedral serves as the willing home base of the Greek Festival every October. Office hours Mon-Fri 8am-5pm.

21 La Colombe d'Or

3410 Montrose (524-7999) Once the baronial residence of Exxon founder Walter Fondren, today La Colombe d'Or is the state's smallest luxury hotel, with just six art-filled suites ($150-$600) upstairs. Downstairs, the restaurant is pure French: superb patés, grilled seafood and birds, delicate filled pastas. The service can sometimes be supercilious, but the restaurant's undeniable charm usually compensates. Houston's only Relais & Chateaux member also boasts a cozy bar. Lunch Mon-Fri 11:30am-2pm, Dinner Sun-Thu 6pm-10pm, Fri-Sat 6pm-11pm. Reservations. Credit Cards, Expensive.

LA COLOMBE D'OR

22 Cody's
3400 Montrose (522-9747) Though it's known as a jazz club, the schedule includes a variety of acts, from folk rockers to rhythm-and-blues artists. Breathtaking views from two huge outdoor patios at either end of the rooftop club, perfect for lounging on breezy evenings. Cody's has always been better known as a jazz club and after-work spot than a restaurant. Still, you can order from a simple American menu, or just graze from the buffet. Mon-Thur 4pm-1am, Fri 4pm-2am, Sat 6pm-2am. Dinner Mon-Thur 6pm-10:30pm, Fri-Sat 6pm-midnight. Credit Cards, Moderate.

Looking west toward the Galleria/Post Oak area from atop Cody's.

23 Grif's Inn
3416 Roseland (528-9912) THE sports bar in Houston, Grif's has been the heart and soul of local team support since 1964, for teams in first place or last. Burgers available as well as the suds. Mon-Sat 10am-2am, Sun 10am-1am.

24 La Mora
912 Lovett (522-7412) Almost from the moment it opened, Lynette Hawkin's Tuscan grill has been a favorite of both the city's glittery trendetti and those who just plain like excellent Italian food. Grilled steaks and rotisserie-roasted birds are fine, but it may be the lavish selection of antipasti that is most seductive of all. Lunch Mon-Fri 11am-2:30pm, Dinner Mon-Thu 6pm-10pm, Fri-Sat 5:30pm-11:30pm. Credit Cards, Moderate.

25 The Ruggles Grill
903 Westheimer (524-3839) The tables are crowded together, the decor isn't much, it's noisy and there's usually a wait. Ruggles is also one of the city's perennial favorites, with an innovative menu offering good value. Chef/owner Bruce Molzan is famous for making vegetables taste delicious (a typical order comes with at least a halfdozen), and desserts are legendary. Noisy but fun, even after all these years. Lunch Tue-Fri 11:30am-2pm, Dinner Tue-Thu 5:30pm-11pm, Fri-Sat 5:30pm-midnight, Sun 5:30pm-10pm, Brunch Sun 11am-2:30pm. Reservations. Credit Cards, Moderate.

26 Felix Restaurant
904 Westheimer (529-3949) The Tijerina family has operated this restaurant, at this location, since 1948. It still has the nice feel of a neighborhood family restaurant, and the food is pretty good, too. Daily 11am-9:45pm. Credit Cards, Inexpensive.

Refer to map on page 54

27 The Lovett Inn

501 Lovett (522-5224) Innkeeper Tom Fricke encountered the Hutcheson estate on a Texas journey that took him through the area and instantly saw its charm. The fine home afforded possibilities for weddings, receptions, even corporate meetings, he pondered. The Lovett Inn's box hedges, winding brick pathways and ornate brass furnishings make this two-story home a favorite meeting place for the well-to-do as well as a coveted site for society locals' most exquisite parties.

28 L'Alliance Francaise De Houston and School

427 Lovett (526-1121) L' Alliance Francaise might not appreciate the comparison, but they're aptly described as a sort of French version of the Goethe Institute. While maintaining no ties with the French Ministry of Culture, L' Alliance promotes cultural events in Houston related to France and all things French; you'll be able to take in lectures on architecture, to attend a wine tasting or to visit an exhibit of Impressionist paintings. And L'Alliance will help in your efforts to deceive the natives on your next trip to Paris with French classes, offered on ten academic plateaus ranging from beginner to near-native. School hours: Mon-Fri 9:30am-5:30pm.

29 La Strada

322 Westheimer (523-1014) Despite its iffy address on lower Westheimer, La Strada packs in serious eaters of many stripes. The menu revolves around a California-Italian heart, including pizzettas, avant-garde pastas, light meats and seafood and a wide selection of appealing appetizers. The pretty setting, with ever-changing art on the walls, is full of light that pours in through the wraparound doors. Lunch Mon-Sun 11am-3pm, Dinner Mon-Thu 5pm-11pm, Fri-Sat 5pm-midnight, Sun 5pm-10pm. Credit Cards, Moderate.

30 Tower Theatre

1201 Westheimer (520-93356) Built after the Great Depression in the 1930s, the Tower sat on the edge of town in those days, showing the latest motion pictures with its new sound-equipped projection gear. Designed by a Dallas architect imported along with the Tower's management, the magnificent old theater survived the decades in good form, its pylon and neon-lit portico intact. The Tower was rehashed discreetly in 1988 and now hosts live music performances. Open for performances only.

31 Dramatika

3224 Yoakum (528-5457) Dramatika's stock of posters, postcards and picture frames is a feast for the eyes, for in this tiny but colorful shop, you'll see James Dean and Jimmy Stewart posters hanging next to beautifully framed works of Matisse, Mondrian and Chagall. Vintage Broadway musical posters stand in rows like record albums, hundreds of them. Don't be let down by mention of James Dean (everybody's got his picture!); this is good stuff. Mon-Fri 11am-7pm, Sat 10am-5pm.

32 Tribal Art

1103 California (522-4795) Tribal masks (and lots of them), pottery, jewelry, ethnic art and clothing. The store is small but chock-full. (Also has a location at 1427 West Gray.) Tue-Sun noon-7pm.

33 Niko Niko's

2520 Montrose (528-1308) Locals drop in for no-frills gyros, souvlaki and dalmas at this greasy spoon á la Athens. Mon-Sat 9am-10pm, Sun 11am-9pm. Inexpensive.

34 Cafe Noche
2409 Montrose (529-2409) This newcomer is Bill Sadler's answer to Mexican food. The former River Cafe owner has new art by old artists and great margaritas, as well as many interesting dishes from the interior of Mexico. The kitchen's use of herbs is unlike anything else in Houston. Open Daily 11:30am-midnight. Reservations for large parties only. Credit Cards, Moderate.

35 Rudyard's
2010 Waugh Dr. (521-0521) In the heart of Montrose, Rudyard's is a popular resting spot for Urban Animals and other downtown skater types. The skaters may look menacing, but they're friendly enough, as long as you don't feed them. The music is mostly rock-and-roll, with a little jazz occasionally thrown in for variety. Open Daily 4pm-2am.

36 Anderson Fair Retail Restaurant
2007 Grant (528-8576) Some of the best songwriters around call this Montrose institution home. Eric Taylor, who wrote many of folkie Nancy Griffith's hits (and used to be married to her), performs here regularly. Serious music fans only. This is a fantastic place to sit and listen and enjoy good music. If you have something else in mind, Houston has a wealth of other options. Cover varies, generally $5. Performances Fri-Sat 8pm-2am.

37 Texas Art Supply
2001 Montrose (526-5221) The largest supplier in the state to the professional as well as weekend artist. Also has one of the finest selections of books in the city, from coffee-table art books to a range of how-to books. Mon-Sat 8:30am-6pm, Sun noon-6pm.

38 The Art League of Houston
1953 Montrose (523-9530) The Art League of Houston began in 1900 to help Texans hang art in public schools, permitting children to "know more about culture." Now the focus of the League has broadened; members include the majority of Houston's full-time artists. The League takes its self-appointed role as focus of the art community in earnest. Exhibits by prominent Texas artists come and go in the 1300-square-foot gallery, and the League holds various workshops, classes, lectures and social events. Gallery: Tue-Sat 10am-5pm.

39 Texas Junk Company
215 Welch (524-6257) This funky 5000-square-foot space harbors the most bizarre collection of memorabilia in Houston, no contest. Primitive Texana is mixed with neon signs, vintage American road maps, first edition books, even cow skulls. This is no antique store, but it's not a dirty junk dealer either, despite its name. You'll also find vintage clothes, framed art and— the hot item with European tourists —real American license plates. Mon-Sat 11am-6:30pm.

40 Golden Room
1209 Montrose (524-9614) Supatra Yooto and Kay Soodjai's little jewel box of a dining room, with lacquered green walls and a spirit house outside the front door, is the spot for extraordinary Thai food. Call ahead for the off-the-menu pot of glass noodles baked with shrimp or the snapper steamed in a foil envelope. Lunch Mon-Fri 11am-3pm, Dinner Sun-Thu 5pm-10:30pm, Fri-Sat 5pm-11pm. Credit Cards, Moderate.

On the lawn behind
The Museum of Fine
Arts at Montrose
and Main

MUSEUM DISTRICT

Focal point for Houston's vibrant visual arts community is the intersection of Montrose Boulevard and Bissonnet, some three miles south of downtown just off Main. Without beating about the bush—or the graceful live oaks that shade the neighborhood—the locals call it simply "The Museum District." Here you'll find The Museum of Fine Arts, with its impressive Impressionists, elegant sculpture garden and adjacent art school. Close by are the Contemporary Arts Museum, Menil Collection and Rothko Chapel, Rice University galleries and some of the better art dealers, restaurants and residential architecture. The Museum District is one of Houston's most

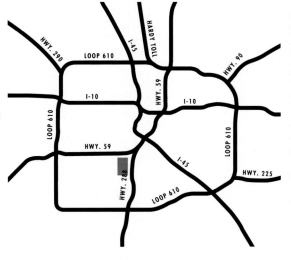

cohesive enclaves, so you may want to consult the *Guide* map and chart a walking tour, comfortable shoes and congenial weather being considered de rigueur.

Refer to map on page 66

1   The Museum of Fine Arts, Houston

1001 Bissonnet at Main (639-7300) (Original building:
William Ward Watkin, 1924; Cullinan Hall: Ludwig Mies van
der Rohe with Staub, Rather & Howze, 1958; Brown Pavilion:
The Office of Ludwig Mies van der Rohe, 1974) Founded in
1900, Texas' first art museum now houses an encyclopedic
permanent assemblage of some 27,000 works
spanning 4000 years, certainly one of the
Southwest's largest and most outstanding collections. Bauhaus master Mies van der Rohe's striking additions to the original structure contain the
Brown Pavilion Galleries of European Art and
Straus Collection of Renaissance and eighteenth-
century masters. Other highlights include the
Beck Collection of Impressionists and Post-
Impressionists and galleries displaying American
and twentieth-century works, photography,
Oriental art and art of Africa, Oceania and the
Americas. The MFA also offers a full calendar of
major exhibitions, book store, gift shop, library
and the popular museum cafe. Admission $3
adults, $1.50 seniors and college students, free to
age 19. Tue-Sat 10am-5pm, Thu 10am-9pm, Sun
12:15pm-6pm.

2   Cafe Express in
The Museum of Fine Arts

The garden cafe of the museum is now run by the
people from the Cafe Annie team. Chicken salad
with pistachios is a passion for many fans, and the
desserts are divine. Just be careful not to over-
order, as it's easy to get carried away. Tue-Sat
11am-3pm. Credit Cards, Inexpensive.

**Portrait of Anton Francesco
degli Albizz**
(Sebaso Del Piombo, 1525)
Oil on canvas, transferred from panel,
53 x 38 7/8 in.

Skizze 160 A (Sketch 160 A)
(Wassily Kandinsky, 1912)
Oil on canvas, 37 1/2 x 42 in.

Refer to map on page 66

**Museum of Fine Arts
Gallery Plan**

*Many of the galleries at
the MFA are used for tem-
porary exhibitions,
collections that are on loan
or traveling shows. The
galleries designated as
permanent are:*

Upper Brown Galleries
European

**Robert Lee Blaffer
Gallery**
Far Eastern

Lower Brown Galleries
*African, Oceania & The
Americas*

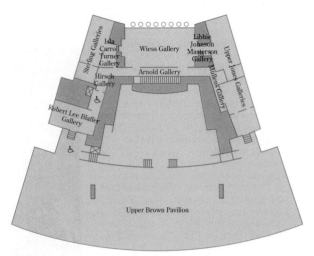

Upper Level

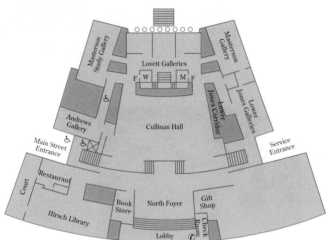

Main Level   Bissonnet Street Entrance

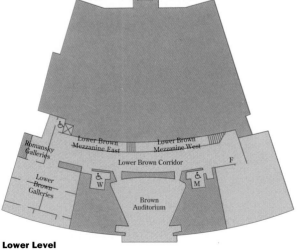

Lower Level

3   The Lillie and Hugh Roy Cullen Sculpture Garden

Bissonnet at Montrose (639-7540) (Isamu Noguchi, 1986) Opposite The Museum of Fine Art's main entrance and fronting the Glassell School of Art, the garden features nineteenth- and twentieth-century sculpture from the MFA's permanent collection. Created by Isamu Noguchi, himself a celebrated sculptor, this plaza-like setting of grassy islands, lush greenery and curved marble walks is perhaps Houston's most popular new art acquisition. On display are major works by Rodin, Matisse, Maillol, Giacometti, Smith, Caro, Kelly, Paladino and Stella. Since the gardens are open late, a very nice time to visit is in the early evening. As the sun and heat go down, the warm light brings out the richness of the sculpture and the garden surroundings. No admission charge. Daily 9am-10pm.

Sculpture in the Lillie and Hugh Roy Cullen Sculpture Garden

A   Spatial Concept/ Nature, No. 1 and No. 2 (Lucio Fontana, 1965) Bronze

B   Two Circle Sentinel (David Smith, 1961) Stainless Steel

C   The Sound of Night (Mimmo Paladino, 1986) Bronze

D   Figure, No. 1, Figure, No. 2, Figure, No. 3 (Robert Graham, 1983) Bronze

E   Adam (Emile-Antoine Bourdelle, 1889) Bronze

F   Flore Nue (Aristide Maillol, 1910) Bronze

G   Untitled (DeWitt Godfrey, 1989) Welded Steel

H   Conversation with the Wind (Pietro Consagra, 1962) Steel Painted Gray

I   Decanter (Frank Stella, 1987) Stainless Steel, Bronze and Carbon Steel

J   Can Johnny come out and play? (Jim Love 1990-19??)

K   Arch Falls (Bryan Hunt, 1981) Bronze on Limestone Base

L   Curved Form: Bryher II (Barbara Hepworth, 1961) Bronze with Stainless Steel Cable

M   The Walking Man (Auguste Rodin, 1905) Bronze

N   The Pilgrim (Marino Marini, 1939) Bronze

O   Argentine (Anthony Caro, 1986) Painted Steel

P   Quarantania I (Louise Bourgeois, 1947-1953) Bronze with Painted Steel Base

Q   Houston Triptych (Ellsworth Kelly, 1986) Bronze

R   Large Standing Woman (Alberto Giacometti, 1960) Bronze

S   Back I, Back II, Back III, Back IV (Henri Matisse, 1909, 1913, 1916-1917, 1930) Bronze

T   Untitled (Joel Shapiro, 1990) Bronze

Sculpture in the garden subject to change.

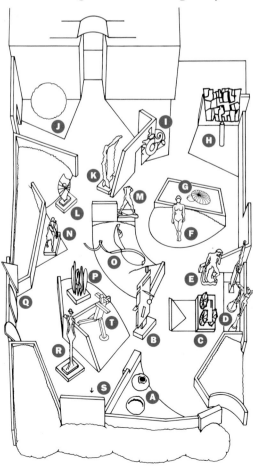

Refer to map on page 66

4 Contemporary Arts Museum

5216 Montrose at Bissonnet (526-3129) (Gunner Birkerts, 1972) The CAM considers itself cutting-edge in more ways than one. Look for the knife-sharp, metal-sheathed parallelogram, then look for the oh-so-subtle entrance. Inside is a "non-collecting museum" displaying changing exhibits of new-direction art and modern-day masters such as Rosenquist and Robert Wilson. Shows are often radical, always exhilarating. Downstairs is a second, smaller gallery and well-curated gift shop. Tue-Fri 10am-5pm, Sat-Sun noon-5pm. Free, $2 donation suggested.

6 The Glassell School of Art

5101 Montrose (639-7500) (S.I. Morris Associates, 1978) This glass-bricked structure adjoining the Cullen Sculpture Garden houses the teaching wing of the Museum of Fine Arts. Glassell's Studio and Junior Schools offer year-round classes for both adults and youngsters, and it sponsors extensive community outreach. The faculty numbers some of the city's best known creatives, and its annual artists-in-residence show and sale attract major attention among Houston's more astute collectors. The short-time visitor should check out the current exhibit in the School's central gallery. Mon-Thu 9am-10pm, Fri-Sun 9am-5pm. Free admission.

5 Manila Palm: An Oasis Secret

Behind the Contemporary Arts Museum (Mel Chin, 1978) The fiberglass, steel, wood, plant fiber and burlap sculpture has been here so long it's now a real part of the neighborhood.

7 The C.G. Jung Educational Center of Houston

5200 Montrose (524-8253) This former art gallery is now a non-profit organization that encourages self-awareness through a "gestalt" of educational courses and expressive arts programs. Also mounts related art exhibits. Mon-Thu 9am-8pm, Fri 9am-5pm, Sat 10am-4pm. Open to the public.

8 Harris Gallery

1100 Bissonnet (522-9116) One of the premier Houston galleries, featuring many Texas artists. Contemporary painting (large selection of landscapes), sculpture and photography. Tue-Fri 10am-5pm, Sat 11am-5pm.

9 The Wyndham Warwick Hotel

5701 Main (526-1991) 12 stories, 307 rooms. Bob Hope once stated on national TV that the view from the Warwick was the most beautiful he'd seen from a hotel room. It is pretty, looking across Hermann Park towards Rice University. Double $145-$175, Suite $175-$1200.

10 Mecom Fountain
Main at Montrose. Oil man John Mecom, living at the time in
the Warwick Hotel, donated funds in 1964 to turn what was a
sunken rose garden on this site into the three circular fountains seen here today.

11 Delia Stewart Dance Center
1202 Calumet (522-6375) An old gray church on Calumet
houses this professional dance company, specializing in
American theater dance. Stewart's dancers are trained in the
Broadway tradition; each performs ballet, tap and jazz, and the
company tours nationally twice a year. A teaching company as
well, Delia Stewart offers beginner and expert instruction.

12 Clayton Library
5300 Caroline (524-0101) The Clayton Center for
Genealogical Research collection holds family histories,
county histories, state and local records, texts on genealogical
research techniques, histories of various patriotic societies
and federal census records dating back to 1790. Mon-Wed
9am-9pm, Thu-Sat 9am-5pm.

13 Genealogy Books and Consultation
1215 Oakdale (522-7444) Proprietor Norma Chudleigh will
assist people interested in finding out about their lineages in
this mine of pedigree know-how. Read how-to books on
genealogical research for Europe and the U.S. or take home
some of the beautiful charts for framing. Mon-Wed and Fri
1pm-5:30pm Sat 10am-5:30pm.

14 Butera's
*4621 Montrose in Chelsea Market and 2946 W. Alabama at
Shepherd (520-8426)* What began as a deli counter in John
Butera's grocery on Bissonnet has become two trendy
meeting places for yuppies and intellectuals dining on salads,
pastas and imported waters. Mon-Fri 7am-10pm, Sat 9am-
10pm, Sun 9am-8pm. Credit Cards, Inexpensive.

15 Anthony's
4611 Montrose in Chelsea Market (524-1922) Restaurateur
Tony Vallone developed the less-tony Anthony's to be a more
casual version of his flagship restaurant Tony's, long
considered Houston's finest restaurant. There's nothing cut-
rate, however, about the exquisite sauces, succoring hearth
cooking or fine wine list. The classic dining room is all rosy
tones, the service taut. Lunch Mon-Fri 11:30am-2pm. Dinner
Mon-Thu 5:30pm-11pm, Fri-Sat 5:30pm-11:30pm, Sun 5:30pm-
9:30pm. Reservations recommended. Credit Cards, Expensive.

16 Spellbinder's Comedy Club
4617 Montrose in Chelsea Market (520-9595) Club features
nationally recognized acts, mostly from Hollywood, L.A., or
San Francisco. Lounge opens at 6:30pm. Shows Tue-Thu and
Sun 8pm, Fri-Sat 7:45pm and 10:15pm.

Refer to map on page 66

Upper Level

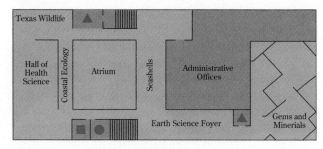

Main Level

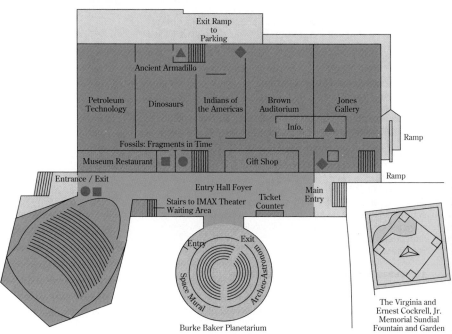

Lower Level

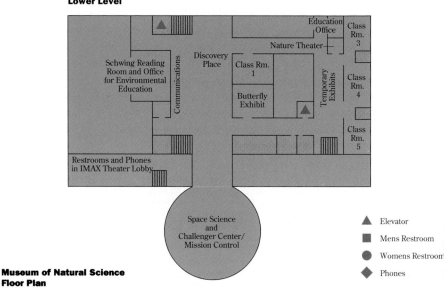

**Museum of Natural Science
Floor Plan**

Refer to map on page 66

17 The Museum of Natural Science

1 Hermann Circle Drive in Hermann Park (639-4600) The
Houston Museum of Natural Science has grown to become
one of the strongest, most respected science museums in the
country. The star attraction in the museum's permanent collection is a $6 million, world class assembly of over 600 mineral
specimens: the Sams Collection of Gems and Minerals in the
Cullen Gallery of Earth Science. The collection displays naturally occurring crystals and cut gemstones in over 50 cases,
housed in total darkness except for the light emanating from
the cases. The most spectacular feature of the exhibit is the
collection of luminescent minerals, whose neon pinks, oranges
and blues—visible only in darkness—transfix the imagination.
In the Alfred Glassell Jr. Hall, a huge, 170-foot-long skeleton
of a 140-million-year-old Diplodocus dinosaur dominates the
room. Nearby stands a life-size Ankylosaurus model, a
Plesiosaur skeleton and a Tyrannosaurus Rex skull. The
McDannald Hall of the American Indian displays cultural
artifacts of Native Americans from South, Central and North
America, including a shrunken head from the Jivaro Indian
culture. Strake Hall of Malacology boasts a collection of over
2500 sea shells displayed in natural settings which mimic the
open sea. Students of the Space Program will leap at the
opportunity to become part of a space station team or part of a
down-to-earth mission control crew at the Challenger Center
affiliate site. In the Arnold Hall of Space Science, models of
future space planes and space stations and ideas on the future
of space travel are presented. Children can see toys that
actually flew with Discovery astronauts, as well as astronaut
training suits like those worn on Gemini missions. Not only
do Houstonians enjoy nature's science of eons past at the
museum, they sample man's vision into his future as well.
Adults $2.50, children under 12 $2. Mon-Sat 9am-6pm,
Sun noon-6pm.

*Above left, a 70-foot-long
skeleton of a 140-million-year-
old dinosaur domiates the
entrance to the galleries of the
museum.The Sundial
Fountain, above, is a favorite
attraction among the younger
set at the entrance to the
Museum of Natural Science.
Below, from the fabulous
collection of gems and minerals from the Museum's Lillie
and Roy Cullen Gallery of
Earth Science.*

18 Burke Baker Planetarium

1 Hermann Circle Drive in Hermann Park (639-4600) The
232-seat planetarium at the Houston Museum of Natural
Science lets you experience the universe, as 5000 stars move
across a dome-shaped screen. The Planetarium presents star
shows weekly, simulating Houston's starfield. The shows may
take you back in time or zoom you into the future from any
spot on earth. Or they might zoom in to view rotating planets,
exploding stars or vistas of alien landscapes. The Planetarium
offers programming tailored specifically for children and families. "Rock" laser shows have included music from the Rolling
Stones and Pink Floyd. In addition, the Planetarium operates
the George Observatory, a satellite facility at Brazos Bend
State Park, where star-gazers can view the night sky through
an observatory or listen to astronomy and natural history
lessons (242-3055 at the George Observatory). Adults $2, chil-
dren under 12 $1.50. Rock laser shows $5 adults and children.
Show schedules are available by phone. Mon-Fri shows hourly
1pm-3pm, Fri evening rock laser shows hourly 7pm-11pm, Sat
shows hourly 11am-5pm, Sat evening shows hourly 7pm-11pm,
Sun shows hourly 1pm-3pm.

Refer to map on page 66

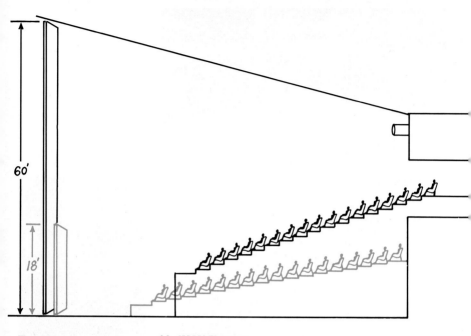

The 60-foot-high screen of the IMAX theater is compared (above) to the average size screen at your neighborhood theater.

19 IMAX Theater

1 Hermann Circle Drive in Hermann Park (639-4600) IMAX films are measured in stories, not feet. The Wortham IMAX Theater at Houston's Museum of Natural Science, opened in 1989, delivers images of extraordinary sharpness and clarity on its six-story screen. The screen is a full ten times larger than your local movie theater's format. The sharp, high-resolution images spread across the 80-foot-wide screen are impressive; *To Fly* debuted with images of a hang glider weaving through the cliffs of California's coast, the Pacific seemingly miles below, and in *The Dream is Alive*, astronaut Kathy Sullivan walked outside the space shuttle 250 miles above the earth. IMAX films tend to be much more engrossing than conventional formats, so the audience often feels a part of the action. The theater seats 394 patrons and is often sold out, so call ahead if you can. Adults $4.50, children 3-11 $3.50. Shows on the hour, Mon-Thu 10am-8pm, Fri 10am-9pm, Sat 10am-10pm.

20 The Children's Museum of Houston

1500 Binz [after November 1992] (52-AMUSE) The newest addition to the Museum District, it is instantly recognizable, thanks to Robert Venturi's whimsical architecture. Inside, children ages 2 to 12 may engage in hands-on art projects and interact with special cultural and scientific exhibitions. If you owe the kids one, this is definitely it. $2 adults, free under 12. Group reservations required. Tue-Thu and Sat 9am-5pm, Fri and Sun 1pm-5pm.

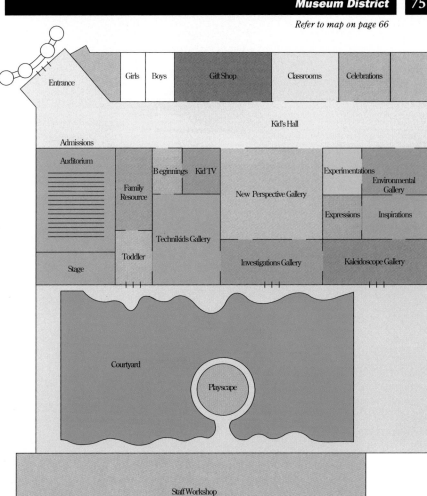

**Children's Museum
Floor Plan**

*The fanciful entrance (left) to
the new museum by architect
Robert Venturi.*

Looking past the
Mecom Fountain
to the Sam Houston
Statue at the
entrance to

HERMANN PARK/RICE UNIVERSITY

Successful civic planning in the early 1900s has imparted a distinctively European aura to the Hermann Park/Rice University district, perhaps Houston's most beautiful area. Bordered by Mecom Fountain to the north, the Texas Medical Center to the south, Rice University campus to the west and Hermann Park to the east, this area is the heart of Houston. The oak-lined esplanades of Main and Fannin were redrawn during World War I, when landscape architect George Kessler laid out his vision of a planned metropolis here. With the Museum of Natural Science, Miller Outdoor Theater and the Houston Zoo, this is by far the city's busiest public space.

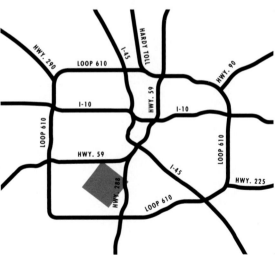

Refer to map on pages 78-79

2 Sam Houston Statue
Enrico Cerraccio's bronze equestrian statue of General Sam Houston imparts a sense of definition to the city. The statue was part of a grand scheme in 1916 to beautify the city—through planning of public green spaces and streets—called the City Beautiful project. Houston's outstretched arm points eastward, toward the San Jacinto battlefield where he defeated the forces of the dictator of Mexico, securing independence for Texas.

1 Hermann Park
Entrance at Main, Fannin and Hermann Drive. In 1914 George Hermann bequeathed to the City of Houston the land that now makes up Hermann Park and part of the Medical Center, including Hermann Hospital on the southern edge of the park.

3 The Museum of Natural Science, Burke Baker Planetarium, IMAX Theater
See Museum District, pages 72-74.

4 Civic Garden Center

1500 Hermann Drive in Hermann Park (529-3960) The Civic Garden Center in Hermann Park is home to over 40 garden clubs and societies, who hold monthly meetings both outside among the rose and bulb gardens and in the center's three meeting rooms. (A 40x60-foot auditorium can seat 250; smaller rooms hold 120 and 35 each.) Flower and plant shows can be taken in on spring and fall weekends. Weddings, receptions and picnics are often held both indoors and out among the center's colorful gardens. A Library, holding member societies' collections, is also available. Mon-Fri 8am-5pm, Sat-Sun available for meetings or events by appointment.

Hidden deep within the park's pines and hardwoods rests an elegant Chinese pagoda, a gift of the citizens of Taipei to the citizens of Houston.

5 Miller Outdoor Theater
Hermann Drive in Hermann Park (520-3291) Since its construction about 20 years ago, the triangular, rust-colored steel roof of the Miller has sheltered annual performances by the Houston Symphony Orchestra, The Houston Jazz Festival, The Shakespeare Festival and myriad other groups. HSO's summer festival plays during June and July; Shakespeare runs throughout midsummer; Jazz happens in the fall, usually mid-September; and Cinco de Mayo, one of Miller's big events, is celebrated on May 5. The open-air theater's seats are covered with the protruding roof, but behind the fixed seats is a hill where viewers take in a concert setting on blankets under the stars. Performance dates and times vary.

7   Train on View
Near the Zoo entrance in Hermann Park. Southern Pacific
Railroad once operated Steam Locomotive #982—built in
1919 —which now stands on display in Hermann Park. The
steam engine and its tender car hauled freight along Texas
and Louisiana lines for years until being retired and donated
in 1957.

8   Train Ride
Near the Zoo entrance in Hermann Park. Children and adults
alike can take advantage of $1 train fares for the Hermann
Park train, which chugs ruefully along its two-mile track 365
days a year. Departures are timed for every eight minutes. $1.
Daily 9:30am-5:30 pm.

9   Boat Rides
Near the Zoo entrance in Hermann Park. Half-hour paddleboat
excursions on the Hermann Park Reflecting Pool are available
365 days of the year as well, barring only bad weather. $5 (for
a two seater) or $8 (for a sedan). Daily 10am-7pm.

10   Teddy Bear
Near Miller Theater on Golf Course Dr. in Hermann Park.
Jim Love's playful Teddy Bear, created in the late '70s, moved
around the city over the years before finding its present home
in Hermann Park. Part fine art, part play thing, the wood and
steel sculpture has been climbed on, played near and generally
enjoyed by park-going Houstonians.

11   Hermann Park Golf Course and Clubhouse
*6201 Golf Course Dr. in Hermann Park (526-0077 or
526-0225)* This narrow, 5966-yard 18-hole golf course has
been hosting regulars from the Medical Center and
surrounding neighborhoods since 1933. Still one of the best
bargins in town (green fees $10-$12.50), the course has been
remolded and improved in recent years. Driving range and
extra large putting green lie in front of the '30s vintage
Mediterranean-style clubhouse. Hours 6:30am-6:30am.

12   Miniature Golf Course
*6201 Golf Course Dr. in Hermann Park (526-0077 or
526-0225)* Recently constructed next to the Hermann
Park Golf Clubhouse. Cost $3 per person for unlimited play.
Daily 7am-8pm.

6   Atropos Key
(Hannah Stewart,
1972) Bronze sculp-
ture on the top of the
hill behind Miller
Outdoor
Theater.

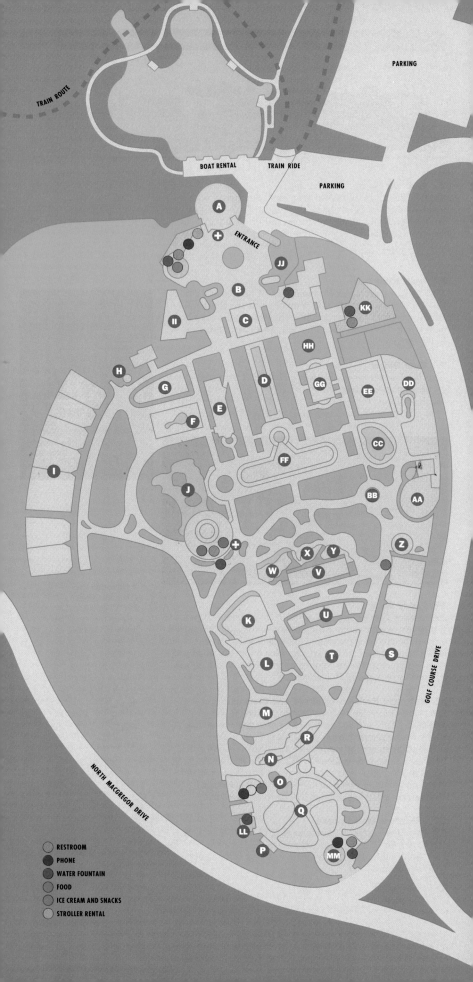

PARKING

TRAIN ROUTE

BOAT RENTAL   TRAIN RIDE

PARKING

A

ENTRANCE

JJ

B

KK

II

C

HH

H

D

GG

G

EE

DD

E

F

CC

I

FF

J

BB

AA

Z

X   Y

W   V

K

U

L

T

S

M

R

N

O

Q

LL

P

MM

RESTROOM
PHONE
WATER FOUNTAIN
FOOD
ICE CREAM AND SNACKS
STROLLER RENTAL

GOLF COURSE DRIVE

NORTH MACGREGOR DRIVE

13 The Houston Zoo

Off Golf Course Drive in Hermann Park (525-3300) The Houston Zoo has been transformed. There once was a time, Zoo people say, when visitors strolled through the gardens like wardens in a prison, but starting with a master plan in 1977, The Houston Zoological Gardens now increasingly reward visitors with animals in realistic habitats. In the Big Cat facilities this new education-based philosophy is reflected, where visitors, protected by Plexiglas partitions, get a close-up look at felines sunning themselves on a savannah-like plain. White tigers roam a virtual fiefdom decked out with waterfall and moat, and the hoofed animal facilities resemble genuine grazing grounds. Primates swing from the new Tree Top Pathway (open 1993). The Discovery Zoo—complete with petting zones—attracts the attention of smaller Zoo visitors.

Popular Attractions

Alligators prey on buckets full of fish at 2pm every Thursday and Sunday from April until September at the Alligator Pond.

Sea lions swim for brunch at 11am and 1pm, for supper every day at 3pm, in the Mammal Marina (near the Zoo entrance).

Zoo Programs

(525-3362 for Zoo programs) "It's Zooperb!" The new George R. Brown Education Center hosts art and science programs in its two classrooms, 300-seat auditorium and the surrounding zoological complex. Discovery Classes run from three-day "Summer Safaris" to two-hour "Discovery Saturdays." Young marine biologists have ventured into the habitats of underwater creatures in "Wet and Wild"; ten- to twelve-year-olds have followed the paths of animal migrations in "Tales of Trails." Prices generally run under $15 for the Saturdays and under $40 for Safaris. The Zoological Society puts on a "Caroling to The Animals" program early every December featuring area students. Other Zoo celebrations, like the "Pumpkin Patch Party" or "Zoobilee,"are limited to Zoological Society members, but the "Adopt an Animal" program buys you joint caretakership for any Zoo animal, with price levels determined by the animals' expense to the Zoo.

Admission to the Zoological Gardens $2.50, children under 13 $.50. *(Admisssion is free to members of the Houston Zoological Society. Membership for two adults: $25, Family memberships: $40.)* Open daily 10am-6pm.

Zoo map legend:

A	Aquarium Administration
B	Macaws
C	McGovern Mammal Marina
D	Reflection Pool
E	Tropical Birds
F	Flamingos
G	Cracids and Pheasants
H	Primates
I	(West) Hoofed Animals
J	Waterfowl
K	Lions
L	Gorilla Habitat
M	Bengal Tiger
N	Jaguars
O	Aquatunnel
P	Hatchery
Q	Discovery Zoo "Petting Zoo"
R	Cheetah
S	(East) Hoofed Animals
T	Rhinoceros
U	Bears
V	Small Cats
W	Siberian Tiger
X	Cougar
Y	Snow Leopard
Z	Hippopotamus
AA	Elephants
BB	Primates
CC	Alligators
DD	Chinese Alligator
EE	Giraffes
FF	Primates
GG	Reptiles
HH	Werler Garden
II	Fischer Bird Garden
JJ	Lemurs
KK	Brown Education Center
LL	Texas Wildlife Building
MM	Discovery Zoo Auditorium

Refer to map on pages 78-79

14 Hermann Park Stables
5716 Almeda Road near Hermann (529-2081) Occasionally you'll see people riding horses through Hermann Park. They have ridden over from the Hermann Park Stables, located just east of the park, and are accompanied by an instructor. Call for information on riding lessons, trail rides through the park or group rides.

16 Autry House
S. Main (524-3168) Autry House leads a double life as weekday cafe and tearoom—serving soups, sandwiches and salads—and as the Episcopal student center for the Rice University campus. Mon-Fri Lunch 11am-1pm.

17 Carl Moore Antiques
1610 Bissonnet (524-2502) European antiques and collectibles. Mon-Sat 9:30am-5:30pm.

18 C.G. Rein Galleries
1700 Bissonnet (526-4916) Contemporary paintings, sculpture, lithographs and serigraphs. Nineteenth-century European paintings and Chinese porcelain. Mon-Fri 9am-5:30pm, Sat 10am-5:30pm.

15 George Hermann
Bronze sculpture of one of Houston's major figures stands at the southwest corner of Hermann Park.

19 Surroundings
1710 Sunset Blvd. (527-9838) Surroundings will widen your eyes with huge bolts of Guatemalan striped fabrics, South American-inspired rugs, clothing, jewelry, glassware, Christmas ornaments and other myriad paraphernalia. This well-known shop's walls burst with upscale goods, like David Marsh handmade and hand-painted furniture, plus carefully selected American made stoneware and table linens inspired by traditional Latin American patterns. Mon-Sat 10am-5pm.

Refer to map on pages 78-79

20 Candlestick Antiques
2206 Bissonnet (524-1722) Furniture and collectibles.
Mon-Sat 10am-4pm.

21 Antique Associates
2214 Bissonnet (529-4497) Furniture and collectibles.
Mon-Sat 10am-4pm.

22 Traditions (Antiques)
2226 Bissonnet (520-1158) Eighteen-century and early nineteenth century English furniture. Mon-Fri 10am-4pm, Sat
2:30pm-5pm (Closed Sat June-August).

23 Que Milagro's
2238 Bissonnet (521-3591) Traditional mexican crafts and
accessories fill the rooms of Que Milagro's former
Southhampton abode. Walls are covered with milagros (evil-
repellent charms), ex-votos (inscribed, illustrated prayers) and
nostalgic Latin paintings. You'll also pore over Que Milagro's
varied collection of Day of the Dead figures, pre-Columbian
artifacts and glassware. Tue-Sat 11am-5pm.

24 Fred's Italian Corner
2278 W. Holcombe at Greenbriar (665-7506) The
Americanized-Italian kitchen takes a retro approach to Italian
food, but this fragrant little Medical Center spot does a brisk
business among the nurses and interns who drop by. Serve
yourself cafeteria-style at lunch, but at dinner it's full service.
Mon-Sat Lunch 11am-3pm, Dinner 5pm-9pm. Inexpensive.

25 Red Lion
7315 S. Main (795-5000) English specialties, such as kidney
pie and roast beef with Yorkshire pudding, and reliable steaks
play second fiddle here to the music venue. For many years,
the Red Lion has been a folk and acoustic music institution.
The upstairs room is so small and intimate it's more like an
attic than a bar. Irish Session Night, a low-key jam on
Wednesdays, is a Houston music tradition—all sorts of musicians show up to play a variety of instruments, from flutes to
mandolins. Shabbily genteel, it's even romantic, in a way.
Good pub. Mon-Fri 11am-11pm, Sat 4pm-11pm, Sun 4pm-
10pm. Reservations. Credit Cards, Moderate.

26 Stables Steak House
7325 S. Main (795-5900) and 3734 Westheimer. A throwback
to the steak 'n' potato days. Still, this is a welcome spot for
many who like their steak well prepared. The atmosphere is a
reminder of the 50s as well—dark, comfortable and friendly.
Mon-Thu 11am-10pm, Fri 11am-10:30pm, Sat 5pm-10:30pm,
Sun 5pm-9pm. Credit Cards, Moderate.

27 The Medical Center
See Medical Center, pages 90-97.

Lovett Hall is the centerpiece of the venerable Rice campus.

28 Rice University
3700 S. Main (528-5731) Rice University, a small (approximately 3200 students) private school, is recognized as one of the Southwest's most respected institutes for higher education. The school was established in 1912, when William Marsh Rice founded the Rice Institute, then a technically oriented school, anchored on "the advancement of letters, science, and the arts." And largely through Rice's endowment—now the ninth largest of any private university—the 300-acre university has grown steadily. Most departments at Rice are strong; a few stand out, Engineering, Architecture, Business Administration and Computer Science among them. The small number of students and the lush campus have created an atmosphere at Rice of a separate community, often referred to as "behind the hedges," where research and investigation are fostered.

Noted architects have contributed to the campus itself, including Cesar Pelli, Ricardo Bofill and the campus' original architect, Ralph Adams Cram. Cram drew up a masterplan for the campus in 1909 and designed the central building, Lovett Hall. At one time the entire student body could meet under the arched entryway—the sally port—of Lovett Hall. And then there's Rice Stadium, with 71,500 seats the largest stadium in Houston. Brown & Root built the stadium within the span of one year after the successful 1949 Rice Owl football season led boosters to act. The Owls won the Cotton Bowl that year, but have yet to do so again since moving into their mammoth stadium.

Galleries at Rice University
Sewall Art Gallery (527-6069) exhibition space for the Department of Art and Art History. Rice Design Alliance (524-6297) sponsors lectures, presentations and tours pertaining to architectural design and execution. Rice Media Center (527-3894) offers film and video arts exhibits. Call the above numbers for current activities, directions and times.

The Shepherd School of Music
Rice University Campus, Entrance 7 off Sunset Blvd.
(527-4854) Alice Pratt Brown Hall, the School's splendid new home, adds one acoustically-impeccable concert hall and three recital halls to Houston's score of music venues. Along with student recitals and the Syzgy new-music series, the halls also host Da Camera Society and Friends of Music chamber concerts. Brown Hall's colonaded entrance faces the football studium, making for an unintentional Texas metaphor. Call for performance dates and prices.

Once dubbed "William Rice's Marsh" because the treeless area would flood during harsh rains, the campus has matured over the years. In 1973, the Rice Prospectus quipped: "Rice has 2465 undergraduates, 611 graduate students, 322 professors, and 4783 trees." All but a few of those were planted by one man, an Italian Immigrant named Tony Martino. Martino planted most of the trees, scrubs and flowers on campus between 1916 and 1926—creating the campus we enjoy today.

Rice University is organized by residential colleges that serve as mini societies, including their own governments. Competition among the colleges can be keen. The annual Beer-Bike race (above) held in the spring on the stadium parking, is one such competition and has become popular enough to draw an off-campus crowd.

Refer to map on pages 78-79

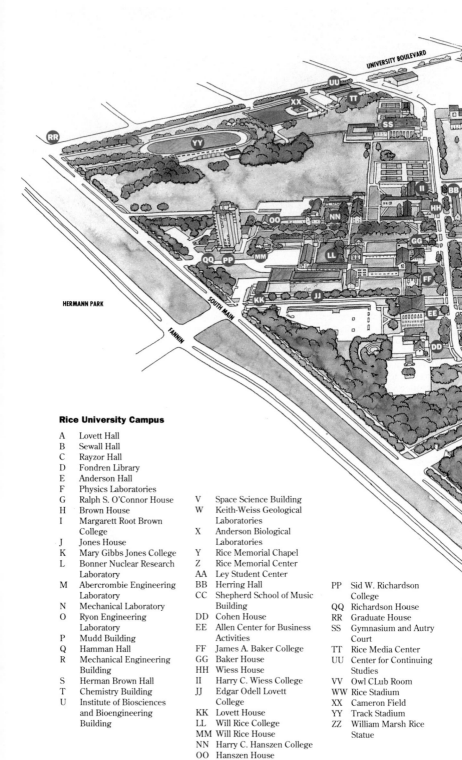

Rice University Campus

A   Lovett Hall
B   Sewall Hall
C   Rayzor Hall
D   Fondren Library
E   Anderson Hall
F   Physics Laboratories
G   Ralph S. O'Connor House
H   Brown House
I   Margarett Root Brown
    College
J   Jones House
K   Mary Gibbs Jones College
L   Bonner Nuclear Research
    Laboratory
M   Abercrombie Engineering
    Laboratory
N   Mechanical Laboratory
O   Ryon Engineering
    Laboratory
P   Mudd Building
Q   Hamman Hall
R   Mechanical Engineering
    Building
S   Herman Brown Hall
T   Chemistry Building
U   Institute of Biosciences
    and Bioengineering
    Building

V   Space Science Building
W   Keith-Weiss Geological
    Laboratories
X   Anderson Biological
    Laboratories
Y   Rice Memorial Chapel
Z   Rice Memorial Center
AA Ley Student Center
BB Herring Hall
CC Shepherd School of Music
    Building
DD Cohen House
EE Allen Center for Business
    Activities
FF James A. Baker College
GG Baker House
HH Wiess House
II Harry C. Wiess College
JJ Edgar Odell Lovett
    College
KK Lovett House
LL Will Rice College
MM Will Rice House
NN Harry C. Hanszen College
OO Hanszen House

PP Sid W. Richardson
    College
QQ Richardson House
RR Graduate House
SS Gymnasium and Autry
    Court
TT Rice Media Center
UU Center for Continuing
    Studies
VV Owl CLub Room
WW Rice Stadium
XX Cameron Field
YY Track Stadium
ZZ William Marsh Rice
    Statue

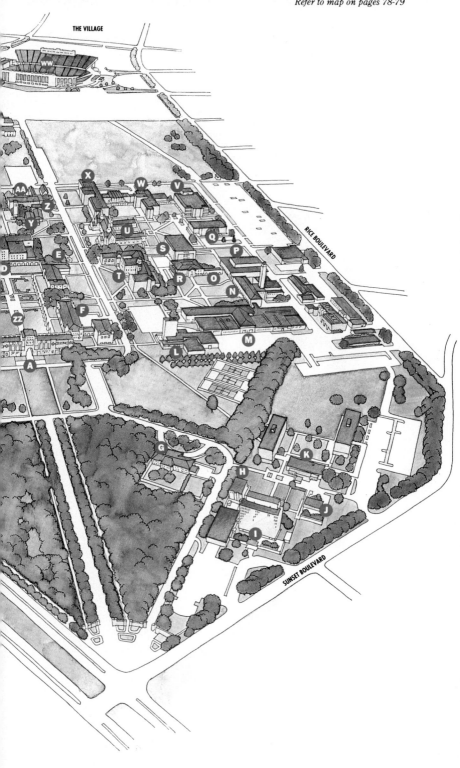

THE VILLAGE

RICE BOULEVARD

SUNSET BOULEVARD

The St. Luke's Tower looms over an ever-expanding Houston Medical Center.

MEDICAL CENTER

The Texas Medical Center is virtually a city within a city. From the 1930s, when Monroe D. Anderson, the wealthy Houston cotton broker, grew concerned over how to best use his fortune, the Medical Center has boomed faster than the surrounding city. Baylor College of Medicine moved here from Dallas in 1943, and since then the Med Center has grown into the largest complex of its kind in the world. It now has 41 member institutions covering more than 600 acres of land, attracting doctors and patients from all over the world and drawing almost $500 million in long-term research funding each year. The Center's importance to Houston is hard to overstate: almost 110,000 people pass through its doors every day; it employs over 51,000 Houstonians; and it indirectly impacts our economy to the tune of $9 billion a year. Its impact on the rest of the world has been felt as well: Dr. Denton Cooley made history at the Texas Heart Institute in 1968 as he performed the U.S.'s first successful heart transplant, and doctors on six continents watched as Dr. Michael DeBakey performed open heart surgery on live closed-circuit television.

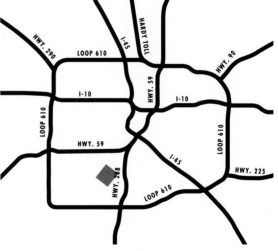

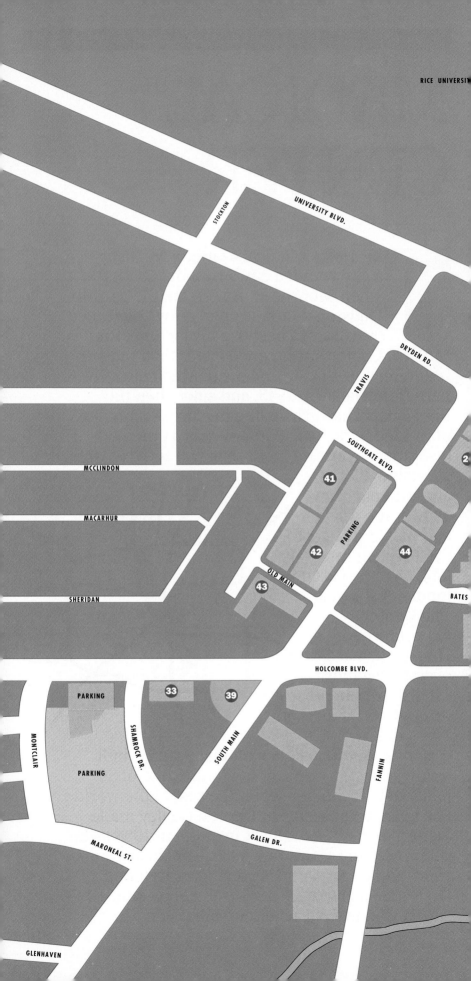

Looking over the vast Texas Medical Center with the Downtown Business District in the background.

1   Baylor College of Medicine

One Baylor Plaza (790-6474) Baylor College of Medicine is a dominating presence at the Texas Medical Center. The complex is affiliated with at least 20 institutions, only a few of which are listed below. Recognized as an institution independent of its parent university in 1969, Baylor appointed the eminent Dr. Michael E. DeBakey president. Now chancellor, Dr. DeBakey helped nurture the college to its present lofty international stature as one of the most respected medical schools in the United States. Admission to Baylor's student body is considered a true honor for any ambitious pre-med student. The college produces academic physicians, clinical specialists and biomedical researchers; most of its students enter primary care fields.

2   Ben Taub Research Center

1200 Moursund

3   Michael E. DeBakey Center for Biomedical Education and Research

1200 Moursund

4   TIRR (The Institute for Rehabilitation and Research)

1333 Moursund (799-5000) The Institute for Rehabilitation and Research opened in 1959 and offers "multi-disciplinary teams" to help patients cope with and overcome disabilities The facility has treated over 40,000 patients from all 50 states.

5   Baylor College of Medicine, Division of Allied Health Services; Jewish Institute for Medical Research

1200 Moursund

6   Fondren Brown Building

6535 Fannin

7   Alkek Tower/Brown Building

6535 Fannin

8   Smith Tower and Garage

6550 Fannin (790-6097)

9   Scurlock Tower and Garage: Sid Richardson Institute of Preventive Medicine

6560 Fannin (790-1198)

Refer to map on pages 92-93

10 Ben Taub General Hospital (old facility)
11 Ben Taub General Hospital (new facility)
1504 Taub Loop (793-2000) Ben Taub served its first indigent patients in the 1960s with funding from Harris County; today its vaunted trauma care facility handles over 93,000 emergencies per year, with a survival rate that's double the national average. As a county facility its emergency room stays hectic 24 hours a day, 365 days a year. Ben Taub's up-to-date 550-bed extension opened adjacent to the original facility in 1989.

12 The University of Texas-Houston Main Building
1100 Holcombe Blvd. (792-2121)
The University of Texas Health Science Center at Houston
1100 Holcombe Blvd. (792-2121) The Health Science Center operates eight units offering undergraduate, graduate and post-doctoral degrees in public health, medicine, dentistry, speech and hearing, nursing and allied health sciences—among others—to 2700 students each year. The center has taken an active role in transmitting research developments into the medical field, forming companies and operating several license agreements and partnerships. The Bioprocessing Research Center focuses on space commercialization of medical research with McDonnell Douglas.

13 The University of Texas Health Science Center Dental Branch
6516 John Freeman (792-4056)

14 The University of Texas Mental Sciences Institute
1300 Moursund (792-4847)

15 The University of Texas School of Public Health
1200 Herman Pressier Blvd. (792-4315) The School of Public Health offers four graduate degrees and serves as a national and international resource for educators, researchers and health professionals who are interested in current health issues such as environmental pollution, access to care, escalating medical care costs, chronic disease, nutrition and health, and violence and injury.

16 The University of Texas-Houston Medical School
6431 Fannin (792-2121) The UT Medical School may be dwarfed in size by the older Baylor institution, but this state school, established in 1969, has grown at quite a rapid rate. Primary teaching hospitals are Hermann and the Lyndon B. Johnson General Hospital, while maintaining relationships with many other area hospitals.

17 The University of Texas Speech and Hearing Institute
1343 Moursund (792-4600)

18 The University of Texas Graduate School of Biomedical Sciences
6901 Bertner (792-4655)

19 The University of Texas M.D. Anderson Cancer Center
6723 Bertner (729-2121) The first official member of the Texas Medical Center, M.D. Anderson Cancer Center was created by the State of Texas with help from the M.D. Anderson Foundation. When founded in 1944, less than 25% of cancer patients could hope for a cure; now the five-year survival rate for all forms of serious cancer at this respected facility surpasses 50%. M.D. Anderson Cancer Center, respected around the world as one of the top three cancer

There are many small restaurants, diners and cafeterias spread throughout the Medical Center.

Chez Eddy
6560 Fannin, on the fourth floor of the Scurlock Tower (790-6474) In the heart of the Texas Medical Center, this restaurant offers health food that died and went to heaven. The good news is that it's not for health nuts only but appeals to gourmands who enjoy seafood and wild game so masterfully prepared you won't even notice the missing salt and fats. Lunch Mon-Fri 11am-2pm, Dinner Mon-Fri 6pm-9pm. Reservations. Credit Cards, Expensive.

Refer to map on pages 92-93

centers in the United States, is a combination of research center, care-giving hospital and active outpatient program. Current studies at the center include "micro-encapsulated drug delivery systems," bone marrow transplant techniques and vaccines against specific kinds of cancer.

20 Methodist Hospital, Main Building

6565 Fannin (790-3311) The largest non-profit private facility in the nation, Methodist Hospital was founded in 1919 as a small, 90-bed facility edging the outskirts of downtown. In 1951, Methodist moved to the Med Center area, and now the 1527-bed hospital, affiliated with 35 health care institutions worldwide, admits over 35,000 inpatients and 800,000 outpatients on an annual basis. Its 3.3-million-square-foot, six-building complex (connected by crosswalks) dominates the Med Center's western fringe. Affiliated with Baylor College of Medicine, Methodist generates more than $30 million each year in research funding, much of it designated for the DeBakey Heart Center. Methodist is a leader in cardiovascular surgery, gastroenterology, internal medicine, organ transplants and neurosciences.

21 Methodist Hospital Patient Center, Dunn Tower

6565 Fannin (797-3311) The new John S. Dunn Tower building provides the most amenable patient environment available; its lobby is more reminiscent of a luxury European hotel than that of a hospital, and its patient rooms are state of the art.

22 Hermann Hospital; Jones Pavilion; Hermann Children's Hospital

6411 Fannin (797-4011) Hermann was established in Houston in 1925 as a private, nonsectarian hospital and later became one of the early members of the Texas Medical Center after M.D. Anderson Cancer Center and Baylor College of Medicine chartered the center in 1942. Life Flight, started by Hermann in the seventies, was the first civilian air ambulance service in the state; it has flown over 38,000 missions to date. The University Clinical Research Center, a University of Texas-affiliated project, makes headway in 17 areas, ranging from osteoporosis to blood clotting problems. Hermann operates a comprehensive burn unit and a significant kidney transplant center as well.

23 Hermann Professional Building

6410 Fannin (797-4890)

24 St. Luke's Episcopal Hospital

6720 Bertner (791-2011)

25 Texas Heart Institute

6655 Travis, Suite 300 (522-6118) St. Luke's Hospital's heart program mothered the Texas Heart Institute in 1962, and together the two facilities have performed countless open-heart and vascular procedures. St. Luke's heart transplant program remains one of the most successful in the nation.

26 St. Luke's Medical Towers

6624 Fannin (791-8081)

27 Texas Children's Hospital

6621 Fannin (770-1000) Texas Children's Hospital operates the most extensive pediatric residency program in the nation, and as it steadily increases its space devoted to critical and outpatient care, this Baylor-affiliated institution aims to become the largest pediatric medical complex in the United States.

28 Texas Children's Hospital Ambulatory Care and Research Facility

6621 Fannin (770-3491)

Refer to map on pages 92-93

29 Texas Children's Hospital Critical Care and Research Facility
6621 Fannin (770-6230)

30 Children's Nutritional Research Center
1100 Bates (798-7000) The center is part of Baylor College of Medicine and engages in research in the improvement of children's dietary regimes and in the needs of pregnant or nursing women.

31 Texas Woman's University
1130 M.D. Anderson Blvd. (794-2000) Texas Woman's University is the largest university for women in the United States. The multi-building facility, established in 1960, enrolls 1200 women in nursing, physical therapy, occupational therapy, nutrition and food sciences projects, plus health care administration, biology and psychology studies.

32 Shriner's Hospital for Crippled Children
1402 North MacGregor (797-1616) Shriner's 40-bed unit offers free care to any child with a treatable orthopedic problem and whose families cannot afford care. This hospital is famous for providing diagnosis and treatment to children of families from Texas, Mexico and Latin America.

33 Texas A & M University Albert B. Alkek Institute of Biosciences and Technology
2121 Holcombe Blvd. (677-7700) This new 11-story building provides facilities for research in biotechnology, human nutrition, comparative medicine and bioengineering.

34 Prairie View A&M University College of Nursing
6436 Fannin (797-0722)

35 University of Houston College of Pharmacy at Texas Medical Center
1411 Moursund (795-8343) The University of Houston College of Pharmacy offers graduate and undergraduate degrees, with an enrollment totalling approximately 240 students. Clinical service with other Med Center Institutions is offered in pharmaceutics, medical chemistry, pharmacology and pharmacy practice.

36 Diagnostic Hospital

37 Diagnostic Clinic of Houston

38 Visitor Information and Assistance Center
1155 Holcombe (790-1136) The center's volunteers give out information and maps and arrange tours of the Medical Center. Tours are by appointment only, and reservations should be made in advance due to the large demand. A seven-minute video on the various institutes and facilities in the Medical Center can be viewed at this location. Mon-Fri 8am-5pm.

39 Wortham Park
Corner of S. Main and Holcombe Blvd. (John Burgee Architects, 1991) Sitting on the grounds of the former Shamrock Hotel, a 650-foot-long rectangular water pool is divided by 23 concrete "water columns" ascending in height from 12.5 to 50 feet. The park, designed by New York architect John Burgee, challenges the imagination.

42 Majors Scientific Bookstore
6640 S. Main (522-1361) Services the professional/technical book needs of the Medical Center but is also a good source for the latest psychology or self-help book. Mon-Fri 8:30am-6pm, Sat 8:30am-5pm.

Medical Center Area Hotels

40 Marriott-Medical Center
6580 Fannin (796-0080)
26 stories, 389 rooms.
Double $99-$120, Concierge Level $120, Suite $225-$500.

41 Plaza Hilton
6633 Travis (524-6633)
19 stories, 420 rooms.
Double $99-$110, Suite $125-$145.

43 Harvey's Suites Hotel
6800 Main (528-7744)
12 stories, 285 rooms.
Double $89, Suite $85-$159.

44 Holiday Inn-Medical Center
6701 Main (797-1110)
10 stories, 301 rooms.
Double $69-$79, Suite $165.

A turquoise Thunderbird soars over the Hard Rock Cafe on Kirby.

KIRBY DRIVE AREA

Kirby Drive, from Westheimer to University Boulevard, is Houston's version of "Restaurant Row." Up-and-coming entrepreneurs have tried out new concepts here that have become some of the city's favorite spots, national restaurant chains have established popular outlets and every possible fast-food name is represented here as well. The street is home to Goode Company, Hard Rock Cafe, Cafe Express, Carrabba's and Dolce & Freddo, to name a few of the more crowded spots. Kirby Drive also takes one to The Village, a shopping area begun in 1938 next to the campus of Rice University. The city's first shopping "mall," The Village has fostered an eclectic group of local shops and restaurants over the years, only recently becoming a target of national retail chains. You can still stroll the streets of The Village, still park in front of the store you are visiting and still feel the small-town atmosphere The Village has always thrived on.

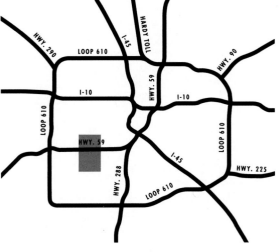

Refer to map on page 100

1   Avalon Drug Store
2518 Kirby (529-9136) It may look like a circa-1950 drugstore
lunch counter, with swivel stools, blue-plate specials and
irritable waitresses, but this Houston institution has long
been used as a second office by many of the city's movers
and shakers. Pecan waffles, grits, burgers and fountain drinks
are favored fare. In keeping with its old-fashioned atmosphere,
many regulars never touch money when they stop in—they
just sign their names. Drugstore: Mon-Fri 7am-7pm, Sat 7am-
5pm, Sun 8am-2pm. Grill: Daily 7am-4pm. Inexpensive.

2   River Oaks Grill
2630 Westheimer (520-1738) Since its takeover by the
Parlante family, the clubby ROG has improved dramatically.
Today it is home-away-from-home for many who come to
sup on the beautiful grilled items and lavish sauces. Keep a
sharp eye out, and you'll spot some serious power-brokering.
Dinner only, Mon-Thu 6pm-10:30pm, Fri-Sat 6pm-midnight.
Reservations. Credit Cards, Expensive.

3   Chuy's Comida Deluxe
2706 Westheimer (524-1700) The yuppied and the restless
meet in this outrageously tacky Tex-Mex cantina, an Austin
import. Despite the din and the inescapable sexual heat,
the food is actually pretty good, with portions the size of a
hacienda. Sun-Thu 11am-11pm, Fri-Sat 11am-midnight.
Credit Cards, Inexpensive.

4   André's Swiss Confiserie and Tearoom
2515 River Oaks Blvd. (524-3863) Breakfast, prix fixe lunch
and dinner with varying menu. Fabulous Swiss bakery, specialty quiche Lorraine. Tue-Fri 8:30am-8pm, Sat 8:30am-5pm.
Inexpensive.

5   River Oaks Country Club
1600 River Oaks Blvd. (529-4321) Seated at the heart of River
Oaks, this exclusive club plays host to The River Oaks Tennis
Tournament every April, its only public event.

6   Brownstone
2736 Virginia off Westheimer (520-5666) The kitchen has seen
a number of defections over the past few years, so it's hard to
say what direction the menu is currently taking. Even so, the
setting—elegant and crammed full of froufrou and antiques
(many of them for sale)—is wonderfully inviting for a ladies'
lunch or intimate evening. Mon-Sat Lunch 11:30am-2:30pm,
Mon-Sat Dinner 6pm-10:30pm, Sun Brunch 11am-2:30pm.
Reservations. Credit Cards, Moderate.

*The flash and dash that is
Chuy's starts at the front
entrance.*

7   River Oaks Garden Club Forum of Civics
2503 Westheimer (523-2483) This 1910 building was updated
in the twenties by John Staub to reflect The Forum of Civics'
role as promoter of urban responsibility. The exquisite gardens behind the building help kick off the Azalea Trail each
year. Mon, Wed and Thu 10am-3:30pm.

8   Shanghai River Restaurant
2407 Westheimer (528-5528) David and Sanne Wang's menu
is fairly traditional in most respects, but many of the Hunan
and Szechuan dishes have a little extra oomph that sets them
above the norm. There's also attention to presentation —
clever carved-vegetable flowers or a fried noodle basket that
might be mistaken for the real thing. Sun-Thu 11am-10:30pm,
Fri-Sat 11am-11:30pm. Credit Cards, Inexpensive.

9   Antique Pavilion
2311 Westheimer (520-9755) The space that was home to
many famous Hart Gallery auctions now houses 90 antique
dealers with a far-ranging selection. Daily 10am-6pm.

Refer to map on page 100

10 French Gourmet Bakery
2250 Westheimer (524-3744) and other locations. This bakery has been producing fresh breads, cakes, pastries and hand-crafted chocolates in Houston for 20 years. They're probably best known for the buttercakes and sponge tortes with delectable fillings and chocolate toppings. Mon-Fri 7am-5:30pm, Sat 8am-5pm.

11 Jalapeño's
2702 Kirby (524-1668) Spinach enchiladas and garlic snapper are two of the out-of-the-ordinary specialties available at this Mexican restaurant that resembles a seaside cantina. It gets boisterous during happy hour, but brunch is very pleasant. Mon-Thu 11:30am-10:30pm, Fri-Sat 11:30am-11:30pm, Sun 11:30am-10pm, Sun Brunch 11:30am-2:30pm. Credit Cards, Inexpensive.

12 The Executive Sweet
2720 Kirby (522-6155) Excellent goodies for those who are feeling thin and in need of chocolate or other sweet things. The chocolate cheesecake is just sweet enough; try the hot fudge sundae if you are in the mood to really binge. Mon-Thu 11am-11pm, Fri-Sat 11am-midnight, Sun 5pm-10pm.

13 Hard Rock Cafe
2801 Kirby, near Westheimer (520-1134) Legions of rock 'n' roll groupies come to study the walls adorned with memorabilia—the guitars of Rusty Hills, BB King and Harry Wilson, early concert posters for the Beatles, clothing worn by John Lennon and such. The next attraction is the shop where the Hard Rock T-shirts, caps and jackets are sold. Finally there is the food, which is good enough: hamburgers and salads, with homemade pie for dessert. Sun-Thu 11:30am- midnight, Fri-Sat 11:30am-1am. Credit Cards, Inexpensive.

14 Beck's Prime
2902 Kirby (524-7085) and 2615 Augusta Drive. This home-grown chain of upscale fast-food outlets offers some of the best burgers, grilled fish sandwiches and milkshakes in town. Drive through like the name says or laze on the deck at one of the picnic tables; the Augusta location, in particular, is a real beauty snuggled under centuries-old oaks. Mon-Sun 11am-midnight.

15 AD Players
2710 W. Alabama (526-2721) The people at AD Players describe themselves as having a "Biblical world view." Box office is open by phone or in person Mon-Fri 9am-5pm, with phone lines open during productions.

16 Carrabba's Italian Restaurant
3115 Kirby (522-3131) The wait for a table at this friendly cucina can be an hour or more. The draw: first-rate pastas, salads, pizza and grilled chicken, and a staff that really hustles. Go before you're hungry—and take earplugs. Mon- Thu 11am-11pm, Fri 11am-midnight, Sat 11:30am-midnight, Sun noon-10pm. Credit Cards, Moderate.

17 Café Express
3200 Kirby (522-3994) and 1800 S. Post Oak in The Pavilion. High-tech delis with full bars and pretty patios from the Cafe Annie team. Chicken salad with pistachios is a passion for many fans, and the desserts are divine. Just be careful not to over-order, as it's easy to get carried away. Sun-Thu 10am-11pm, Fri-Sat 10:30am-midnight. Credit Cards, Inexpensive.

Refer to map on page 100

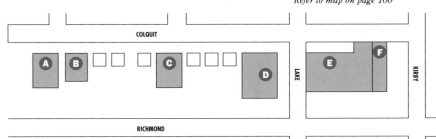

18 Colquitt Area Galleries

Often when one gallery in this cozy little arts enclave has an opening, they all do. It makes for a nice evening, walking from one gallery to the next.

A   Moody Gallery
2815 Colquitt (526-9911) Presents paintings, sculptures, photographs and works on paper by contemporary American artists with emphasis on Texas artists. Tue-Sat 10am-5:30pm.

B   Artables Craft Gallery
2811 Colquitt (528-0405) Fine crafts gallery featuring clay, wood, fiber and glass. Tue-Sat 10am-5pm.

C   Lynn Goode Gallery
2719 Colquitt (526-5966) Contemporary painting and three-dimensional art. Tue-Sat 10am-5:30pm, except Thu 10am-7pm.

D   McMurtrey Gallery
3508 Lake (523-8238) Exhibits by regional artists specializing in still life, narrative, abstract and some photography. Tue-Fri 10am-5:30pm, Sat 10am-5pm.

D   Parkerson Gallery
3510 Lake (524-4945) Specializing in nineteenth- and twentieth-century European and American art. Tue-Fri 10am-5pm, Sat noon-5pm, Mon by appointment.

D   Robinson Gallery
3514 Lake (526-0761) Specializing in nineteenth- and twentieth-century American art. Tue-Fri 10am-5:30pm, Sat 10am-4pm.

E   New Gallery
2639 Colquitt (520-7053) Gallery featuring nationally and internationally prominent contemporary artists, predominately painters and sculptors. Tue-Sat 10:30am-5pm.

E   Judy Youens Gallery
2631 Colquitt (527-0303) Houston's only major exhibitor of glass works of art. Also showings by national painters, photographers and some wood sculptors. Tue-Fri 10am-5:30pm, Sat 11am-5pm.

E   Davis/McClain Gallery
2627 Colquitt (520-9200) Dealers of contemporary American and European painting, sculpture and photography including works by major international artists and emerging artists. Mon-Fri 10am-5:30pm, Sat 11am-5pm.

F   Radio Music Theater
2623 Colquitt (522-7722) Comedy club with a local flavor. The troupe that acts here puts on routines that more times than not incorporates local people and issues. Nice club and quality acts. Thu-Fri 8:30pm, Sat 8:30pm and 10:50pm. Reservations necessary. Box office open Tue-Sat 11am-7pm.

19 Bertolotti Cucina Italiana
2300 Richton off Kirby (524-3354) Stefano Bertolotti's Northern Italian eatery handles seafood beautifully, as well as gnocchi, filled pastas and veal. Good choice for business entertaining; the Richton location is romantic as well. Lunch Mon-Fri 11am-2:30pm, Dinner Mon-Thu 5pm-10pm, Fri-Sat 5pm-midnight. Credit Cards, Moderate.

Refer to map on page 100

20 Little Pappasito's
2536 Richmond (520-5066) Flavorful, tender fajitas are their specialty, with wonderful borracho beans and huge servings. One of the best margaritas in town. Sun-Wed 11am-10:30pm, Thu 11am-11pm, Fri-Sat 11am-midnight. Credit Cards, Moderate.

21 Ninfa's
3601 Kirby Drive (520-0203) and other locations. Many have tried, but none have equaled Mama Ninfa's original green sauce. Loaded on chips or dribbled over the combination platter, it manages to be both cool and incendiary at the same time. Mon-Thu 11am-10pm, Fri 11am-11pm, Sat 8am-11pm, Sun 8am-10pm. Credit Cards, Inexpensive.

22 McGonigel's Mucky Duck
2425 Norfolk (528-5999) Though it started out as mostly a folk venue, a lot of well-known local and regional rockers play here as well. The louder bands can be a little overwhelming in such a small club, but the quieter folk singers create an atmosphere conducive to a quality dating experience. An outdoor patio has added some needed breathing space, and for those who don't like to sit still, you can play darts in a small room behind the main bar. Covers on Friday and Saturday approximately $5. Mon-Fri 11am-2am, Sat noon-2am.

23 Houston's
4848 Kirby (529-2385) and other locations. This small national chain practices a red-white-and-blue variety of edible ethnicity. The menu is even innocent of most California and Cajun influences, offering a short list of lavish entree-sized salads, classic burgers and decadent desserts. The air is always buzzing, the place full of life. Sun-Thu 11am-11pm, Fri-Sat 11am-midnight. Credit Cards, Inexpensive.

24 Goode Company Seafood
2621 Westpark near Kirby (523-7154) Set back off Kirby a bit, this seafood diner is every bit as good as its two nearby siblings. The daily crowds—expect a long line and a parking hassle, especially at lunch—are more proof of this city's insatiable appetite for mesquite-grilled shrimp, gumbo, catfish and oyster po'boys. Mon-Thu 11am-10pm, Fri-Sat 11am-11pm, Sun noon-10pm. Credit Cards, Inexpensive.

25 Goode Company Hamburgers and Taqueria
4902 Kirby (520-9153) Breakfast-lovers create a traffic jam most weekends trying to squeeze in here for the migas (Mexican-style scrambled eggs), quail and eggs, and chocolate cinnamon shakes. The rest of the time, the grill serves up some of the best burgers around, along with Tex-Mex basics. Sit outside on the patio long enough, and you'll see most of Houston drop by eventually. Mon-Fri 11am-10pm, Sat-Sun 7:30am-10pm. Credit Cards, Inexpensive.

Refer to map on page 100

26 Goode Company Barbeque
5109 Kirby (522-2530) Jim Goode looks the way Yankees think a good ol' boy Texan should look, but he cooks better than your mother. Out-of-towners who want to eat real Texas food should be accompanied to one of his two barbecue outposts (the other at 8911 Katy Freeway) for irresistible chicken, brisket, duck and pork. Don't pass on the jalapeno cheese bread or pecan pie, either. Daily 11am-10pm. Credit Cards, Inexpensive.

27 Actors' Theatre of Houston
2506 South Boulevard (529-6606) Chris Wilson's troupe does well by the classics and takes all the dramatic risks it can afford. Office hours Mon-Sat 10am-10pm. Call for programming information.

28 Murder by the Book
2342 Bissonnet (524-8597) "Where a good crime is had by all" is their motto. This small specialty bookstore has a monthly meeting of the Murder by the Month Club. Mon-Sat 10am-6pm, Sun noon-5pm.

29 Kay's Lounge
2324 Bissonnet (528-9858) Watering hole for local academic, corporate, media and medical personalities, not to mention the average blue collar. Mon-Sat 2pm-2am.

30 Jack Meier Gallery
2310 Bissonnet (526-2983) Presenting contemporary paintings, sculptures and works on paper by predominantly regional artists. Tue-Fri 9am-5:30pm, Sat 10am-4pm.

31 Detering Book Gallery
2311 Bissonnet (526-6974) Deals in used, rare and out of print hardback books of general humanities. Daily 10am-6pm.

32 The Volcano
2349 Bissonnet (526-5282) Local bar down the street from Kay's and behind more sheet metal than should be allowed in the neighborhood. Mon-Fri 5pm-2am, Sat-Sun 8pm-2am.

33 Brazos Bookstore
2421 Bissonnet (523-0701) Many say this is the finest bookstore in Houston. Owner Karl Kilian pays special attention to Houston's writers and photographers, often hosting book signing parties in this homey, gallery-style shop on Bissonnet. Great art and fiction sections. Often discounts bestsellers by 25%. Mon-Fri 10am-6pm, Sat-Sun 10am-5pm.

34 Third Planet Books
2439 Bissonnet (528-1067) Collectibles, and lots of them. Every grown child's dream of old baseball cards, rare comic books and lots of Trekkie memorabilia. Mon-Wed and Sat 10am-7pm, Thu-Fri 10am-8pm, Sun noon-6pm.

Refer to map on page 100 and page 107

35 Sunset Tea Room
2606 Sunset Blvd. (666-9032) In its early days, this quiet spot drew mostly ladies for light lunches and tea. Today, the menu is broader, and there are plenty of men among the diners. King Ranch casserole, quiche, fresh fish and beef regularly turn up on the rotating menu. Daily Lunch 11am-2:30pm, Dinner Tue-Sat 5:30pm-9:30pm. Inexpensive.

36 Onyx Books & Other Unearthly Delights
2502 Sunset Blvd. near Kirby (522-6699) New Age tomes on the shelves and baskets of crystals surround you, while the lunch-only kitchen sends out daily vegetarian specials. Inexpensive. Mon-Fri 10am-6pm, Sat 10am-5pm.

37 Gremillion & Co.
2501 Sunset Blvd. (522-2701) Contemporay American art. Tue-Fri 9am-5pm, Sat 10am-5pm.

38 Dolce & Freddo
5515 Kirby near Sunset (521-3260) and 7595 San Felipe near Voss (789-0219) If you're hip enough, these sleek espresso bars are the place for cappucino, unpronounceable gelati and enough attitude dancing to last the week. Popular way to finish off an evening on the town. Sun-Thu 11am-midnight, Fri-Sat 11am-1am. Inexpensive.

39 Crown & Serpent
5731 Kirby (528-1158) The college crowd sometimes gets so loud that the rock-and-roll is hard to hear, but a few of the local bands that play at the Crown & Serpent manage to rise above the roar. It's a hoppin' singles scene on weekends. Covers when applicable are in the $2-$5 range. Mon-Fri 4pm-2am, Sat-Sun 5pm-2am.

40 Stop, Look and Learn
2415 Robinhood (528-6508) Tucked away on this side street is a terrific bookstore for children and their parents. Some toys as well as supplies for teachers. Mon-Fri 9:30am-5:30pm, Sat 9:30am-4:30pm.

41 The Village
Houston's first "mall," the Village was established in 1938 next to Rice University. Today it is a diverse group of homegrown shops and restaurants.

A French Gourmet Bakery & Cafe
2484 Bolsover (528-3647) Try not only the delicious cakes and pastries here, as at the Westheimer location, but also the freshly prepared soups, salads and quiches. Mon-Fri 7am-6pm, Sat 8am-5:30pm, Sun 9am-2pm.

B House of Coffee Beans
2520 Rice Blvd. (524-0057) A cornucopia for the senses awaits coffee and tea lovers at House of Coffee Beans, one of Houston's oldest and finest gourmet coffee shops. Behind aromas of 80 home-roasted coffees and 40 tea varieties lies an excellent selection of coffee-addict's paraphernalia: porcelain mugs, the best European coffee makers, teapots and an array of imported shortbreads. Mon-Fri 10am-6pm, Sat 10am-5pm.

C The Bagel Manufactory
2438 Rice Blvd. (520-ROLL) Need a little nosh? More than a dozen varieties of jaw-massaging bagels, as well as cream cheese spreads and sandwich fillings (e.g., pastrami, egg salad, corned beef), are the raison d'être at this industrious Village deli. Mon-Fri 7am-6pm, Sat 8am-6pm, Sun 8am-3pm. Inexpensive.

Refer to map on page 100 and page 107

TANGLEY

DUNSTAN

Ⓐ

BOLSOVER

Ⓑ Ⓒ Ⓓ Ⓔ

RICE BOULEVARD

Ⓕ Ⓖ Ⓗ Ⓘ Ⓙ

KIRBY   KELVIN   Ⓞ   MORNINGSIDE   CHAUCER   GREENBRIAR

Ⓚ Ⓛ Ⓜ Ⓝ

TIMES BOULEVARD

Ⓟ Ⓡ Ⓣ

Ⓠ

Ⓢ Ⓧ

AMHERST

Ⓤ

Ⓥ Ⓦ

UNIVERSITY BOULEVARD

Ⓨ Ⓩ

SHAKESPEARE

D   Iowa and Guatemala

2422 Rice Blvd. (520-5650) Iowa/Guatemala boasts an eccentric display of handcrafted items; half the store's floor space is reserved for the finest Americana—quilts, rag dolls and wooden cutouts from the heartland—while the remainder is a showplace of handwoven cotton sweaters, linens and hand-made toys from Central America. The proprietor of this happily schizophrenic boutique hails from (you guessed it) Iowa. Mon-Sat 10am-6pm, Sun noon-4pm.

E   British Market

2366 Rice Blvd. (529-9889) If it's made in England, the British Market probably carries it. You'll find everything from Walker's shortbread, tea biscuits, cottled cream and Yorkshire pudding to Spode china, Irish linen tablecloths and obligatory Royal Family photographs. Mon-Sat 9am-6pm, Sun noon-5pm.

F   Croissant-Brioche

2435 Rice Blvd. (526-9188) Breakfast is the real draw here, taken on an outdoor table with a stack of newspapers. At lunch or dinner, try a soup, salad or ham-and-cheese croissant. Mon-Sat 7am-7pm, Sun 7am-3pm. Credit Cards, Inexpensive.

G   Houston Potters Guild Shop

2433 Rice Blvd. (528-7687) A group of Houston potters has formed a co-op to market their handmade work. High-quality functional and decorative crafts. Special commissions can be ordered. Mon-Sat 11am-6pm.

H   Kahn's Deli

2429 Rice Blvd. (529-2891) The sandwiches are thick and the meat is always fresh at this old-fashioned spot. Although it's almost too small to support its many loyalists, at least one ex-New Yorker says Kahn's is his favorite Houston deli. Mon-Fri 10am-3pm, Sat 10am-4pm. Inexpensive.

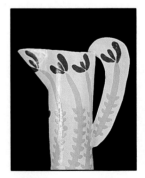

A Ritva Grunberg pitcher from the Houston Potters Guild.

Old Dolph's location

2525 Rice Blvd. across from the House of Coffee Beans. On the site of this now-defunct restaurant is a small bit of sports memorabilia left over from a former sports bar. Next to the sidewalk is a row of concrete squares with the shoe and hand impressions of former sports stars Earl Campbell, Bum Phillips, Ralph Sampson, Nolan Ryan, Robert Brazile, Calvin Murphy, Elvin Bethea and Artis Gilmore (whose size 18 basketball shoe prints are worth standing in).

I   Variety Fair 5 & 10

2415 Rice Blvd. (522-0561) Owner Ben Klinger has helped Houstonians celebrate every holiday from Halloween to President's Day for over 40 years. Paper and plastic turkeys, heart-shaped stickers and paper doilies, tiny American flags and cards for every occasion overflow from the shelves of this tiny dime store year round. One never knows what might pop up from along the narrow aisles. A sift through the Valentine cards might uncover a love token that's been hiding 20 years. Great toys and candy too. Mon-Sat 9am-6pm.

J   The Allegro Italian Bakery & Cafe

2407 Rice Blvd. (526-4200)and other locations. The original Village location of this expanding chain is a busy place on weekend mornings as joggers, *New York Times* readers and groups of friends crowd this little bakery for croissants and cappucino. The menu is limited to baked goods, sandwiches and omelettes, and the service is often slow, but any location is reliable for take-out. Mon-Sat 7am-9pm, Sun 8am-6pm. Credit Cards, Moderate.

K   Ovations

2536 Times Blvd. (522-9801) A tiny two-story club, in a 1930s-era building, manages to draw the elite from Houston's jazz and classical music communities. The beautiful lighting and thoughtful interior design make the space feel much larger than it is. This is the place for a truly classy night on the town. Covers are $4-$7. Sun-Thu 7pm-1am, Fri-Sat 7pm-1:30am.

L   Main Street Theater

2540 Times Blvd. (Box Office 524-6706) Tries everything from the Bard to broad comedy with varying degrees of success. Box office: Tue-Sat 11am-6pm, Sun noon-4pm.

M   G&G Model Shop

2522 Times Blvd. (529-7752) G & G is the model maker's paradise, the land of milk and honey for imaginary engineers of miniscule trains, assemblers of Stealth Fighter replicas, drafters of plans for lilliputian utopias and drivers of small-world cars and boats. The knowledgeable staff at G & G takes the trade perfectly seriously, handing out helpful advice to model builders at no charge. Mon-Wed and Fri 10am-6pm, Thu 10am-7pm, Sat 10am-5pm.

N   Shiva Indian Restaurant

2514 Times Blvd. (523-4753) Solid, good-value Indian specialties have more variety here than at most Indian restaurants. The setting is colorful, too, with purple predominating and cozy red banquettes curtained with strands of seashells. Lunch Mon-Fri 11:30am-2:30pm, Sat noon-3pm, Brunch Sun 11:30am-3pm, Dinner Sun-Thu 6pm-10pm, Fri-Sat 6pm-11pm. Credit Cards, Moderate.

O   The Bead Shop

2476 Times Blvd. (523-9350) The Bead Shop specializes in unusual beads from around the world, from Austrian crystal to tiger's eye, in every imaginable size, shape and price. Create your own earrings, design your own necklaces and craft unique bracelets; the Bead Shop will even assemble your masterpieces upon request, if you wish. So many rows of glass cases bursting with beads in this tiny shop titillate the imagination. Mon-Sat 10:30am-6pm.

P   Le Peep

6128 Village Parkway (523-PEEP) and other locations. Serving just breakfast and lunch, this Denver-based chain of country-cottage cafes has been called the perfectly executed concept. Huge portions suggest the menu was written by giants, though the home-style pancakes, waffles and sausage taste as though they were prepared by someone's grandma. Mon-Fri 6:30am-2:30pm, Sat-Sun 7am- 2:30pm.

Q   Cafe Chino

6140 Village Parkway (524-4433) Popular, small Chinese restaurant that can take a while to get seated in. Tasty corn soup, chicken with cashews. Mon-Thu 11am-10pm, Fri 11am-10:30pm; Sat noon-10:30pm, Sun noon-10pm. Credit Cards, Moderate.

Refer to map on page 100 and page 107

R Nash D'Amico's Pasta and Clam Bar
2421 Times Blvd. (521-3010) Tiny local Italian spot with a friendly crew, enjoyable fare and a very busy bar. More talking than eating during the early evening hours. Mon-Thu 11am-10pm, Fri-Sat 11am-11pm. Credit Cards, Moderate.

S Prego's
2520 Amherst (529-2420) Imagine a California-Italian menu with Southwestern overtones. That's the offering of chef John Watt at this comfortable and trendy little eatery. Lunchtime parking can be scarce. Mon-Thu 11:30am-10pm, Fri 11:30am-11pm, Sat noon-11pm, Sun 5pm-11pm. Reservations. Credit Cards, Moderate.

T Calypso
5555 Morningside (524-8571) Pan-Caribbean cuisine is the calling here. Try the jerk chicken (Jamaica), stamp & go (Trinidad), coconut-battered shrimp (Caymans) or picadillo (Cuba). Nice patio and occasional live steel band music, too. Mon-Thu 11:30am-10pm, Fri 11am-midnight, Sat 10am-midnight, Sun 10am-10pm.

U La Madeleine French Bakery & Cafe
6205 Kirby (942-7081) and other locations. These popular bakery/restaurants serve an eclectic crowd who've come to dine on a great Caesar salad, traditional quiches and French pochettes. Cappuccino and fresh pastries as well. Daily 6:30am-10pm. Moderate.

V Iconography
2552 University (529-2630) It's back to the drawing board at Iconography, where unique postcards, stationery items, colorful printed papers, greeting cards, unusual pens and personalized rubber stamps greet customers. A hallmark of this idiosyncratic shop is its highly specialized cards for every conceivable occasion — like one in particular spotted recently: "congratulations on your new car!" Mon-Fri 10am-7pm, Sat 10am-6pm, Sun noon-5pm.

W World Toy & Gift Shop
2404 University (522-9257) The greatest attraction in World Toy & Gift remains a fascinating (and very extensive) array of dollhouse furniture and miniatures—like tiny chandeliers, miniscule oriental rugs, even diminutive claw-footed porcelain bathtubs. Assuredly the finest such collection in Houston. Maintains a china and porcelain repair service as well. Mon-Sat 9am-6pm.

X Aquarian Age Bookshelf
5603 Chaucer (526-7770) Here you'll find the most comprehensive collection of new age literature in town, including volumes on shamanism, the Hindu Vedas, Bhagavad Gita interpretations, holistic medicine journals and general works on philosophy and meditation. A western text might even catch your eye here or there. Also an excellent selection of cookbooks. Mon-Sat 11am-7pm.

Y Fu's Garden
2539 University (520-7422) George and Jenny Phou now have two Fu's Gardens (also at 5866 San Felipe), both swathed in acres of floral wallpaper and offering a rich, lacquered elegance. Terrific Hunan menu and a friendly staff that is kind to children. Mon-Thu 11am-10pm, Fri 11am-11:30pm, Sat noon-11pm, Sun noon-10pm. Credit Cards, Moderate.

Z Trattoria Pasquale
2325 University (665-6116) Owner Pasquale Bosco is from Sicily, and the kitchen at this unpretentious little cafe reflects that regionalism. Seafood and pastas are always reliable, and there's a good use of garlic. Lunch Mon-Fri 11am-2pm, Dinner Mon-Thu 5:30pm-10:30pm, Fri-Sat 5:30pm-11pm. Credit Cards, Moderate.

The world-famous
Astrodome during an
Astro baseball game.

ASTRODOME AREA

The Astrodome put Houston on the map. *The* map. No longer would Walter Cronkite feel compelled to utter "Texas" after mentioning "Houston," no longer was our town seen as an old-west backwater. Houston had little to call attention to itself before NASA in the mid '60s, before the Med Center took on its prominence. That is, until two local power brokers—Judge Roy Hofheinz and R.E. "Bob" Smith—got together to develop some raw land on south Kirby. The result was the "Eighth Wonder of the World," and indeed, it was a wonder. The Harris County Domed Stadium was the largest indoor arena ever built and retained that title for a decade while sparking a nation-wide building

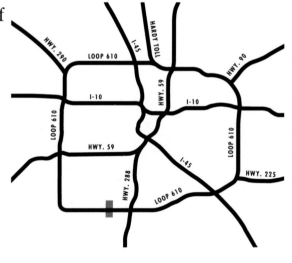

spree in covered stadiums. The Dome also sparked the building of a major entertainment complex: Astrohall and Astroarena are adjacent to the stadium, while theme parks AstroWorld and WaterWorld are just a walk away.

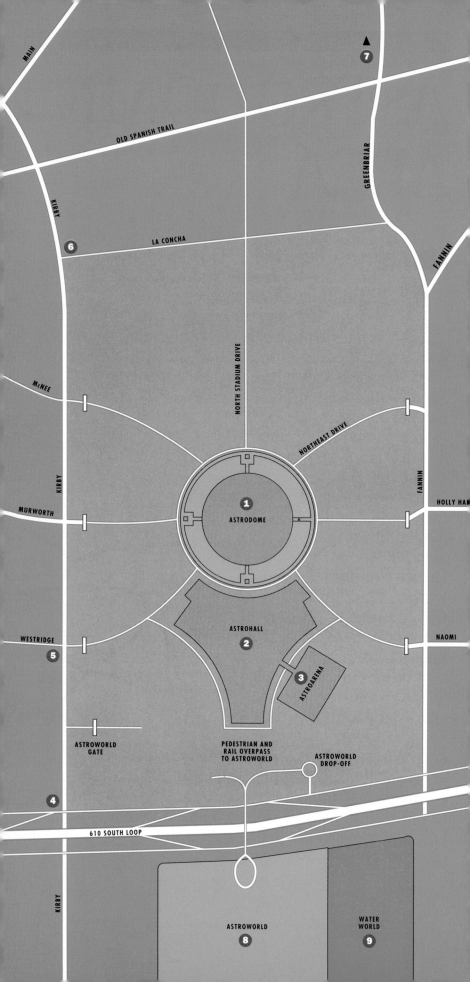

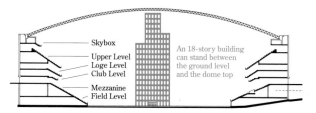

Skybox
Upper Level
Loge Level
Club Level
Mezzanine
Field Level

An 18-story building
can stand between
the ground level
and the dome top

1 The Astrodome

8400 Kirby at Loop 610 (799-9595 or 799-9555) (Hermann Lloyd & W.B. Morgan and Wilson, Morris, Crain & Anderson, 1965) The Harris County Domed Stadium, known as the Astrodome, was labeled the "Eighth Wonder of the World" when it opened in 1965. The Astrodome was the brainchild of local entrepreneur, politician and promoter Judge Roy Hofheinz who championed the idea of a domed stadium and who saw it to realization with the ample backing of Robert E. "Bob" Smith. A brochure prepared for the grand opening of the Dome praised "the biggest project of its kind ever built, the largest indoor arena in the world, the largest clear-span building ever constructed, the world's largest air-conditioned stadium, the first major league stadium with a roof over it, and the first all-purpose, weather-free combined sports stadium and convention center." The structure revolutionized stadium design and put Houston solidly on the nation's sports map. (And began the never-ending argument about grass vs. synthetic turf.) Given our heat and humidity, not to mention the occasional mosquito, the Dome made watching baseball and football games in Houston downright comfortable. The fear of a sudden downpour washing out a game was also eliminated. (Of course, there is always an exception to every rule: on June 15, 1976, a game between the Pittsburgh Pirates and the Houston Astros was called because heavy rains and street flooding kept all but 800 souls away from the game.) When the stadium opened, one of the main attractions was a 474-foot-long scoreboard that literally exploded with sound and lights when something good happened to the home team. The scoreboard was destroyed in a 1989 remodeling of the Dome when additional seats were added. **AstroTurf** When the Astrodome first opened, it had a traditional grass field. Everyone was convinced that the sunlight coming through the Dome's glass-paneled roof would be sufficient to cultivate a regular field of grass. As with other aspects of the Dome, no one *really* knew, because no one had ever tried it before. While the grass was struggling to make it inside, the outfielders who were playing on it were struggling even more. Routine pop flies to the out-field were routinely dropped as the fielders had trouble seeing the ball amid the tremendous glare caused by the sun shining through the panels. To rectify the situation, thin coats of gray paint were sprayed over the panels, cutting the glare while keeping the panels translucent. The fielders could see the ball well, but the grass died. To cover up this new problem, the dying brown grass was spray-painted green. As luck would have it, however, Judge Hofheinz heard of a synthetic turf that had just been invented and was being tested on a very small scale at a school in Rhode Island. The company developing the turf had been in no rush to put their new product on the market before being contacted by Hofheinz. Pushed by the Judge, the infant product was refined and installed for its first real test on the floor of the Dome in three short months. Two and a half months later, March 30, 1966, the first major league game—an exhibition game between the Dodgers and the Astros—was played on what was to be called AstroTurf.

Astrodome Tours A one-hour tour that includes the press facilities, sky boxes, a trip out onto the field and an 18-minute film on the history of the Dome. Daily (except when pre-empted by event) 11am, 1pm, 3pm (also 5pm summer). Admission $3.25, seniors $2.75, children under 4 free. (Add $4 to park at the Dome.)

The first baseball game played indoors: the opening exhibition game between the Houston Astros and the New York Yankees, April 9, 1965. Mickey Mantle hit the first home run; however, the Astros won the game 2-1.

First indoor football game: September 11, 1965, the University of Houston Cougars played the University of Tulsa.

A bloodless bullfight took place in the Astrodome in February 1966.

On January 20, 1968, the University of Houston defeated UCLA 71-69 in the Dome before a record crowd to see a basketball game: 52,693. The nationally televised game featured a legendary matchup between future NBA all-stars Elvin Hayes and Lew Alcindor (Kareem Abdul Jabbar).

Evel Knievel survives a record jump of 13 cars in the Dome before 41,857 tense patrons on January 9, 1971.

Refer to map on page 112

**Astrodome Seating—
Baseball**

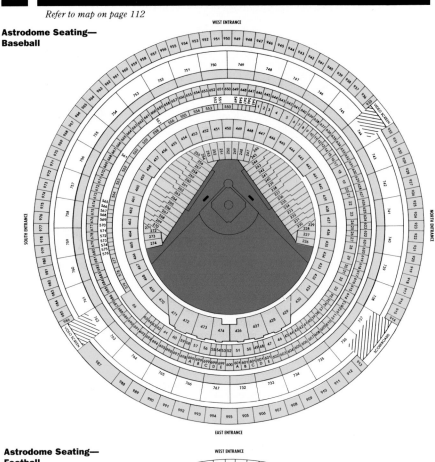

**Astrodome Seating—
Football**

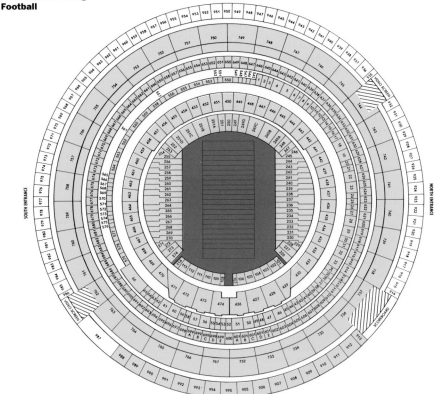

Refer to map on page 112

Houston Astros

The Astrodome, 8400 Kirby at Loop 610 (799-9500) The major league Houston Astros baseball team plays an 82-game season in the Western Division of the National League, 41 of the games at home in the Astrodome.

The Astros began in 1961 when the Houston Sports Association bought the minor league Houston Buffs ball club and after a national contest drawing over 12,000 entries, changed the name to the Houston Colt 45s. The team played for a year in the minor league American Association before entering the National League in 1962. The team won their first game in the major leagues, defeating the Chicago Cubs 11-2 in Houston. While the name was a natural for a Texas team, the company that made Colt .45 pistols objected, and in 1965 the name was changed to the Astros to coincide with their new stadium. The Astros—at press time—have never made it to the World Series. In 1980 the team won their division for the first time with a one-game playoff victory over the Los Angeles Dodgers. The Astros eventually lost to the Philadelphia Phillies three games to two in one of the most exciting playoff series ever played. The Astros won their division again in 1986 when Mike Scott threw a no-hitter against the San Francisco Giants to clinch the title. They eventually lost to the New York Mets in the National League playoffs.

Houston Oilers

The Astrodome, 8400 Kirby at Loop 610 (797-1000 or 799-9555) The Houston Oilers football team plays a 16-game schedule in the National Football League's AFC Central Division. Eight of the games, plus some pre-season and hopefully post-season games, are played at home in the Astrodome.

The Oilers were founded in 1959, one of the six charter members of the American Football League. K.S. "Bud" Adams, who still owns the team, contracted to play the team's first games in Jeppesen Stadium on the University of Houston campus. The Oilers won their first regular season game—37-22 over Oakland—and eventually the first championship of the fledgling AFL by defeating the Los Angeles Chargers 24-16 at Jeppesen Stadium on January 1, 1961. The Oilers were flush with success during the early days of the AFL, winning the championship the first two years and their division the third year before losing the title to the Dallas Texans in an historic six-quarter game (20-17). In 1966 the American Football League and the National Football League agreed to merge, which led to the creation of the Super Bowl, a game the Oilers have yet to play in. The Oilers won their division for the first time as part of the NFL in 1991. (Even during the "LuvYaBlue" period from 1978-1980, the Oilers failed to win their division.)

2 Astrohall

Next to the Astrodome, 8400 Kirby at Loop 610. Astrohall is a 550,000-square-foot exhibition area used for a variety of conventions and trade shows. It is the home of the various livestock during the annual Houston Livestock Show & Rodeo.

3 Astroarena

Next to the Astrodome, 8400 Kirby at Loop 610. Astroarena is a stadium-type facility that hosts events ranging from horse shows to tennis matches.

6 Sports Page

8111 Kirby (790-1900) A very lively sports bar in the Holiday Inn, where fans go before and after games at the Dome, or while the game is on if they were not lucky enough to snag a ticket. Eight screens help the crowd keep up with various games. Mon-Sat 11am-2pm (food service stops at midnight), Sun noon-midnight.

Astro All-Stars

Dick Farrell, 1962, 64, 65
Hal Woodeshick, 1963
Joe Morgan, 1966, 70
Claude Raymond, 1966
Mike Cuellar, 1967
Rusty Staub, 1967, 68
Jimmy Wynn, 1967
Larry Dierker, 1969, 71
Dennis Menke, 1969, 70
Don Wilson, 1971
Cesar Cedeno, 1972, 73, 74, 76
Lee May, 1972
Bob Watson, 1975
Ken Forsch, 1976
Joaquin Andujar, 1977, 79
Terry Puhl, 1978
Craig Reynolds, 1979
Joe Niekro, 1979
Joe Sambito, 1979
Jose Cruz, 1980, 85
J.R. Richard, 1980
Bob Knepper, 1981, 88
Nolan Ryan, 1981, 85
Ray Knight, 1982
Dickie Thon, 1983
Bill Dawley, 1983
Jerry Mumphrey, 1984
Mike Scott, 1986, 87, 89
Kevin Bass, 1986
Glenn Davis, 1986, 89
Dave Smith, 1986, 90
Jeff Bagwell, 1991
Craig Biggio, 1991

Retired Oiler Jerseys

Jim Norton, #43
Record-setting punter and safety for nine seasons (1960-68) and a part of the 1960 championship team.

Elvin Bethea, #65
Played 135 consecutive games as defensive end starting in 1968, eventually playing 210 games in his 16 seasons. This team leader was honored with an "Elvin Bethea Appreciation Night" in 1983.

Earl Campbell, #34
The team's all-time favorite player, Earl rushed for more than 1000 yards his first three seasons, winning the NFL's rushing and MVP awards. Adding his pro career to his outstanding Texas high school and college accomplishments, the Texas Legislature saw fit to designate Earl a Texas Legend, joining Davey Crockett, Sam Houston and Stephen F. Austin.

The Texa
roller co
Astrowo
attractio

Refer to map on page 112

8 AstroWorld and WaterWorld

Loop 610 at the Fannin exit (799-1234) Six Flags' Astroworld sits just across the freeway from the Astrodome complex. The 75-acre amusement park attracts about 2.5 million visitors (with WaterWorld) each year, making it Houston's largest tourist attraction. The huge Texas Cyclone roller coaster is Astroworld's most popular ride, drawing thousands of riders a year. According to "experts," it's among the very best of the country's wooden coasters. Certainly Astroworld's great inventory of speedy, thrilling rides ranks among the best: The Greezed Lightnin', Ultra Twister, The Looping Starship, XLR-8 (read: accelerate), The Condor and The Viper are each nerve-wracking in its own way. Calmer souls might enjoy the puppet show by Hollywood producers Sid and Marty Krofft or maybe a film on the domed screen of The Horizons Theater. The Southern Star Amphitheater supports the park's appeal to older fun-seekers with contemporary, country and Christian music performances, held throughout the year. "Fright Nights," gentle (but spooky) family-oriented evenings in the Halloween spirit, are hosted in October. Astroworld openings vary with Houston's unpredictable weather, but count on a weekend in March. Everyday operations stretch from Memorial Day to Labor Day, and the general closing falls in late October/early November. Ticket prices hover around $20.95 plus tax for adults and $14.95 plus tax for children 54 inches tall and under; two-day tickets are $23.95 plus tax for children three years of age and older, and children under three are admitted free. Season tickets are also available. Staffers at Guest Relations will escort disabled visitors through the park. Summer hours Mon-Sat 10am-10pm, Sun 10am-8pm.

9 WaterWorld

Loop 610 at the Fannin exit (799-1234) WaterWorld, a 14-acre park neighboring Astroworld, brings heat relief and "imitation beach" to a young Houston clientele every summer. Assorted water-laden rides run the gamut. One of the more thrilling experiences—The Edge—flings visitors from a tower hundreds of feet down into a blue, water-filled pool below. Breaker Beach creates beach-like waves with a man-made wave system. Thunder River gives paddlers a whitewater experience with 20-foot-wide rafts running on an artificial Colorado River. Volleyball or tanning by the pool are options as well. The facilities at WaterWorld include Men's and Women's locker rooms and a restaurant, The Beachcomber. It's a summer park, so wait until May for weekend openings; weekday openings generally coincide with the end of the school year. If you are going to Astroworld, you may upgrade your ticket to include WaterWorld for $5 plus tax. Otherwise, single-day tickets hover around $11.95 plus tax for adults, $10.12 plus tax for children 54 inches tall and under; two-day tickets are $23.95 plus tax, and children under three are admitted free. Staffers at Guest Relations will escort disabled visitors. Summer hours Mon-Sat 10am-10pm, Sun 10am-8pm.

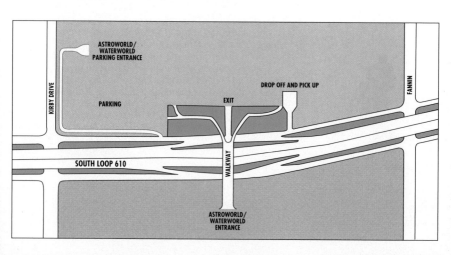

SHEPHERD AREA

This is an area of shopping plazas. Next to the enclave of River Oaks mansions, the River Oaks Center offers one of the city's few commercial areas that invites outdoor walking and window browsing. Shows and restaurants bring people here as well, who then stroll along the palm-tree-lined plaza. Further south, the freshly built Shepherd Square at Westheimer contrasts with the 1950s Alabama Plaza across the street. This plaza's Alabama Theater building now houses Bookstop, the city's largest bookstore. Even further south, the Shepherd Plaza houses an eclectic mix of trendy restaurants, roadside diners, art boutiques and specialty stores.

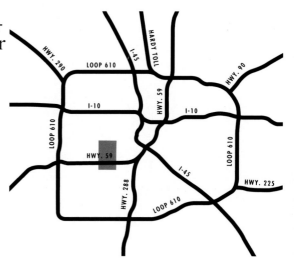

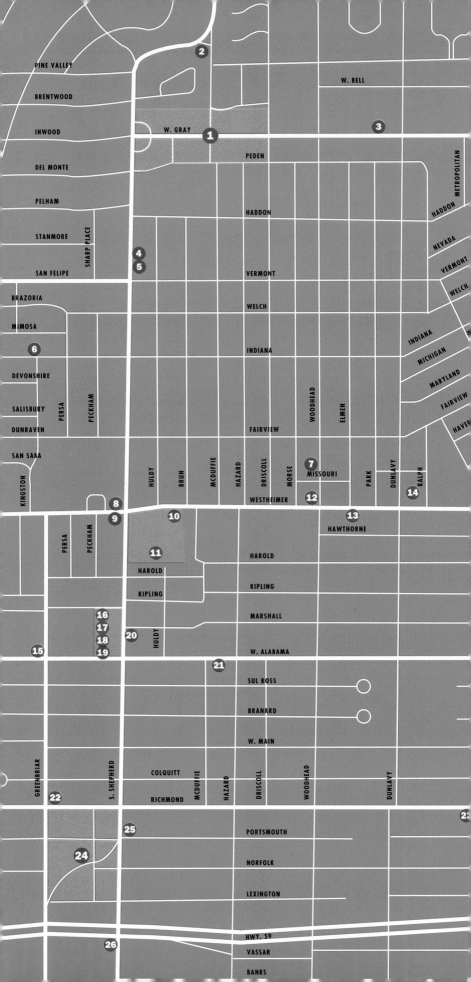

Refer to map on page 120

5 Armando's
1811 S. Shepherd (521-9757) A flashy crowd eats at this
lively semi-Mexican, semi-Italian restaurant on River Oaks'
southern border. Cozy and a little boisterous inside, on a nice
night you might prefer to sit outside next to the busy street
and watch the valets park the procession of designer cars.
Good food, better people-watching. Lunch Mon-Fri 11am-2pm,
Dinner Sun-Tue 5pm-10pm, Wed-Sat 5:30pm-11pm.
Reservations recommended. Credit Cards, Moderate.

6 The Women's Institute of Houston
2202 Avalon Place (529-7123) Academic and Liberal Arts eso-
terica are pursuits in the Women's Institute curriculum; the
non-profit organization heralds from times when intellectual
women's curiosity enjoyed less welcome than today. Institute
classes study Florentine architecture in "Florence, an anatomy
of the Athens on the Arno" and anticipate "Fiscal Fitness in the
90s." These are mostly daytime classes, not limited to women.
Mon-Thu 9am-4pm, Fri 9am-noon. Call for information.

7 John Holt Antiques
2416 Woodhead (528-5065) Elegant Spanish and Italian
antique furniture pieces, silver objets d'art from South
America and elsewhere. One room of the Holt enterprise is
reserved for santos, carved and painted devotional statues
replicating the family of Catholic saints. Mon-Thu 11am-10pm,
Fri-Sat 11am-11pm, Sun 11am-9pm.

8 St. Anne's Church and School
*Church 2120 Westheimer, School 2140 Westheimer (Church
526-3276, School 526-3279)* Site of the annual Italiana Fiesta,
a three-day celebration of food and games. Alcohol is served,
but this is a family picnic and the crowds come to eat and
people watch.

9 Cafe Adobe
2111 Westheimer (528-1468) This Mexican restaurant
featuring unremarkable Tex-Mex and some regional Mexican
dishes is known less for its food than as an after-work meeting
spot. On fine days, ask to be seated on the lovely, plant-filled
patio. Lunch Mon-Fri 11:30am-2pm, Dinner Mon-Thu 6:30pm-
10pm, Fri-Sat 6:30pm-10:30pm. Reservations. Credit Cards,
Moderate.

10 Churrascos
*9788 Bissonnet, US 59 and Beltway 8 (541-2100) and 2055
Westheimer at Shepherd (527-8300)* Opening at their original
Bissonnet location, Nicaraguan brothers Michael and Glenn
Cordua introduced a new wrinkle in Houston's love affair
with Latin food, proving there is life beyond Tex-Mex. Even
if beef doesn't ordinarily move you, order the namesake
churrascos, a simple centercut tenderloin sauced with the
robust chimichurri sauce of olive oil, parsley and garlic.
Equally remarkable is the wine list, which will appeal to
pennypinchers with sophisticated tastes. Mon-Fri Lunch
11:30am-2pm, Mon-Thu Dinner 6pm-9:30pm, Fri- Sat 6pm-
10pm, Sun 6pm-8:30pm. Reservations. Credit Cards, Moderate.

11 Brentano's
*2055 Westheimer in Shepherd Square (523-4011) and The
Galleria (961-1091)* This bookstore stands out among
Houston booksellers by offering special ordering services
customarily found only with small "college town" book
handlers. If you're looking for hard-to-find or one-of-a-kind
cookbooks, historical treaties or photography glossies,
then this well-stocked retailer will handle your needs, even
including greeting you with a cup of gourmet coffee for your
browsing pleasure. Mon-Sat 10am-9pm, Sun noon-6pm.

11 Randall's Flagship
*2055 Westheimer in Shepherd
Square (284-1200).* This is
not your run-of-the-mill grocery store. This is a bakery,
deli, coffee bar, pharmacy,
meat and fish market, floral
shop, cosmetic center, video
store and restaurant all inside
a very large grocery store.
During the Christmas season
a large grand piano graces the
entrance area, filling the store
with seasonal music. Their
slogan "your remarkable
store" is true. Open 24 hours.

12 Pasternak's Emporium

2515 Morse at Westheimer (528-3808) Architectural remnants and antiques, from stained-glass windows to brass plumbing fixtures, large one-of-a-kind fireplace mantels to delicate, Victorian gingerbread trim. Great place for a weekend browse. Mon-Sat 10am-6pm, Sun noon-5pm.

13 Antique Co-Op Area

1700 block of Westheimer. An area of antique shops that has grown up around a building holding a co-op. The stores here change often, but there is always a big enough collection of shops to make stopping worthwhile.

14 Dream Merchant

1658 Westheimer (520-0076) Vintage '60's and look-alike contemporary threads are a throwback to those radical times; this is the place to get your Easy Rider biker get-up, including anything in leather—boots, vests, studded jackets, hats, even tanned underwear—and authentic chain jewelry, sunglasses, etc. Mon-Wed 11am-7pm, Thu-Sat 11am-8pm, Sun noon-6pm.

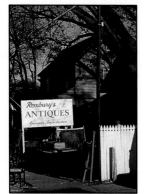

Along the Antique Co-op area on Westheimer.

15 A Moveable Feast

2202 W. Alabama near Greenbriar (528-3585) It's a good name, for this health-food restaurant/store really has moved around a bit since starting in 1971. Pimento-cheeseless sandwiches, vegetarian Tex-Mex, no-meat "happy burgers" and smoothies are among the possibilities. Daily 9am-10pm. Inexpensive.

16 Whole Foods Market

2900 S. Shepherd (520-1940) Whole Foods Market, an Austin-grown company, landed in Houston in 1984. The stores bill themselves as merely a "natural foods supermarket," but the hordes of yuppies and housewives flocking to this store testify that something different is up here. Everything at Whole Foods is strictly organic; you'll encounter the best pesticide-free produce, only hormone-free beef, an extensive line of natural vitamins and a deli and coffee counter that's to die for. Daily 9am-10pm.

17 Bookstop

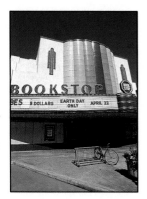

2922 S. Shepherd (529-2345) Bookstop's main home in Houston's old Alabama Theater makes this giant book warehouse worthy of note. An erstwhile grand matron of local movie houses, and one of only a handful of silver screens in town in the forties and fifties, the old theater today houses what is easily the largest bookstore in Houston, a discount bookseller that at any one time may have over 100,000 volumes in the store. Also features very large magazine and computer sections. Daily 9am-midnight.

18 Whole Earth Provision Company

2934 S. Shepherd (526-5226) Whole Earth Provision Co. stands apart among outdoor equipment suppliers; the roots of this funky, eclectic nature store stretch back to the late sixties in Austin, when owners Jack and Linda Jones began selling camping gear to Hill Country hippies. Now Whole Earth sells the best brands of tents, backpacks, telescopes, street clothes and outerwear—like Moss, the North Face, Dana Designs, Celestron, Patagonia and Royal Robbins— mixed in with a maddening potpourri of toys, children's books, maps, travel guides and incense burners. Mon-Fri 10am-9pm, Sat-Sun 10am-6pm.

19 Butera's

2946 S. Shepherd (528-1500) What began as a deli counter in John Butera's grocery on Bissonnet has become two trendy meeting places for yuppies and intellectuals dining on salads, pastas and imported waters. Mon-Sat 10:30am-10pm, Sun 10:30am-8pm. Inexpensive.

20 Little Pappas Seafood Kitchen
3001 S. Shepherd (522-4595) and other locations.
Straightforward fried-seafood chain, also from the Pappas
family (Pappasito's, Pappadeaux, Pappamia, etc.). Exceptional
Greek salads. Lunch Mon-Fri 11am-2:30pm, Sat-Sun 11am-
4pm, Dinner Sun-Thu 5:30pm-10pm, Fri-Sat 5pm-11pm.
Credit Cards, Inexpensive.

21 West Alabama Ice House
1919 W. Alabama (528-6874)
Ice houses have been a Houston
staple for years and have followings that are usually neighborhood oriented. If you're
hankering to visit one of these
open-air bars, the West Alabama
Ice House, opened in 1927,
would be a good place to start.
In good weather, the bar is completely open, with people standing near or sitting on bar stools,
picnic tables and parked cars.

22 The Pig Live
2150 Richmond at Greenbriar (524-0696) Formerly the Pig 'n'
Whistle. A couple of bartenders pooled their money, bought
the club themselves and simplified the name. Located in a
charming old house with big windows, The Pig is roomy
enough so that you can converse upstairs even when a loud
rock band is playing downstairs. The local and regional acts
usually draw a mid-twenties crowd. $5 cover on the weekend.
Weekday cover depends on band. Daily noon-2am.

23 Munchies
1617 Richmond (528-3545) For the most eclectic open-mike
night in town, don't miss Tuesdays at Munchies. From country
to folk to blues (and from terrible to fantastic), the open-mike
acts are often surprisingly good. Some weeknights are devoted
to small-ensemble classical music, but weekends are usually
reserved for good ol' rock-and-roll. Regardless of the music,
the atmosphere is always extremely laid back. Mon-Fri 11am-
2am, Sat-Sun 4pm-2am.

24 Shepherd Plaza
At Richmond, Shepherd and Greenbriar
Remodeled and restocked with some
very interesting shops and restaurants.
A Blue Water Grill
2181 Richmond (526-7977) The whole
point at this jazzy, boldly designed
newcomer is seafood, and the East-
meets-West kitchen handles it well,
offering a satisfying slate that ranges
from grilled escalare to barbecued
oysters to scallops with a to-die-for
curry sauce. Sun-Thu 11am-10pm,
Fri 11am-11pm, Sat 5pm-11pm. Credit
Cards, Moderate.
B Cent'Anni
*2128 Portsmouth, between Greenbriar
and Shepherd (529-4199)* It's been
accused of trendiness, but there's no
denying the good pizzas from the
wood-burning oven and terrific pastas
turned out by owner Walter Aymen's
kitchen. One of the city's most beautiful
bars is also here, as is a very civilized
weekend brunch. Mon-Thu 11am-
11pm, Fri-Sat 11am-midnight, Sun
11am-10pm. Credit Cards, Moderate.

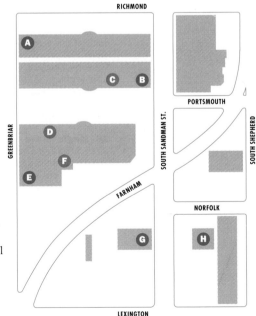

Refer to map on page 120

C   The Yoga Institute
2150 Portsmouth (526-6674) Since 1974, The Yoga Institute has offered competent instruction in mental house-cleaning to willing Houstonians. Body movement, stretching, breath, exercise, meditation and relaxation will "bring out the mellow" after the Institute's six-week seminar. A classical bastion of Hinduism The Yoga Center isn't, however: the Institute lays claim to the disciplines of Buddhism, American Indians, Shintoism and Christianity following the tradition of St. Augustine. An eclectic mix. Bookstore: Daily 7am-9pm. Classes (at different levels of skill—call for details): Mon-Fri 9am, 5:30pm, 7pm; Sat 9am, 10:30am.

D   Deep Texas
2173 Portsmouth (526-2464) Forties and fifties western furniture and accessories and some foodstuff. The perfect place to pick up a Texas gift package for those who aren't so lucky to live in the great state. Mon-Wed 10am-6pm, Thu-Fri 10am-8pm, Sat 10am-7pm.

E   8.0
3745 Greenbriar (523-0880) Spandex on the women and ponytails on the men is practically de rigueur at this self-righteously hip scene. Happily, the prices are low and the pop-eats food is fairly healthful—the menu ranges from steamed veggies with brown rice to very good burgers to chili—but in the end, 8.0 is more about after-dark cruising than dining. Whatever, just don't take this place too seriously. Daily 11am-2am. Inexpensive.

F   The Compleat Gardener
3810 Farnham (942-8880) A one-stop gardening experience; perennials, tropical and exotic plants, birdfeeders, baskets, birdbaths and plenty of gardening gifts. Wonderful Saturday morning stop. Daily 10am-7pm.

G   59 Diner
3801 Farnham (523-2333) Good roadside food and a culinary trip down memory lane have equal appeal at this 1950s-style diner that features plastic booths, old-fashioned soda fountain and daily blue-plate specials. Smart choice for kids. Sun-Thu 6:30am-11pm, Fri-Sat 7am-midnight.

H   Star Pizza
2111 Norfolk (523-0800) and 140 S. Heights Blvd. It's true Star offers everything from calzone to lasagna, but it's the pizza—and more particularly Joe's Pizza, a spinach-and-garlic favorite—that has ensured its fame. Mon-Thu 11am-9:30pm, Fri-Sat 11am-10pm. Credit Cards, Inexpensive.

25   Rockin Robin Guitars and Music
3619 S. Shepherd at Richmond (529-5442) The single Mecca for Houston's gear and equipment-seeking musicians. The walls of this warehouse-style building on Shepherd, open since 1972, are decked out with hundreds of hanging guitars—Gibsons, Fenders, Ovations and some vintage classics—so it's little wonder the store enjoys an exclusive reputation. Drums, cymbals, keyboards and amps can also be found in this throwback to the seventies. Mon-Wed and Fri 10am-7pm, Thu 10am-9pm, Sat 10am-6pm, Sun noon-6pm.

26   Magic Island
2215 Southwest Freeway (526-2442) More of an entertainment experience than a restaurant, Magic Island has various magic shows and up-close demonstrations. The acts and the format change, but if you like disappearing birds or sleight-of-hand card tricks, this is the place. Shows Mon-Thu 9:30pm; Fri 8:30pm, 9:30pm and 10:30pm; Sat 8pm, 9pm, and 10pm.

HIGHLAND PARK-GREENWAY PLAZA

During Houston's go-go years, Kenneth Schnitzer's Century Development Company was busy building a complex on the Southwest Freeway that would rival some downtowns. Greenway Plaza was conceived as a master-planned office, residential, shopping and entertainment complex, and although such grand plans are rarely fulfilled, this project came close. The Summit, the 17,000 seat sports stadium that houses the Houston Rockets, is the focal point of Greenway Plaza. A little north is a project typical of development in Houston's earlier days: Highland Village's '50s style arrangement of stores along Westheimer that boast some of the city's more interesting shops and restaurants.

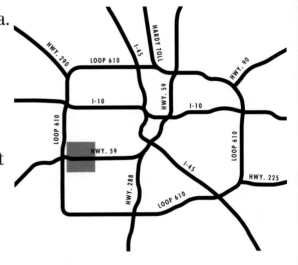

Refer to map on pages 128-129

Rocket Retired Jerseys
Hanging from the rafters at the Summit are two banners with retired Rocket jersey numbers:

Calvin Murphy, #23
The Rockets' all-time favorite player, Calvin had a spectacular 12-year career in Houston. Although the smallest man in the league for much of his career, Murphy averaged more than 20 points a game in five seasons, set free-throw shooting records and made the All-Star Team in 1979.

Rudy Tomjanovich, #45
A five-time All-Star, Rudy T was a scoring leader for 11 seasons as a Rocket, averaging over 50% shooting for his career.

1   The Summit

10 Greenway Plaza (961-9003) (Kenneth Bentsen, Lloyd, Jones Associates, 1976) Built in 1976 as part of the Greenway Plaza master plan by Kenneth Schnitzer's Century Development Corporation. Because the arena is part of a large office and retail development, there is plenty of free parking for sporting and entertainment events. Access is easy as well, from the Southwest Freeway (US 59) exiting at Kirby, Edloe or Wesleyan. The Summit seats 16,275 for basketball games and 17,000 for concert events; as many as 2 million patrons come to see 175-185 events every year.

Houston Rockets

10 Greenway Plaza (627-2115 or 627-0600) The Houston Rockets basketball team, a member of the Western Conference of the major league National Basketball Association, plays an 82-game schedule, 41 games being played at home in Houston in The Summit.

    The Rockets were founded in 1967 in San Diego, the twelfth team to join the NBA. The team was moved to Houston in 1971 and began playing in The Summit in 1975. The team has never won the NBA championship but has played in the finals twice, losing to the Boston Celtics 4-2 in the 1981 finals and again by the same score in 1986. Moses Malone led the team in 1981, the twin towers of Hakeem Olajuwon and Ralph Sampson were the team leaders in 1986.

Rocket All-Stars

Elvin Hayes, 1969, 70, 71, 72
Don Kojis 1968, 69
Moses Malone 1978, 79, 80, 81, 82
Jack Marin 1973
Calvin Murphy 1979
Hakeem Olajuwon 1985, 86, 87, 88, 89, 90, 91, 92
Ralph Sampson 1984, 85, 86, 87
Rudy Tomjanovich 1974, 75, 76, 77, 79
Otis Thorp 1992

The Summit Seating

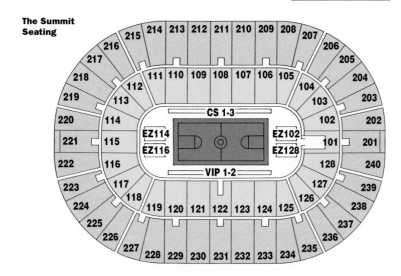

2 Stouffer Presidente Hotel

6 Greenway Plaza East (629-1200) 20 stories, 389 rooms. Double $120-$155, Suite $245-$525. Easy access to The Summit and the rest of Greenway Plaza.

3 Greenway Theater

5 Greenway Plaza East in the Underground (626-0402) A three-screen theater specializing in foreign-language and out-of-the-mainstream films. Home base to WorldFest, the international film festival held in Houston every spring.

4 Maxim's

3755 Richmond in Greenway Plaza (877-8899) This swanky Archi-Digest spot appeals to the city's bluebloods and old money. The Creole-American kitchen is not all that it might be—though the Charlie Belle salad is excellent—but most regulars, many of whom eat here several times a week, don't seem to mind. Mon-Sat 11:30am-10:30pm, Sat 6pm-11pm. Reservations. Credit Cards, Expensive.

5 INNOVA

10 Greenway Plaza (961-9003) (Cambridge Seven and Lloyd Jones Brewer & Associates, 1984) A gleaming headquarters to interior and furnishing suppliers, the home of the local chapter of the AIA and a popular meeting and conference center.

6 Bering's

3900 Bissonnet (665-0500) Bering's carries everything one expects to see in an everyday hardware store but offers one of the best gift and housewares departments in Houston. Limoges boxes, Herrend china, Lalique crystal and unusual picture frames sit under the same roof that shelters hoes, rakes, fertilizers and lawn loungers. And Bering's gourmet section offers high-end blenders and kitchen toys, like Braun coffee makers and coveted Kitchen Aid blenders. Also: myriad flavors of coffee beans, chocolates and bonbons. Mon-Sat 8:30am-6:30pm, Sun 11am-6pm.

7 Cleburne Cafeteria

3606 Bissonnet (667-2386) Fans who mourned Cleburne's disastrous fire a few years ago were much relieved when the owners decided to rebuild this popular family-run cafeteria from the ground up. Today, yet another generation is developing a habit for the wholesome American food that includes squash casserole, broiled chicken, carrot salad and turkey with dressing. Popular among the older set. Mon-Fri Lunch 11am-2:30pm, Dinner 4pm-8:30pm, Sun 11am-8:30pm (Closed Sat). Inexpensive.

8 Luby's Cafeteria

5215 Buffalo Speedway (664-4852) This San Antonio cafeteria chain has many outlets in the Houston area, all with large and loyal followings. The Buffalo Speedway location has a constant line, day in and day out. Daily 10:45am-8:30pm, Inexpensive.

9 Molina's Mexican Restaurant

5227 Buffalo Speedway (432-1626) and other locations. Molina's began in Houston in 1941 when founder Raul Molina left James Coney Island (where he was a cook and dishwasher) to start his first restaurant. The various Molina's are owned by different family members today, but all serve a familiar brand of Tex-Mex. Mon-Fri 11am-10pm, Sat 9am-11pm, Sun 9am-10pm. Credit Cards. Inexpensive.

10 Buffalo Grille

3116 Bissonnet at Buffalo Speedway (661-3663) The patio has become a popular see-and-be-seen spot for locals from West University Place who flock here for enormous pancakes (one is enough), peppered bacon and French toast. Lunch is also served, but no dinner. Mon-Fri 7am-2pm, Sat-Sun 8am-2pm. Credit Cards, Inexpensive.

Refer to map on pages 128-129

11 Houston Camera Exchange

4014 Richmond (621-6901) Carries some new equipment, but an extensive selection of used photographic paraphernalia has made this co-op style outlet famous; from 35mm to 4x5 formats, you'll be exposed to tripods, lenses, camera bodies and even darkroom gear, including brands like Leica, Nikon, Mamiya and Schneider. The knowledgeable and genuinely helpful sales staff will assist you with all photographic projects —including equipment rental. They're also buyers of used photo equipment. Mon-Wed and Fri 9am-6pm, Thu 9am-8pm, Sat 10am-6pm.

12 Ragin' Cajun

4302 Richmond (623-6321) Shrine to LSU, as well as a restaurant, this loud, sometimes rowdy spot crammed with Cajun kitsch is famous for its red beans and rice, as well as muffalettas and gumbo. When you need a crawfish fix, this is the spicy spot for it. Mon-Thu 10:30am-9pm, Fri 10:30am-10pm, Sat 11am-10pm. Inexpensive.

13 Altermann and Morris Galleries

3461 W. Alabama (840-1922) Specializing in Southwestern art and artists. Primarily painters and sculptors. Mon-Fri 9am-5pm, Sat 11am-4pm.

14 Stables Steak House

3734 Westheimer (621-0833) and 7325 S. Main. A throwback to the steak 'n' potato days. Still, this is a welcome spot for many who like their steak well prepared. The atmosphere is a reminder of the '50s as well: dark, comfortable and friendly. Lunch Mon-Fri 11:30am-2pm, Dinner Sun-Thu 5:30pm-10pm, Fri-Sat 5:30pm-11pm. Credit Cards, Moderate.

15 Highland Village

A varied mix of up-scale shops and restaurants in a rambling set of buildings that is promoted as a shopping village.

A Grotto

3920 Westheimer (622-3663) This was Tony Vallone's third creation in his ever-expanding empire of restaurants. Here he designed a rustic Neopolitan menu and serves it up in a noisy, frenetic dining room (figure out the players in the bawdy mural) where patrons spend as much time checking out one another as they do eating. It's so well liked by its regular patrons, it sometimes feels like a private club, especially on Sunday evenings. Expect to wait for a table. Mon-Thu 11:30am-11pm, Fri-Sat 11:30am-midnight, Sun 11:30am-10pm. Credit Cards, Moderate.

B The Antiquariam Antique Print Gallery

3930 Westheimer (622-7531) Wide range of antique prints and museum quality framing. Mon-Sat 10am-5pm.

C James Avery Craftsman

3960 Westheimer (621-0135) The legendary Texas Hill Country jewelry craftsman began as a shaper of Christian symbols and has since expanded his silver and gold jewelry studio to include literally hundreds of motifs and symbolic precious-metal gestures, like friendship rings, trinkets abstracted from wildlife profiles and simple (but charming) geometric designs. Mon-Wed and Fri 10am-6pm, Thu 10am-8pm.

Refer to map on pages1286-129

D   La Madeleine French Bakery & Cafe
4002 Westheimer (623-0644) and other locations. These popular bakery/restaurants serve an eclectic crowd who've come to dine on a great Caesar salad, traditional quiches and French pochettes. Cappuccino and fresh pastries may be savored in the crowded dining area or on an attractive patio. Daily 6:30am-10pm. Moderate.

Fresh-baked bread from La Madeleine.

E   Casablanca Moroccan Restaurant
2514 Suffolk (621-0863) Most exotic restaurant in River Oaks invites you to sit on the floor and eat with your fingers while enjoying the belly dancer. For the best time, go with a group and be sure to order the kitchen's outstanding b'stilla, a chicken-filled powder-sugared North African pie that is the house specialty. Credit Cards. Mon-Sat 6pm-11pm. Moderate.

F   Confederate House
4007 Westheimer (622-1936) The South rises again. This is as Old Guard Houston as you'll find outside the city's private country clubs. With its Tara-like decor, discreet staff and the best bartender in the city (according to many), the Confederate House is the place to spot Houston's bluest bloods dining in multi-generational groups under portraits of rebel generals. Lunch Mon-Fri 11:30am-2:30pm, Dinner Mon-Sun 6pm-10:30pm. Reservations. Credit Cards, Expensive.

G   Tootsies
4045 Westheimer (629-9990) It's got an air about it, Tootsies does. Strut (you must) through its glass double doors and soak in the atmosphere exuded by designer Thierry Meugler's exquisite suits, by Isaac Misrahi's front-echelon casual wear or by myriad masterpieces of Tom and Linda Platt. Local jewelry crafter Mariquita Masterson displays her sterling serrano pepper-styled cufflinks and beautiful gold necklaces dotted with glass "stones" extracted from carcasses of Tanquerray bottles. Owner Mickey Rosmarin's staff tends to clients' every whim: a procession of designer shoes will fall at your feet when a dress is pondered; proper tones of blush and eyeliner will naturally be recommended; a purse and striking jewels might be submitted for your perusal. Either exit Tootsies metamorphosed or feign satisfaction with having feasted your senses on the very best. This Highland Village boutique has evolved into the one-stop shopping destination for Houston's rich and famous. Mon-Sat 10am-7pm.

H   Little Tootsies
4037 Westheimer (629-9990) Another of the parent boutique's offspring, Little Tootsies offers designer clothes and accessories for kids. Possibly the best special occasion clothes rack for kids in Houston. Mon-Sat 10am-7pm.

I   Tootsies Takes Off
4081 Westheimer at Suffolk (552-0190) The discount outlet boom convinced Tootsies owner Mickey Rosmarin to open his own "outlet" in 1990, his price cutting cleverly alluded to in the store title. Snap up sale items from the big store here. Mon-Sat 10am-7pm, Sun noon-5pm.

16   Romeros
2500 Mid Lane (961-1161) A comfortable little Italian restaurant in a neighborhood-style setting, just minutes from the busy Galleria area. Excellent grilled fish. Mon-Fri Lunch 11am-2:30pm, Mon-Thu Dinner 5:30pm-10pm, Fri-Sat 5:30pm-11pm, Sun 5:30pm-9pm. Credit Cards, Moderate.

17   Wooden Star Gifts
4344 Westheimer at Mid Lane (840-8832) A Texas souvenir hunter's paradise. Mostly tasteful stuff here, attempting to capture the essence of life (with a big L) in the Lone Star State. Mon-Wed and Fri 10am-5pm, Thu 10am-8pm, Sat 10am-6pm; Sun 11am-5pm.

Memorial Park's tree-lined, three-mile track draws joggers from all around Houston.

MEMORIAL PARK/BUFFALO BAYOU

For as small as Buffalo Bayou is as a waterway, it has been a central element in the development of Houston. The city was established where the bayou meets White Oak Bayou; the bayou was widened to become the Houston Ship Channel; and in 1917 a camp was set up along the bayou to train soldiers for duty in World War I. That camp ground would later become Memorial Park, one of the largest city parks in the country. Today thousands of Houstonians jog, play golf, tennis, softball and volleyball, swim, hike, canoe, picnic and just relax in the 1503-acre Memorial Park and Buffalo Bayou Park, the land that extends along the bayou near downtown. Buffalo Bayou Park is also the site of many large public gatherings, such as Fourth of July fireworks displays and the historic *Rendezvous Houston*, a laser light-fireworks-and-music extravaganza by artist Jean-Michel Jarre that drew over a million viewers in 1986.

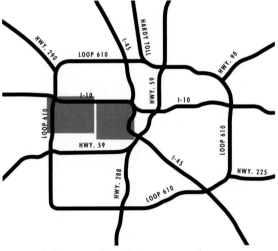

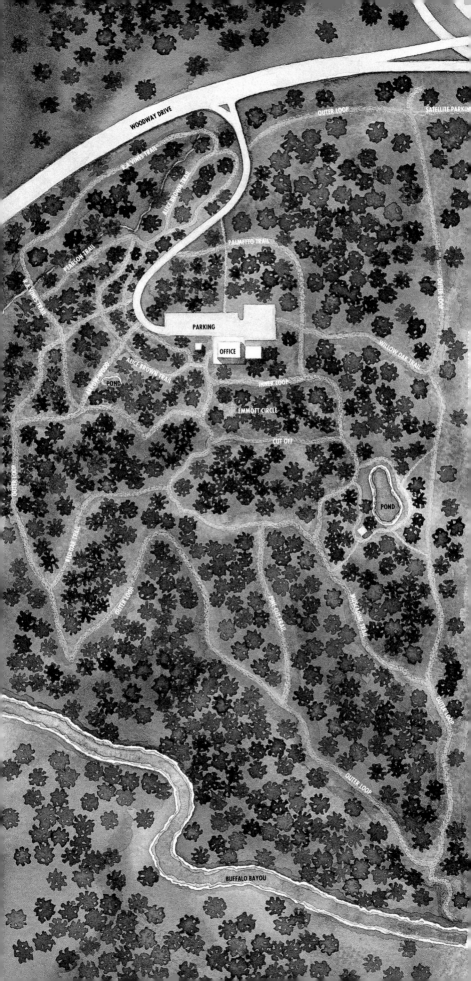

Refer to map on pages136-137

Memorial Park
One of Houston's greatest treasures, Memorial Park consists
of 1503 acres straddling Buffalo Bayou. The park was created
in 1924 as a memorial to the soldiers of World War I, especially those that were stationed at Houston's Camp Logan,
which was situated on this site from 1917-1919. In the 20
months that this camp was active, more than 25,000 soldiers
trained here. After the camp was decommissioned, local citizens and the *Houston Chronicle* led a campaign for the land to
become a public park. With the backing of the Hogg family—
Miss Ima, Will and Mike—the land was purchased and sold
to the city at cost, to be used forever as a public park by the
citizens of Houston.

**1   Houston Arboretum
& Nature Center**
*4501 Woodway Drive in Memorial Park
(681-8433)* The Houston Arboretum &
Nature Center is a 155-acre enclave dedi-
cated to preserving Houston's native tree,
plant and animal species. Located on the
western fringe of Memorial Park, the
Arboretum occupies 10% of the park,
providing respite to almost 160 species
of native and migrating birds like the
red-shouldered hawk and the red-bellied
woodpecker. Over five miles of nature trails
lead through second-growth forests of
mixed hardwood and pine, including a half
mile interpretive path and a longer loop
trail. Formal environmental education programs have been the Arboretum's hallmark
for years; outdoor classes in horticulture,
nature photography, native landscaping
and bird watching are conducted year
round. Special events are celebrated within
the preserve, including Texas Arbor Day
(the third weekend of every January) and
Texas Wildflower Day (the fourth weekend
of every April). Field trips to the wilder
regions of Texas, like High Island, the Big
Thicket and Brazos Bend, are led by envi-
ronmentalists and Arboretum staff; excursions leave the parking lot around 6am and
cost from $10 to $15. "Tyke Hikes" are

nature story walks for children 3-4 years old and their parents,
held Tuesdays at 1pm in June and July. Older kids can find
solace in the Arboretum's Summer Nature Programs: the
week- long "Discovery Classes" from 9:30am to noon are tailored for age groups from 5-15 years. "Saturday Happenings"
are two-hour workshops on specialized natural science topics
for children ages 5-12, held from September through May.
Free public tours are conducted most Sunday afternoons at
2pm and 3pm. Admission to the grounds is free. Open Daily,
8:30am-6pm.

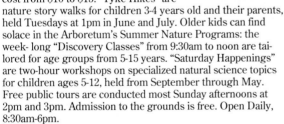

*A word of warning: All of the
Houston-area arboretums and
nature areas are "all-natural,"
so for a more comfortable visit
take along some mosquito repellent when the weather has been
wet and warm.*

Early morning at Memorial Park: on the golf course, above, and at the Seymour-Lieberman Exer-Trail, below.

2   The Seymour-Lieberman Exer-Trail

Memorial Drive Loop in Memorial Park. This cushy three-mile loop makes a superb training ground for athletes—miles are clearly marked for timing—while at the same time it's something of a social phenomenon, a destination of choice for young and old alike. Water fountains are placed at each mile marker and stretching apparatus is frequently found along the trail. Someone is always on the track, save bad weather or late nights, and it is very crowded on pleasant weekend mornings.

3   Memorial Park Tennis Center

Memorial Drive Loop in Memorial Park (861-3765) Eighteen Laycold courts decked out with windscreens await tennis aficionados at the public Memorial Park Tennis Center. Private and group lessons are held at the center, plus the Houston Tennis Association sponsors spring, summer, and fall leagues for men and women in singles as well as doubles. The largest amateur tennis tournament in the world, The Coca-Cola Open, begins every Easter weekend. Runners from the trail as well as tennis players crowd the clubhouse on clear afternoons, for its bulletin boards are an exhaustive source of info on fun-runs, triathlons, marathon warm-ups and tennis events.
Pro shop and Tennis Center: Mon-Fri 6am-9pm, Sat 7am-6pm, Sun 7am-4:30pm. Can vary with the seasons and the weather.

4   Memorial Park Golf Course and Clubhouse

Memorial Drive Loop in Memorial Park (862-4033) The 1936 vintage Memorial Park Clubhouse opens onto the grand old 7333-yard municipal golf course, once the site of the Houston Open. Red Spanish tile graces the roof of the tiny clubhouse, once warmed by a fireplace and enlivened by golf-talk from the nearby restaurant. This eatery, the showers and the fireplace were swept out in a 1965 "renovation." The public golf course stays busy, as it is one of the best bargains around. Driving range and lessons available. Pro shop and clubhouse open dawn to dusk, weather permitting.

5   Houston Polo Club

8552 Memorial (681-1171 or 681-8571) Polo easily qualifies as the fastest contact sport in the world, and you can view it, plus the stables holding upwards of 200 fine horses, at The Houston Polo Club during the spring and fall seasons. Matches are on Sunday evenings at 5pm or 5:30pm and last approximately 1-1/2 hours. Spring season is April to July and fall season is September to November. Open to the public. Admission is $15

Refer to map on pages 136-137

6   Rainbow Lodge

1 Birdsall Street off Memorial (861-8666) Bavarian-style hunting lodge, perched on the edge of Buffalo Bayou, is crammed with hunting and fishing trophies and a cozy rabbit warren arrangement of tucked-away rooms. Simple dishes are often the most satisfying, and brunch (with harpist) is among the city's most civilized. You're welcome to wander the beautiful grounds, site of many Houston weddings. Lunch Tue-Fri 11:30am-2pm, Dinner Tue-Fri 6:30pm-10:30pm, Sat 6pm-10:30pm, Brunch Sun 10:30pm-2pm. Reservations. Credit Cards, Expensive.

7   Otto's

5502 Memorial Drive (864-2573) Self-service barbecue (burgers are served on the other side of the building) that made a name for itself long before George Bush was spotted eating here, Otto's has been family run since 1950. Fans must approve of the old-shack decor, for it is consistently selected as one of the city's best barbecue joints. Mon-Sat 11am-9pm. Inexpensive.

8   One's A Meal

5525 Memorial Drive (861-8300) and 2019 West Gray next to River Oaks Theatre. Breakfast with character and big biscuits, as well as burgers and plenty of satisfying home-style food, are the ticket at Haritos Bibas' two around-the-clock cafes. Best bet: the Western omelette. Great people-watching in the wee hours. Daily 24-hours. Inexpensive.

9   Beer Can House

222 Malone Avenue. One more terrific example of Houston's folk art, this home is covered with the cardboard from six packs and has a lace-like curtain of beer can tops sparkling in the breeze, all behind a fence of—you guessed it—empty beer cans. Retired owner John Milkovisch claims to have drunk the contents of every decorative item on the house. Just drive by; it is not open to the public.

10 Roznovsky's

5719 Feagan (864-1492) On the weekends this is a crowded, noisy beer and hamburger hall. Favorite stopping-off place for Memorial Park devotees. It gets pretty crowded weekdays at lunch with businessmen looking for a good hamburger, fries and a game of pool. Tue-Sun 11am-10pm.

11 Westcott Drive Inn

6603 Westcott in Memorial Park (862-0958 or 861-3267) Your standard icehouse with roll-up garage doors, pool tables and dusty softball trophies but with a classic motto: "Hangovers installed and serviced." Also serves up hamburgers, cold beer and pinball. Daily 11am-midnight.

MEMORIAL DRIVE

PARKING

ENTRANCE

BUFFALO BAYOU

GAZEBO

OFFICES

MUSEUM

GREENHOUSE

A

B

I

H

G

C

D

F

E

Refer to map on pages 136-137

6 Bayou Bend Collection and Gardens

1 Westcott Street off Memorial Drive (529-8773) A beautiful 14-acre tract along Buffalo Bayou was Will, Mike and Miss Ima Hogg's selection for the site of their new home in 1927. Miss Hogg lived in Bayou Bend's Eden-like setting for 40 years, as she sculpted the gardens and selected the antiques her home is famous for. She passed away in 1975, after bequeathing the estate to The Museum of Fine Arts, which now maintains the property—with the River Oaks Garden Club—in park-like condition. The grand white home, fronted with Ionic columns and festooned with pairs of forest-green shutters, reminds one of gracious Southern living. Leading art historians have ranked the Hogg collection of American Decorative Arts one of the three most respected in the nation, and it's no wonder. Among the elegant possessions are an eighteenth century men's writing desk that towers almost six feet and an original Paul Revere sterling silver teapot, its spout curved in the shape of an elephant's trunk. You'll see notable paintings, portraits by Stuart, as well as works by Peale and Copley. In all, Miss Hogg's collection numbers some 1200 items and flows from 27 rooms, more than enough to impart a real sense of the arts and everyday life in early America.

Reservations required: House Tours, every 15 minutes, Tue-Fri, 10am-11:45am, 1pm-2:45pm. Minimum age 14 years., maximum group size four people, $4 per person, seniors $3.

No reservation required: Garden Tours, self-guided, Wed-Sat 10am-5pm, Sun 1pm-5pm, $2 per person, children under 12 free.

Free admission: Second Sun of every month, except March and August, House and Garden Tours, 1pm-5pm.

[Closed until fall 1993 for renovations]

The three statues of Diana (above), Euterpe and Clio gracing the gardens grew from a visit by Miss Hogg to the Vatican, where she spotted two of the white marble statues. While in Antonio Frilli's studio having replicas made, a third statue caught Miss Hogg's attention, and she commissioned all three in Carrara marble.

Bureau Table
(John Townsend, c. 1785-95)
Mahogany with yellow poplar and chestnut, 34.5x38x20.5 inches

The Bayou Bend Gardens
Nine of the English gardens are followed here in roughly a circular pattern, starting with the Clio Garden.

A The Clio Garden
Miss Hogg pioneered the culturing of azaleas in Houston. This parterre-style garden blooms in a geometric imitation of seventeenth-century English manor plantings.

B The Diana Garden
A Texas State Historical plaque graces the crown terrace of this, the largest garden in the park, designed with steps to serve as an amphitheater for social gatherings. Water jets placed on the edges of a reflecting pool frame the statue dubbed Diana, the centerpiece of the garden.

C The East Garden
Flanks of a rare Camellia Japonica bloom beneath hedges of wax leaf ligustrum, while myriad varieties of azaleas, pruned to form three tiers, form a dynamic, semi-circular background for a misty round fountain, the focal point of this garden, the first to be landscaped at Bayou Bend.

D The Bicentennial Topiary Garden
A Lone Star-shaped topiary garden, where perennials are trained in shapes of the indigenous Texas wildlife of 1776.

E The White Garden
Ivory blossoms greeted Miss Hogg along a winding driveway each time she arrived; now bronze deer, placed there as a tribute to her gardener of thirty years, overlook white rows of tulips and azaleas.

F The Butterfly Garden
A giant-scale rendition of a flying butterfly. Clipped Boxwood trim the wings, while 30 foot-long beds of pink and lavender azaleas imitate its colorful camouflage. Bricks form a torso; antennae reach towards a figure of Cupid.

G The Waterfall Garden
Legend has it that this waterfall was built after a water leak streamed water down the bank. A pool with figures of fawns was installed.

H The Carla Garden
In 1962 hurricane Carla levelled trees and plants near the waterfall. Ms. Hogg took advantage of the natural clearing to begin a garden-in-the-round, now home to an almost-antique painted wooden carousel peacock figure, guarding the low-cut rings of azaleas.

I The Euterpe Garden
A statue of the muse of poetry and music appears rested here, with Indica azaleas and ivy encircling the pedestal.

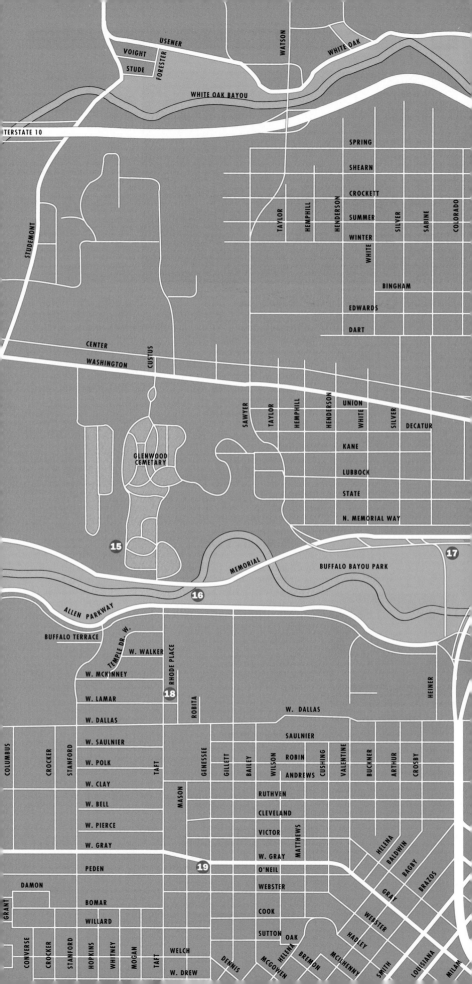

Refer to map on pages 144-145

1 Hofbrau Steaks
1803 Shepherd (869-7074) University of Texas alumni have made this rowdy steakhouse their unofficial headquarters in Houston. Fans recommend the T-bones with grilled onions, special wilted salad and ranch-cut potatoes. Great jukebox. Mon 11am-9:30pm, Tue-Fri 11am-10:30pm, Sat-Sun 5:30pm-10:30pm. Moderate.

Buffalo Bayou Park
This greenbelt provides miles of mountain biking, distance running and picnicking pleasure to Houstonians year around. Every day downtowners break to get in a few miles at lunch or to picnic on the banks. The park was developed in the 1930s when a street called Buffalo Bayou Parkway, now Allen Parkway, was laid to connect the new River Oaks development with downtown.

2 Cadillac Bar
1802 Shepherd at I-10 (862-2020) Covered with graffiti, this boisterous border-town cantina (the original is in Nuevo Laredo) echoes with cries of "arriba, arriba!" Shooter girls roam with tequila in hand, while tourists don oversized sombreros and have their picture made. A favorite spot for impressing Yankees. Mon-Thu 11am-9:30pm, Fri 11am-midnight, Sat-Sun noon-10pm. Credit Cards, Inexpensive.

3 Cyclone Anaya's
1015 Durham near Washington (862-3209) and 9347-1/2 Richmond. Outstanding nachos and margaritas, along with blaring ballgames on the TV, crying babies and a rather bizarre birthday ritual (let's just say celebrants usually wind up drenched), make this a great place to meet friends to kick off an evening of partying. The Tex-Mex food is actually pretty humdrum—though enchiladas can be very good—but it's great loud fun, if you can handle it. Mon-Thu 11am-11pm, Fri-Sat 11am-midnight, Sun noon-10pm. Inexpensive.

4 The Bon-Ton Room
4216 Washington (863-0001 or 863-7383) A top contender for most exciting bar in the Heights, the Bon Ton Room catches its stride about midnight every Friday. Normally uptight young professionals shed their suit coats and dance to some of the best rhythm and blues on the planet. It's a small club, and it seems seedy from the outside, but good sweaty fun awaits within. Doors open at 7pm and admissions range from free to around $10.

5 Old Bayou Inn
216 Heights Boulevard. (861-6300) Atmospheric spot for good burgers and Mexican food, as well as a chicken-fried steak that is everything it should be. Mon-Fri 11am-midnight, Sat-Sun 9am-8:30pm. Inexpensive.

9 Gus Wortham Memorial Fountain
Allen Parkway at Waugh. The fountain's flower-like spray wets down joggers as they pass by this memorial to Gus Wortham, founder of American General and one of Houston's major benefactors.

6 Rockefeller's
3620 Washington (861-9365) Housed in an ornate old bank building, Rockefeller's hosts some of the best touring acts in the country. Though ticket prices are often steep, this is the only club in town to see big names in such an intimate setting. Doors open at 7pm and showtimes vary depending on the act. Admission prices are $10-$20.

7 Sam Segari's
77 Harvard at Washington (880-2470) Fabulous skin-on fries, plump shrimp that snap when you bite them and good stiff drinks are three reasons why this lowkey eatery on a nondescript stretch of Washington (next to Rockefeller's) is a favorite of many of the city's most discreet well-to-do. Mon-Thu 11:15am-10:15pm, Fri-Sat noon-11:15pm, Sun noon-10:15pm. Reservations. Credit Cards, Inexpensive.

Refer to map on pages 144-145

8   Black Forest Tavern (formerly Bavarian Gardens)
3926 Feagan (861-2968) Mid-level touring bands and a lot of
local talent make the Black Forest a dynamic music scene. It's
mostly a large sit-and-watch room, but spontaneous dancing
does occur. Also one of the friendliest bars in town. Covers
when applicable: $3-$20. Mon-Fri 4pm-2am, Sat-Sun 2pm-2am.

10 Stages Repertory Theater
3201 Allen Parkway (527-8243) New works and an occasional
taste of avant garde drama comprise most of Stages
Repertory's menu. The double-stage complex is on Allen
Parkway (watch for possible move). Summertime sees a Texas
Playwrights Festival at Stages. Call for programming.

11 Allbritton's Cafeteria
905 Waugh (524-4908) This cafeteria's roots were established
in 1907 when Luther Allbritton started his first eating estab-
lishment. His son Sonny opened here in 1938 and has been
serving to an unpretentious crowd since. Daily 10:45am-8pm.

12 Nino's
2817 W. Dallas (522-5120) Vincent Mandola's cozy dining
room—next to his newer Vincent's—is standing-room-only
most nights. It's terrifically popular for hearty Italian classics,
as well as several original Mandola dishes. Lunch Mon-Fri
11am-2:30pm, Dinner Mon-Thu 5:30-10pm, Fri-Sat 5pm-11pm.
Reservations. Credit Cards, Moderate.

13 Vincent's
2701 W. Dallas (528-4313) Vincent Mandola's recent addition
of a rotisserie is the source of succulent roasted chicken, perhaps the juiciest in town. Roasted peppers with olive oil,
capers and anchovies are a great starter. Noisy and friendly.
Lunch Mon-Fri 11am-3pm, Dinner Mon-Thu 5pm-10:30pm, Fri-
Sat 5pm-11:30pm. Reservations. Credit Cards, Moderate.

14 Museum of Printing History
1324 W. Clay (522-4652) The focus here is how printing has
changed through the centuries. Classes are available, and
antique presses are still inked up and used. Everything from
vintage printing equipment to historical newspapers and beautifully printed antique documents are here. Free admission
(Donations welcomed). Tues-Sat 9am-5pm.

17 Fonde Recreation Center
110 Sabine (223-9106) The place where serious basketball
players go at it. Stars of the street and the NBA shoot it up
here, including the likes of Moses Malone and John Lucas.
A Pro-Am Summer League lets amateurs trade elbows with
some of NBAs best. Mon-Fri 9am-9pm, Sat 9am-5pm.

18 Antone's
807 Taft (526-1046) and other locations. In 1962 the late Jalal
Antone opened the first Antone's at this Taft location; today,
his po'boy is a Houston tradition, either made to order or pre-
wrapped for the lunch crowd that lines up daily in these
casual, under-designed delicatessens crowded with barrels of
olives, bulk grains, crates of wines and imported meats.
Though famous for its original salami and ham filling—the
chain sells more than 100,000 every month—today you
can also get "the nature boy," a tabouli and feta cheese
sandwich. Mon-Sat 8am-6:30pm. Inexpensive.

19 This Is It
239 West Gray (523-5319) Those peripatetic food writers
Jane and Michael Stern have made This Is It's meatloaf
nationally famous, and for good reason. It is rich and
wonderful and has a restrained hand with the seasonings.
The restaurant is probably Houston's most prominent soul
food emporium. Mon-Thu 6:30am-10pm, Fri-Sat 6:30am-mid-
night, Sun 6:30am-6pm. Inexpensive.

15 Howard Hughes' Grave
Glenwood Cemetery The eccentric multi-billionaire, born and
raised in Houston, is laid to
rest in the family plot here.
Worth a drive by, as the hilly
and heavily wooded Glenwood
Cemetery is one of Houston's
prettiest areas. Cemetery open
7am-5pm.

16 Large Spindle Piece
(Henry Moore, 1968/74) A
massive bronze sculpture
along the jogging path
between Buffalo Bayou and
Allen Parkway.

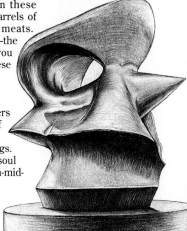

The Transco Tower looms over the Post Oak area.

POST OAK-GALLERIA

The Post Oak area is a medium-sized city all by itself. Large office complexes are surrounded by shopping, restaurants and high rise condominiums. And in the middle of this city stands a tower—the Transco Tower—that serves as a beacon, both literally and figuratively, to help motorists find their way here. That is Post Oak today. In the late '60s it was just another area of urban sprawl before an enterprising Houston developer built the Galleria and forever changed the make-up of the city. The Galleria has expanded over the past twenty-plus years to a 2.1-million-square-foot retail mall that attracts an average of 10,000 shoppers a day. It is famous for being a place to buy outrageously expensive items, but it is also a

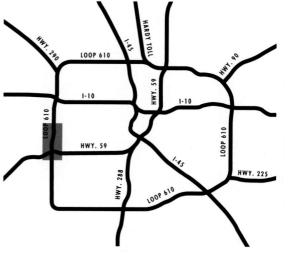

place to just stroll, to people watch. The Galleria sparked the growth of an entire shopping area as high-end stores, restaurants and hotels crowded in around the mall, turning the area into a national and international destination.

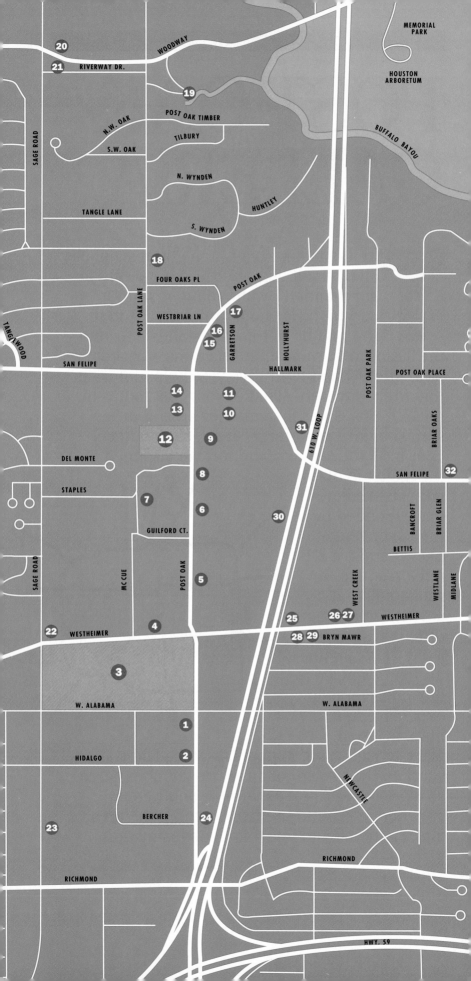

Refer to map on page 150

1 The Transco Tower

2800 South Post Oak Blvd. (Philip Johnson and John Burgee, 1983) There are not too many cities that could have—or would have—built this building as it was here in Houston. While one of the taller buildings in the world at 64 stories, it is more extraordinary because of where it is: outside the central business district. What makes this building so stunning is that it is out in the open, a symmetrical monument. It is the tallest building in the world not in a downtown area and, real trivia here, the tallest building in the world surrounded by grass. Noted architect Philip Johnson and his partner John Burgee designed the tower for developer Gerald Hines with the backing of the building's major tenant, Transco Energy Company. As the building was being completed, a new idea surfaced from this team, that of putting a beacon on the top. Now, every night from dusk until midnight, a high-powered lamp rotates atop the building, sending out a beam of light that can be seen miles away.

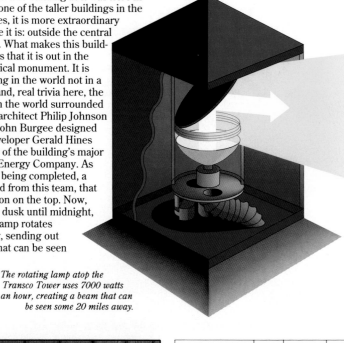

The rotating lamp atop the Transco Tower uses 7000 watts an hour, creating a beam that can be seen some 20 miles away.

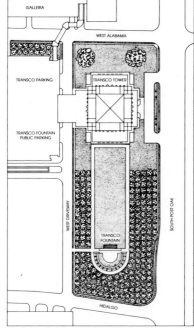

2 The Transco Fountain

2800 South Post Oak Blvd. (Philip Johnson and John Burgee, 1985) After the completion of the Transco Tower, Gerald Hines presented the city with a real gift, the Transco Fountain. Designed by the same team that produced the Transco Tower, the fountain has become a public park although it is squarely on private property, solely a privately owned structure. The public doesn't seem to mind, as the fountain has become the most photographed spot in the city. Originally the idea was to build a "Mountain Fountain," a pyramid-like mound with water cascading down one side and with tree-covered terraces. But the design that won out was the fountain as it is today, save for one major change. The original design called for a reflecting pool between the fountain and the tower, but eventually that idea gave way to a recessed lawn. The lawn is now popular with frisbee-throwers and picnickers. The fountain itself is in the shape of a U with water rushing down the outside and inside surfaces. On the interior of the fountain the falling water makes an engulfing sound, while the movement of the water creates an almost levitating experience. The fountain is lit in the evenings.

The ever-popular ice skating rink at the Galleria.

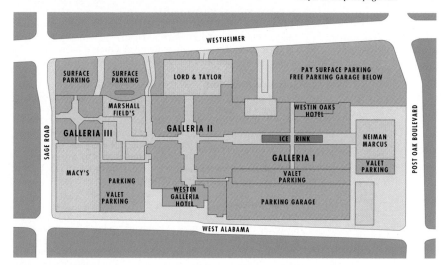

1 The Galleria

Westheimer between South Post Oak Blvd. and Sage (622-0663)
(Hellmuth, Obata & Kassabaum and Neuhaus & Taylor, 1969-1971, 1979) The pride and joy of Milan in the 1860s was the "Galleria," a select group of cafes and boutiques grouped in a translucent glass-covered atrium. One hundred and ten years later, on November 16, 1970, another Galleria opened, this time in Houston. Gerald Hines fathered this version amid mounting skepticism that it would be a success. At $70 million to construct, the original Galleria proved to be not only a revolutionary idea but a relative bargain as well. The massive center was designed by Hellmuth, Obata & Kassebaum of St. Louis with Neuhaus & Taylor of Houston to house shops, hotels, movie theaters and even office towers, centered around a Central Park-style ice skating rink. The mall has grown to encompass the entire block it is on, and plans have the Galleria expanding across to adjoining blocks in the near future.

1969 Neiman Marcus opens
1970 Galleria opens
1974 Galleria II and Lord & Taylor opens
1986 Galleria III and Macy's complete

Ice Skating Rink

Galleria I, ice rink level (621-1500) The ice skating rink drew a great deal of attention when the Galleria opened: just the thought of cutting across the ice on a nice 102° Sunday afternoon was enough to turn a few Texas heads. It is still a very busy place during prime shopping hours and impossible during the Christmas season when the skaters share the ice with a mammoth Christmas tree. Classes available. Admission $7.00 for all ages. Mon-Fri 9am-5pm and 8pm-10pm, Sat 1pm-10pm, Sun 1pm-6pm.

Sam Houston Book Shop

Galleria I, ice rink level (626-1243) Named for our city's most famous figurer, this locally owned bookstore boasts an impressive Texana collection, notable art book selection and extensive travel department. A favorite browsing spot for a spouse stranded in the Galleria.Mon-Sat 10am-9pm, Sun noon-6pm.

Texas Souvenirs

Galleria I, ice rink level (961-4244) The ultimate Texas souvenir shop has chili pepper, bluebonnet and longhorn-shaped everything, plus scads of Texas-themed T-shirts in every size. Out-of-state visitors may want to pick up a bottle of Texas Champagne (hot pepper sauce), jalapeno ketchup or Margarita mix. Mon-Sat 10am-9pm, Sun noon-6pm.

The Best of The Galleria:

A PEA IN THE POD
ACCENTE
ACCESSORY LADY
BARNEY'S
BOARDWALK GALLERY
GOLDSMITH'S
CHARLES JOURDAN
CRABTREE & EVELYN
CRATE & BARREL
FENDI
GALLERY OF GOLF
GIANNI VERSACE
GUCCI
HANSON GALLERIES
KITES UNLIMITED
KNOTS
KRISPIN
LA CICOGNA
LAURA ASHLEY
LORD & TAYLOR
LOUIS VUITTON
MACY'S
MARSHALL FIELD
MILIEUX
NEIMAN MARCUS
NORTH BEACH LEATHER
POLO RALPH LAUREN
SAM HOUSTON BOOK SHOP
SOMETHING'S AFOOT
SOUTHERN FABRICS
T & TOMATO
TIFFANY & CO.
TRENDY TOTS
TURQUOISE LADY
ZOE COSTE

Refer to map on page 150

Houston Sports Exchange

Galleria I, ice rink level (552-1882) T-shirts, sweatshirts, caps and jackets bearing the colors and names of virtually every sports team in the U.S. can be found or ordered from this sports fan's paradise. Mon-Sat 10am-9pm, Sun noon-6pm.

Barney's New York

Galleria I, street level (622-3636). Nestled among the high-end boutiques by Neiman Marcus is this couturier department store. Unlike the sprawling, jam-packed superstores Texans have come to expect, this artfully planned small space offers a carefully selected sampling of the finest jewelry, accessories, men's and women's fashions and housewares by the hottest (and most expensive) designers, plus Barney's own label. Mon-Sat 10am-9pm, Sun noon-6pm.

Gianni Versace

Galleria I, street level (623-8220) The flamboyant Italian designer whose trademark is layers of bold prints in body-conscious fashions for men and women opened this funky boutique in 1990. But take heart; calmer, solid brights coexist peacefully with the ultra-trendy prints for individuals who want to wear the famous maker's label without shouting to the whole world about it. Mon-Sat 10am-9pm, Sun noon-6pm.

Crate & Barrel

Galleria III, street level (621-775) Stylish, affordable housewares, including an extensive array of glassware for any occasion, stock the shelves of this popular shop. Brides-to-be register for every kitchen need, as well as bed linens, office accessories and picnic baskets. Mon-Sat 10am-9pm, Sun noon-6pm.

Fred Joaillier

Galleria I, street level (960-9441) Fred Joaillier of Beverly Hills' Rodeo Drive fame brought their contemporary fine jewelry designs to Houston in the late 1970s. The salon also carries a selection of designs from other jewelers, including Rolex, Piaget and Cartier. Shoppers will enjoy refreshments from the fully stocked bar and the solitude of a private viewing room. Mon-Sat 10am-9pm.

Tiffany's

Galleria I, street level (626-0220) World-famous jewelry and gift proprietor features the finest designer wares, including Paloma Picasso's gold and gem-studded trinkets, Baccarat crystal, Limoges boxes and Faberge eggs. Complete china, crystal and silver bridal registry available with Tiffany's own wedding and special occasion books. Mon-Sat 10am-5:30pm.

Sharper Image

Galleria III, street level (961-0123) Promising the most innovative and environmentally friendly products on the market, this high-tech grown-ups' toy store has built its business with yuppies who can't wait to be the first on the block to own the latest fitness, video or stereo equipment, recreation gear or office gadget. Mon-Sat 10am-9pm, Sun noon-6pm.

Refer to map on page 150

Kites Unlimited

Galleria II, level 2 (960-0608) With more than 30 varieties of dual- and single-line deltas, diamonds and boxes, all made of neon-bright ripstop nylon, kite fanciers will find the perfect windy day companion at Kites Unlimited. Parrots, fish, sharks and airplane shapes mingle with traditional kites and an array of windsocks. Mon-Sat 10am-9pm, Sun noon-6pm.

Something's Afoot

Galleria II, level 2 (552-1818) This shop offers socks for every occasion for men, women and children. You'll find rhinestone-studded tennis socks, toddler's Mickey Mouse-decorated socks and unusual dress socks to wear with a tuxedo. Small collection of ladies' hosiery and special-occasion boxer shorts as well. Mon-Sat 10am-9pm, Sun noon-6pm.

Babbage's

Galleria II, level 2 (961-0005) Computer and video games for kids of all ages abound in this entertainment software store. Like other software retailers, Babbage's offers a good selection of programs for office use, but their Nintendo games are definitely the bigger draw. Mon-Sat 10am-9pm, Sun noon-6pm.

Hanson Galleries

Galleria II, level 2 (522-1242) Handmade crafts by American artisans fill the shelves at Hanson Galleries. Jewelry made of titanium, iridescent hand-blown glass perfume bottles and goblets, kaleidoscopes and beautifully carved wooden boxes are just a few of the one-of-a-kind items always in demand here. Mon-Sat 10am-9pm, Sun noon-6pm.

Milieux

Galleria II, level 3 (439-7495) In a word, this home furnishings boutique is eclectic. With the focus on accessories, the shopkeepers are careful to represent every style from traditional to contemporary and Southwestern to safari, and they can special order almost anything. Shopping tip: look no further for those Holstein-upholstered bar stools you've been wanting; Milieux keeps a steady stock. Mon-Sat 10am-9pm, Sun noon-6pm.

Neiman Marcus

Galleria I, all levels (621-7100) Texas' own specialty department store is seen as the place to shop in the state, judging by all the movies that include scenes in the restaurant and on the escalators. And they do offer the state's finest collection of designer labels for women, men and children, plus exquisite linens, tableware and gifts. Mon-Sat 10am-9pm, Sun noon-6pm.

Roof, Westin Oaks

5011 Westheimer (623-4300) This small rooftop club has a wonderful view of the Galleria area. The performers (mostly jazz and soul) and the decor here are smooth and clean. Since the club is above a major hotel, the crowd is usually an interesting mix of foreign tourists, traveling business people and locals. Mon-Sat 4:30pm-2am.

Galleria Area Hotels

3   Westin Galleria
5060 W. Alabama in the Galleria (960-81500) 24 stories, 492 rooms. Double $190-$225, Suite $350-$1200.

3   Westin Oaks
5011 Westheimer in the Galleria (960-81500) 21 stories, 406 rooms. Double $190-$250, Suite $350-$1200.

8   The Doubletree Post Oak
2001 Post Oak Blvd. (961-9300) 14 stories, 448 rooms. Double $135-$155, Suite $185-$1000.

19 Omni (formerly Inn on the Park)
Four Riverway (871-8181) 11 stories, 381 rooms. Double $180-$220, Suite $425-$1175.

22 JW Marriott-Galleria
5150 Westheimer (961-1500) 23 stories, 485 rooms. Double $145, Concierge Level $155, Suite $155-$500.

25 Sheraton Grand
2525 West Loop South (961-3000) 15 stories, 321 rooms. Double $65-$109, Luxury Level $215-$500, Suite $475-$1750.

30 Houston Marriott-West Loop/Galleria
1750 West Loop South (960-0111) 14 stories, 302 rooms. Double $109-$139, Suite $129-$139.

31 Holiday Inn Crowne Plaza-Galleria
2222 West Loop South (961-7272) 23 stories, 447 rooms. Double $99-$148, Luxury Level $148, Suite $100-$250.

32 Ritz-Carlton (formerly The Remington)
1919 Briar Oaks Lane (840-7600) 12 stories, 232 rooms. Double $175-$250, Luxury Level $215-$500, Suite $475-$1750.

Refer to map on page 150

4 Cafe Continental

5016 Westheimer (623-4666) In a lonely strip center next to the defunct Sakowitz store, the kitchen here is purely classical French of a kind very common (and old hat) in New York but not so often seen in these parts. Francophiles gather in the comfortable dining room for the rich cream-and-butter sauces that, if you're not a slave to your cholesterol count, instills a radiance of well-being. Terrific seasonal offerings (e.g., bouillabaisse), too. Mon- Thu 11:30am-10:30pm, Fri 11:30am-11:30pm, Sat noon-11:30pm, Sun noon-10:30pm. Credit Cards, Moderate.

5 Ta Hua

2405 Post Oak Blvd. (621-1763) The homeliest restaurant in the chic Post Oak area is the cheapest too, but fans know you come here for one thing only: dumplings. Steamed or fried, filled with pork, shrimp or vegetables—
you can build a meal around them, all seasoned up with the do-it- yourself sauce kit. Daily 11am-10pm. Cheap.

6 Oshman's

2131 Post Oak Blvd. (622-4940) Al Lubetkin has nurtured his Oshman's sporting goods stores through some tough years in the hyper-competitive market and somehow emerges healthy every time. This venerable Houston retailer of every sort of sporting equipment has at times made itself famous with in-store skiing lessons (moving carpet) and a computerized golf course simulator. A new, mammoth location on the west end of town boggles the mind. Mon, Thu, Fri 10am-9pm, Tue, Wed, Sat 10am-6pm, Sun noon-5pm.

7 Uncle Tai's

1980 Post Oak Blvd. (960-8000) Restaurant namesake Wen-Dah Tai is the godfather of high-end Chinese restaurants in Houston. This elegant dining room has not received much attention in recent years, but it is always a reliable standard for business dining — and excellent Hunan food. Mon-Thu 11:30am-10pm, Fri-Sat 11:30am-10:30pm, Sun 5pm-10pm. Reservations. Credit Cards, Expensive.

9 Tony's

The inimitable Tony Vallone at Tony's Restaurant on Post Oak Boulevard.

1801 Post Oak Blvd. (622-6778) More business deals and beautiful moments have been sealed at Tony's than in Houston's board rooms and mansions. Tony Vallone's legendary kitchen—the city's best known, bar none —is continental, with a strong Italian accent. But don't let that stop you if you're in the mood for gumbo. The bottom line is you can get just about anything you want to eat here. Sight'ems by news–paper columnists keep the local grapevine twisting and turning. Lunch Mon-Fri 11:30am-2pm, Dinner Mon-Sat 6pm- 11:30pm. Reservations. Credit Cards, Expensive.

10 Leslie & Co.

1749 Post Oak Blvd. (960-9113) Leslie & Co. is a genteel sort of place; this shop's preppy, conservative, semi-Bostonian look never loses currency. Leslie offers latest variations of these classic themes—argyle print socks, V-neck golfing sweaters, narrow pinstripe ties, herringbone twill jackets—promoted by a staff seemingly pulled straight from the yearbook of Choate Rosemary Hall. Mon-Sat 10am-6pm, Thu 10am-9pm.

11 La Mer

1717 Post Oak Blvd. (621-0404) Despite its name, Walter Aymen's stylish La Mer is not strictly seafood. Fish-phobes will find grilled beef medallions, roasted chicken breast and a vegetarian casserole. Still, seafood is generally the way to go, with reliable bouillabaisse, steamed mussels, seafood-and-pasta dishes and tenderest crabcakes. Mon-Thu 11am-10pm, Fri-Sat 11am-11pm. Moderate.

Refer to map on page 150

12 Saks Fifth Avenue Pavilion
1800 Post Oak Blvd. (627-0500) Houston's
most elite shopping center was built around
Saks Fifth Avenue in 1989; upscale merchants
include Hermes, Ungaro, Sonya Rykiel, David
Webb Jewelers, Luomo, Pierre Deux and
Victoria's Fine Linens. Several of the more
interesting stores include:

Janice Rudy
1800 Post Oak in The Pavilion (960-1073) The
antithesis of preppy, the wild and colorful contrast to the conservative. So don't come to this
trendy china, crystal and silver boutique in
hopes of finding Waterford or Lennox, because
you won't. Floor lamps spring from the
ground; funky artist-designed platters, bowls,
goblets and flatware line the shelves and
tables. Everything at Janice Rudy—everything
—is among the very best, most polished and
most aesthetically balanced avant garde
furnishings around. Mon-Sat 10am-6pm.

Louis Tenenbaum Estate Jewelers
1800 Post Oak in The Pavilion (629-7444)
Offers, according to some, the best collection
of antique and near-antique jewelry in Houston. Hark back to
British Empire times with beautiful, hand-set diamond and
ruby settings in white gold or platinum; take a step back
to 1930s America when you see Tenenbaum's extensive
collection of art deco wedding rings. Mon-Sat 10am-6pm.

Walzel's
1800 Post Oak in The Pavilion (627-7495) Tacks opposite
Houston's other master jeweler, Louis Tenenbaum. She
selects simple, elegant, and abstract creations for her contemporary gold and silver collection, then throws in a rare pre-
cious gem for punctuation. Local artists contribute their
costume jewelry creations, sprucing up the selection with the
most upscale faux-gems in town. Mon-Fri 10am-5:30pm, Sat
noon-4pm.

Sfuzzi
1800 Post Oak in The Pavilion (622-9600) Like its counter-
parts in Dallas and New York, this trendy neo-Italian is as well
known for the crowd that frequents it as for the menu. Good
pizzas, grilled fish and pastas. Forget the "s" and pronounce it
foo-zee. Mon-Wed 11am-11pm, Thu-Sat 11am-1pm, Sun
10:30am-10pm. Reservations. Credit Cards, Moderate.

Cafe Express
1800 Post Oak in The Pavilion (963-9222) and 3200 Kirby.
High-tech delis with full bars and pretty patios from the Cafe
Annie team. Chicken salad with pistachios is a passion for
many fans, and the desserts are divine. Just be careful not to
over-order, as it's easy to get carried away. Sun-Thu 10:30am-
11pm, Fri-Sat 10:30pm-midnight. Credit Cards, Inexpensive.

Hunan
1800 Post Oak in The Pavilion (965-0808) Said to be George
Bush's favorite Chinese restaurant, this elegant Pavilion dining
room features savory squab packages (eat them like a taco)
and excellent stir-fried green beans. Despite its relative
tameness overall—many other local Hunan restaurants
offer more exciting food—the dramatic setting and tuxedoed
service make it special. Mon- Thu 11:30am-10:30pm, Fri
11:30am-11:30pm, Sat noon-11:30pm, Sun noon-10:30pm.
Reservations. Credit Cards, Moderate.

13 Cafe Annie
1728 Post Oak Blvd. (840-1111) Sophisticated Euro-Southwest
bistro setting and chef/co-owner Robert Del Grande's cutting-
edge kitchen make this one of the city's most highly regarded
restaurants year after year. Beautifully plated food looks more
like art than nourishment. Excellent wine list, too. Lunch Mon-
Fri 11:30am-2pm, Dinner Mon-Thu 6:30pm-10pm, Fri-Sat
6:30pm-10:30pm. Reservations. Credit Cards, Expensive.

Refer to map on page 150

14 Gugenheim's Delicatessen
1708 Post Oak Blvd. (622-2773) Even chicken-fried Texans like this crisply designed outpost of New York's Carnegie Deli. Here you can sample such exotica as borscht, pickled herring, smoked whitefish and most of the Eastern European dishes associated with Jewish cuisine, and the towering sandwiches present an etiquette challenge. There's breakfast, too, and a large selection of bottled beers and sodas, including Cel-Ray tonics. Mon-Thu 10am-9pm, Fri 10am-10pm, Sat 9am-10pm, Sun 9am-9pm. Credit Cards, Inexpensive.

15 Willie Gs
1605 Post Oak Blvd. (840-7190) Cajun food, and lots of it. Crawfish fixed any way you like in a noisy, festive atmosphere. Mon-Fri 11am-11pm. Sat 11:30am-11pm. Sun 11:30am-10pm. Credit Cards, Moderate.

16 The Drive Inn
1503 Post Oak Blvd. (623-6060) Like its namesake in Matamoros, Mexico, The Drive Inn offers Mexican food for gringos. Unfortunately, the quality of the original is lacking in this knock-off. Still, it offers a casual and less-expensive alternative in the Galleria area, home to so many of the city's more ambitious restaurants. Sun-Thu 11am-10pm, Fri-Sat 11am-11pm. Credit Cards, Moderate.

17 McDonald's
1405 Post Oak Blvd. (963-0647) The largest McDonald's in the state, it's said, with designer-suit types lined up for breakfast holding their *Wall Street Journals*. Mon-Fri 6am-11pm, Sat-Sun 7am-11pm.

18 Post Oak Grill
1415 Post Oak Lane (993-9966) An American bistro with a tasteful, if not fashionable, crowd serves grilled fish, Wienerschnitzel, pastas and entree salads. There's live music in the adjacent bar, as well as a pretty terrace for dining outdoors. Nice lunch spot. Mon-Wed 11am-10pm, Thu 11am-12:30am, Fri 11am-1am, Sat Lunch 11am-3pm, Dinner 6pm-1am, Sun Brunch 11am-3pm, Dinner 6pm-10pm. Credit Cards, Moderate.

19 Omni (formerly Inn on the Park)
Four Riverway (871-8181) One of the most beautiful settings in Houston, this hotel sits back in a wooded area.
Cafe on the Green Mon-Sun Breakfast 6:30am-11:30am, Mon-Sat Lunch 11:30am-2:30pm, Dinner 5pm-11pm, Sun Brunch 11am-2:30pm. Moderate
La Reserve Mon-Fri Lunch 11:30am-2pm, Mon-Sat Dinner 6:30pm-10:30pm. Expensive.

20 Jags
5120 Woodway at Sage (621-4766) The brainchild of super-caterer Jackson Hicks is open to the public, although the Decorative Center in which it is set is a to-the-trade-only designer's emporium. Fantastically pretentious lunch-only restaurant, where the food is very good (occasionally sensational), beautiful to look at and rather pricey. Mon-Fri Lunch 11:30am-2:30pm. Reservations. Credit Cards, Moderate.

21 Jack's on Woodway
5055 Woodway (623-0788) Veteran restaurateur Jack Ray seems to have exorcized the jinx that cursed this location through so many restaurant incarnations. The current inspiration is clearly Santa Fe, and the menu reveals a fascination with native Southwestern foods that are done up into busy platters of stimulating fare. For dessert, order Jack's Sack, a chocolate sack filled with pound cake and berries that will satisfy four. Mon-Fri Lunch 11am-2pm, Mon-Thu Dinner 5pm-10pm, Fri-Sat 5pm-11pm. Reservations. Credit Cards, Moderate.

Refer to map on page 150

23 The Men's Club
3303 Sage Road (629-7900) This is the largest "gentlemen's club" in town and a place visitors like to talk about back home because of its sheer size and uninhibited style. Mon-Fri 11am-2am; Sat-Sun 6pm-2am.

24 Stelzig's of Texas
3123 Post Oak Blvd. (629-7779) Stelzig's opening date back in 1870 merits its inclusion in a litany of "old west" artifacts, but it's a survivor, not a thing of the past . This is now Houston's most upscale western wear store. (One might argue that strains of Kentucky blue-blood racing society have crept into the picture here.) Lucchesse, Nocona and Justin boots in ostrich, cowhide or antelope. Stetson hats in various gallon denominations. Belt buckles appear in forms crafted from prairie memorabilia; you'll see relics like buffalo nickel cuf-flinks and old-time Texas sheriff's badges. Mon-Wed, Fri-Sat 9:30am-6pm; Thu 9:30am-8pm.

26 LePeep
4702 Westheimer (629-7337) and other locations. Serving just breakfast and lunch, this chain of country-cottage cafes has been called the perfectly executed concept. Huge portions suggest the menu was written by giants, though the home-style pancakes, waffles and sausage taste as though they were prepared by someone's grandma. Mon-Fri 6:30am-2:30pm, Sat-Sun 7am-3pm.

27 On The Border
4608 Westheimer (961-4494) This Dallas-based chain has put together a real Texas-flavored bar and restaurant. Chicken faitas served sizzling with margaritas served in a mug. Great place for a lazy Sunday afternoon on the patio. Mon-Thu 11am-midnight, Fri 11am-1am, Sat 10am-1am, Sun 10am-midnight, Bar open Sun-Thu til 1am, Fri-Sat til 2am.

28 Captain Benny's Half-Shell Oyster Bar
4715 Westheimer (877-1028) and other locations. These boat-shaped oyster bars are all over town now, but the Main Street location near the Astrodome is still the most authentic. Most of Houston stops in eventually, from pro athletes to oil field trash to staffers from the nearby Medical Center. As you might expect, the oysters (raw or fried), shrimp and catfish are terrific, the people-watching excellent. Mon-Sat 11am-11:45pm, Sun 1pm-9pm. Credit Cards, Inexpensive.

29 Tokyo Gardens
4701 Westheimer (622-7886) Sushi-lovers argue over the mer-its of the raw fish served here, but there's no denying the exotic charm of the huge koi so friendly to kids or the Japanese dancers who regularly perform in the evenings. Mon-Fri Lunch 11:30am-2pm, Dinner 5:30pm-10:30pm, Sat 5:30pm-11pm, Sun 5:30pm-10:15pm.

30 Ritz-Carlton Dining Room (formerly the Remington)
1919 Briar Oaks Lane (840-7600) A bit stuffy, perhaps, the light-filled restaurant is certainly one of the most beautiful in the state. Across the hall, the Grill, swathed in dark wood and rich tones, provides the kind of men's club ambiance that is classic American. Either choice guarantees an excellent meal of classic choices with a slight Southwestern accent. In the afternoons, English-style tea is served in the living room. Restaurant: Mon-Sat 6:30am-2:30pm, Dinner 6:30pm-10pm, Sun 6:30am-11am, Sun Buffet Brunch 11am-2:30pm. Reservations. Credit Cards, Expensive. Bar & Grill: Mon-Sat 4pm-2am, Sun 4pm-midnight. Credit Cards, Expensive.

Looking east on Westheimer towards the Transco Tower.

WESTHEIMER CORRIDOR

Heading west from the Galleria area, Westheimer Road cuts a six-lane path through the middle of the largest concentration of strip centers, apartment complexes and neon signs in Texas. At night Westheimer resembles a great white way, with wall-to-wall cars, flashing signs and brightly lit storefronts. But this street is only the middle of what is a much larger corridor of restaurants and shops supported by the hundreds of thousands of people who live and work in this area. While there are restaurants that offer some of the finer dining experiences in town, the emphasis in this area is on fun, and lots of it. On the outside edge of this area is a large, loosely organized area of warehouse outlets known as the Harwin Area Wholesale District. It is worth a Saturday morning, but go prepared for an experience that more resembles a border town than a shopping mall.

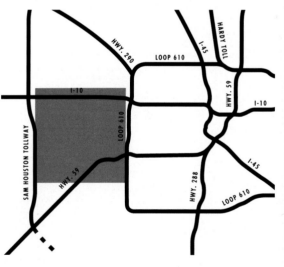

Refer to map on pages 162-163

1 James Coney Island
5745 Westheimer (652-3819) Houston's original chili dog emporium is fondly referred to as a "grease pit" by its many fans. Walk through the cafeteria-style line, take your mess to a table, close your eyes and enjoy. But caution: Go only if your digestive track is in good shape. Mon-Fri 5:30am-7pm, Sat 6am-6pm. Inexpensive.

2 Beck's Prime Drive-Thru
2615 Augusta (266-9901) and 2902 Kirby. This homegrown chain of upscale fast-food outlets offers some of the best burgers, grilled fish sandwiches and milkshakes in town. Drive through like the name says or laze on the deck at one of the picnic tables; the Augusta location, in particular, is a real beauty, snuggled under centuries-old oaks. Mon-Sun 11am-midnight. Inexpensive.

3 Cité Grill
5860 Westheimer at Augusta (783-1566) Chef/co-owner Herve Glin is doing California-French food, but you'll detect many Southwestern influences, too, at this lively bistro. The menu changes seasonally, but keep an eye out for long-cooked dishes from Glin's home province of Brittany. Better yet, just put yourself in the chef's hands and let him orchestrate dinner. Lunch Mon-Fri 11:30am-2:30pm, Dinner Mon-Thu 5:30pm-10:30pm, Fri-Sat 5:30pm-11pm. Reservations. Credit Cards, Moderate.

3 Houston's
5888 Westheimer (975-1947) This small national chain of fern bars practices a red-white- and-blue variety of edible ethnicity. The menu is even innocent of most California and Cajun influences, offering a short list of lavish entree-sized salads, classic burgers and decadent desserts. The air is always buzzing, the place full of life. By night it's something of a singles hangout. Mon-Thu 11am-11pm, Fri-Sat 11am-midnight.

3 Orvis Houston
5848 Westheimer (783-2111) Orvis is the fly fisherman's par-adise. It's one of the few places in Houston where you can go to get a book on how to tie your own trout-catchers, and it's probably the only place where you can actually get the stuff to do it. Also at Orvis: duck hunter's equipment, including well-made waders, thigh boots and an ample selection of top quality guns. Nice sport clothes too. Mon-Fri 9am-6pm, Sat 9am-5pm.

4 Spectrum Bookstore Inc.
5868 Westheimer (789-2269) Beyond your favorite fiction, Spectrum has always had a large selection of photography, cooking and travel books. Mon-Sat 10am-7pm, Sun 1pm-6pm.

5 Cineplex Odeon
2660 Augusta (781-3233) There are multi-theaters every-where in town, but this large, glitzy and extremely clean movie house seems to be the place to date on Friday and Saturday nights. Call for recording of showtimes.

6 Studebaker's
2630 Augusta (783-4142) Civilized dancing for those old enough to remember seeing the Beatles. Tue-Fri 5pm-2am, Sat 7pm-2am.

7 Fuddrucker's
3100 Chimney Rock (780-7080) While Fuddrucker's may be as much a miracle of marketing as it is of hamburger grilling, there's no arguing with the results. Among the great gimmicks: a glassed-in butcher shop so customers can watch the steak being cut and ground, an on-premises baker where the buns are made daily and a long condiment stand. You

Refer to map on pages 162-163

serve yourself, moving through a cafeteria-style line. Grab a
couple of longnecks, stroll on out into the beer garden and
proceed to get your hands and face greasy. Sun-Thu 11am-
10pm, Fri-Sat 11am-11pm. Inexpensive.

8   Dirty's
3230 Chimney Rock (781-1655) A place for burgers and beer
after the softball game. Mon-Fri 11am-midnight, Sat 11:30am-
midnight, Sun 11:30am-11pm. Inexpensive.

9   The Rivoli
5636 Richmond (789-1900) The art nouveau-accented design
and a contemporary/continental menu appeal to the many
business diners who regularly come here, as well as socialites
who lunch. The kitchen is famous for its lobster bisque. Lunch
Mon-Sat 11:30am-2:30pm, Dinner Mon-Sat 6pm-11pm, Sun
noon-10:15pm. Reservations. Credit Cards, Expensive.

10   Sammy's
5825 Richmond (780-0065) A little wood house on a busy strip
of Richmond near the Galleria is an incongruous setting for
Lebanese dining, but the cognoscenti come here for falafel,
kibi and the addictive mezza platters. Warm proprietorship.
Mon-Thu 11am-10:30pm, Fri-Sat 11am-11pm, Sun noon-10pm.
Reservations. Credit Cards, Inexpensive.

11   India's
*5704 Richmond near Chimney Rock (266-0131) and 2416 Bay
Area Blvd.* High-caste Indian restaurant features a low-key,
rather impersonal dining room, but elegant cuisine. Noon
buffet is a bargain, too. Lunch Mon-Fri 11am-2:30pm, Sun
noon-3pm, Dinner Sun-Thu 5pm-10pm, Fri-Sat 5pm-11pm. Bay
Area Blvd. Reservations. Credit Cards, Moderate.

12   Sam's Place Del Norte
5710 Richmond (781-1605) Sam's is like a
non-stop giant frat party. And it keeps growing.
Right next to the main Sam's is Sam's Boat and
the latest addition is Sam's Ice House. The bands
play mostly cover tunes, but paradoxically, the
real draw seems to be the crowd itself — people
come in droves because they know tons of other
fun-seekers will be there. Mon-Sat 11am-2am,
Sun noon-2am.

Sam's Place Del Norte.

13   Sam's Boat
5710 Richmond (781-BOAT) Next door to Sam's Place is
Sam's Boat, offering up seafood with their outdoor party.
Together these two clubs seem like an ongoing street party.
Mon-Sat 11am-2am, Sun noon-2am.

14   Rick's Cabaret
3113 Bering Drive (785-0444) The first Houston "gentlemen's
club" that drew a following around the country. The name
Rick's would show up on visitor surveys right next to the more
predictable Houston amenities. Mon-Fri 11am-2am, Sat-Sun
7pm-2am.

15   Magnolia Bar & Grill
6000 Richmond at Fountain View (781-6207) Upper-scale
Cajun restaurant features plantation shutters, enormous
antique mahogany bar and lazy ceiling fans. The food is
dependably good (and very like its sibling, Louisiana Don's);
the Sunday buffet is outstanding. Mon-Thu 11am-10pm, Fri-Sat
11am-11pm, Sun 10:30am-11pm. Reservations. Credit Cards,
Moderate.

16 Dave & Busters

6010 Richmond (952-2233) They call this warehouse-sized club a "53,000-square-foot restaurant and entertainment facility," but that doesn't come close to describing what D&B really is. The club that began in Dallas has packed in all the activities they must have liked as kids and then added a restaurant and bar. It is a nutty combination, but now you can play indoor golf, video games, billiards, shuffleboard, bowl and shoot baskets while holding a longneck beer. A show room to watch large-screen sports telecasts, Las Vegas-style card games and a dance floor where you can "bop" round out the club. Children are welcome here, to a point, that point being 10pm. Mon 11am-1am, Tue-Fri 11am-2am, Sat 11:30am-2am, Sun 11:30am-1am. Credit Cards, Moderate.

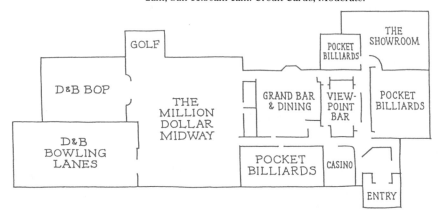

17 Ginza

5868 San Felipe near Fountain View (785-0332) Some Westerners have complained of feeling unwelcomed here, but for an authentic Japanese meal it's hard to beat this Tanglewood spot. The sushi is sparkling fresh, and lunch is a bargain. Lunch Mon-Fri 11:30am-2pm, Dinner Sat-Sun 6pm-10:30pm. Reservations. Credit Cards, Moderate.

18 Fountain View Cafe

1842 Fountain View (785-9060) What the Avalon is to River Oaks and the Buffalo Grille is to West U., the Fountain View Cafe is to Tanglewood. Top-notch breakfasts are worth a visit in and of themselves, but don't overlook terrific burgers, deli sandwiches and full-fountain service. Mon-Fri 7am-3pm, Sat-Sun 8am-3pm. Inexpensive.

19 Bering's

6102 Westheimer (785-6400) Bering's carries everything one expects to see in an everyday hardware store but offers one of the best gift and housewares departments in Houston. Limoges boxes, Herrend china, Lalique crystal and unusual picture frames sit under the same roof that shelters hoes, rakes, fertilizers and lawn loungers. And Bering's gourmet section offers high-end blenders and kitchen toys, like Braun coffee makers and coveted Kitchen Aid blenders. Also: myriad flavors of coffee beans, chocolates and bonbons. Mon-Fri 8am-6pm, Sat 8:30am-6pm, Sun 11am-5pm.

20 Palm

6100 Westheimer near Fountain View (977-2544) Speakeasy-style steakhouse, with thick steaks and lobsters as big as a poodle. It's part of the New York chain, right down to the rude waiters and caricatures covering the wall. Mon-Fri 11:30am-10:30pm, Sat-Sun 5:30pm-10:30pm. Credit Cards, Expensive.

21 Fuads
6100 Westheimer (785-0130) This intimate little Continental-style spot will cook whatever you are in the mood for. Just don't ask for a menu; they won't give you one. This is a place for regulars, and as such can seem like you're in someone else's club. But the fare is enjoyable. Mon-Fri 11am-2am, Sat-Sun 6pm-2am. Credit Cards, Expensive.

22 Pappadeaux
6015 Westheimer (782-6310) and other locations. The Pappas family's Cajun branch is known for loud Dixieland music, crawfish in the fountain and plenty of things blackened. Try the gumbo, fried alligator, frog legs and softshelled crabs. Sun-Thu 11am-11pm, Fri-Sat 11am-midnight. Moderate.

23 Mama's Cafe
6019 Westheimer near Fountain View (266-8514) Down-home breakfasts (and plenty of newspapers), burgers and chicken-fried steaks make this roadhouse-like diner a favorite of both families and weekday working people. Cheerful, efficient ambiance. Mon-Thu 6:30am-midnight, Fri 6:30am-1am, Sat 8am-1am, Sun 8am-midnight. Reservations. Credit Cards, Inexpensive.

24 County Line
6159 Westheimer (784-8777) and *13850 Cutten.* These two outposts of an Austin chain are done up to resemble 1940s roadhouses, with big band music and plenty of memorabilia on the walls. The culinary draw: excellent barbecued brisket, ribs, sausage and chicken, along with slow-smoked prime rib. The side dishes don't live up to the meats, unfortunately, but the homemade milkshakes partially compensate. Lunch Mon-Fri 11am-2pm, Dinner Mon-Sat 5:30pm-10pm, Sun noon-9:30pm. Credit Cards, Inexpensive.

25 El Patio
6444 Westheimer (780-0410) Inside this nondescript restaurant along the Westheimer strip is one of the more famous bars in town, known as "Club No Minors" for the small sign on the door. After-work meeting place where you might not leave till closing time due to the strongest magaritas in town. Mon-Sat 11am-10:45pm, Sun 11am-9:45pm. Credit Cards, Inexpensive.

26 LaTrattoria
6444 Westheimer (780-0410) Chef-owner Carlo Moliaro's friendly little spot serves Northern Italian dishes to a discriminating clientele. One of the city's best and still a well-kept secret. Mon-Sat 11am-10:45pm, Sun 11am-9:45pm. Credit Cards, Inexpensive.

27 Montesano's
6009 Beverly Hill, off Fountain View (977-4565) Recent renovations have made Antonio Mingalone's dining room even more beautiful, with painstakingly hand-finished walls, gorgeous wine racks and acres of modern art. When Mingalone himself is in the kitchen, it's hard to find a better Italian meal in town. Don't even bother with the menu; just put yourself in the chef's capable hands. Fine wine list, too. Lunch Mon-Sat 11:30am-2:30pm, Dinner Mon-Sat 5:30pm-11pm. Reservations. Credit Cards, Moderate.

28 Ruth's Chris Steak House
6213 Richmond (789-2333) Ghosts from Houston's oil boom hover in this ageless steakhouse, where the steaks are big and come sizzling in butter (hold up a napkin to shield your tie when served). Good ol' boys with Rolex watches and sipping bourbon gather here to chew the fat. Sun-Fri 11:30am-11pm, Sat 5pm-11pm. Reservations. Credit Cards, Expensive.

Refer to map on pages 162-163

29 Yucatan Liquor Stand

6353 Richmond (789-6055) A party — and a big one — every night of the week. The bands usually play in the parking lot, drawing fun-loving masses second only to Sam's. There is a disco inside and a huge sandbox of a volleyball court outside. The sign above the entryway, "Mercado de Carne" (meat market), pretty much says it all. Mon-Thu 4pm-2am, Fri-Sun 3pm-2am.

30 Al Basha

6374 Richmond at Unity (784-2727) This tiny storefront restaurant in a strip center has rose-colored tablecloths, soft Arabic music and simple Lebanese food. Good lunch choice for dining on the mezze (or mazah, as it's spelled here), tiny plates of exotica that include hummus, stuffed grape leaves, falafel, babaganouj and such. The action heats up on weekend evenings when a bellydancer entertains. Sun-Thurs 11am-10pm, Fri-Sat 11am-midnight. Inexpensive.

31 Back Alley

6400 Richmond (952-2559) A cavernous club decorated to look vaguely like a seedy alley. Both up-and-coming acts and big stars trying something new (such as David Bowie's Tin Machine) pack them in at this raucous party house on Richmond Street's rockin' west end. Covers $3 weekdays, $5 weekends. Wed-Sun 8pm-2am.

32 Pappasito's

6445 Richmond (784-5253) and other locations. Mind-numbingly loud and with a wait that often runs an hour or more, these Tex-Mex cantinas turn out some of the city's best-loved Mexican food. The fajitas are terrific. Sun-Thu 11am-11pm, Fri-Sat 11am-midnight. Credit Cards, Moderate.

33 LaBare

5447 Richmond (780-0930)) If Rick's is a "gentlemen's club," then this must be a "ladies' club." The chain of male stripper clubs is for ladies only. Cover. Tue-Sat 6pm-2am.

34 Akbar (formerly Bombay Grill)

3640 Hillcroft, between Richmond and Westpark (977-1272) It looks more like an American steakhouse than a curry parlor, but this popular Northern Indian restaurant is set square in the middle of an Indian commercial district and boasts the clientele to prove its authenticity. The cooks who work with the tandoor oven are masters of their art, pulling out moist red-hot chicken, chunks of swordfish and little rolls of minced lamb. Vegetarians will also be happy here. Lunch Daily 11am-2pm, Dinner Daily 5:30pm-10:30pm. Credit Cards, Moderate.

35 Carrabba's

3115 Kirby (522-3131) and 1399 S. Voss (468-0868) The newer Voss location siphoned some of the crowds off the original Kirby restaurant, but the wait for a table at either of these two Italian cucinas can still be an hour or more. The draw: first-rate pastas, salads, pizza and grilled chicken, and a staff that really hustles. Go before you're hungry—and take earplugs. Kirby: Mon-Thu 11am-11pm, Fri 11am-midnight, Sat 11:30am-midnight, Sun noon-10pm. S. Voss: Mon-Thu 11am-10:30pm, Fri-Sat 11am-11:30pm, Sun 11:30am-10pm. Credit Cards, Moderate.

36 Third Coast

6540 San Felipe (783-6540) The Brennan family's long-awaited second Houston outpost is a wavy-gravy diner with rotisserie-grilled chicken and pork loin, meatloaf, buttery mashed potatoes and supernal macaroni and cheese. Save room for desserts, for they are truly decadent. Mon-Thu 11am-10pm, Fri-Sat 11am-11pm, Sun 11am-9pm. Credit Cards, Moderate.

Refer to map on pages 162-163

37 Dolce & Freddo
7595 San Felipe near Voss (789-0219) and 5515 Kirby Drive.
If you're hip enough, these sleek espresso bars are the place
for cappucino, unpronounceable gelati and enough attitude
dancing to last the week. Popular way to finish off an evening
on the town. Sun-Thu noon-midnight, Fri-Sat noon-1am.
Inexpensive.

38 Doneraki
7705 Westheimer (975-9815) The original Fulton location is
the real thing—a good Mexican restaurant in the heart of a
Hispanic neighborhood. The interior is just tacky enough, with
beer signs tacked about, mariachis and good margaritas, too.
The newer and larger Westheimer location, though less
authentic, still brings in droves of fajita-loving customers.
Noisy. Mon-Thu 11am-midnight, Fri-Sat 11am-3:30am, Sun
11am-10pm. Credit Cards, Inexpensive.

39 Vargo's
2401 Fondren north of Westheimer (782-3888) The setting
here is glorious, with acres of azaleas, a beautiful pond and
plenty of wildlife (e.g., peacocks, geese, swans) to keep the
view ever moving. The kitchen is resolutely middle-of- the-
road American, but you'll feel satisfied just devouring the
scenery. Lunch Mon-Fri 11am-2pm, Dinner Mon-Thu 6pm-
10pm, Fri-Sat 5pm-11pm, Sun 11am-2:30pm. Reservations.
Credit Cards, Moderate.

40 Atchafalaya River Cafe
8816 Westheimer (975-7873) and other locations. Spicy
crawfish, boudin, gumbo and etouffee are the calling cards
at these ersatz Cajun roadhouses, where the loud party
atmosphere rarely lags. When you tell your friends to meet
you there for the lively happy hour, pronounce it uh-CHAF-ul-
LIE-uh. Mon-Thu 11am-11pm, Fri-Sat 11am-midnight, Sun
11am-10pm. Credit Cards, Moderate.

41 Nam
2727 Fondren at Westheimer (789-6688) A definite contender
for the best eggrolls award, this mainstream Vietnamese
restaurant also serves poultry, seafood and beef dishes.
Courteous staff is happy to show you the ins and outs of
Vietnamese dining. Mon-Thu 11am-11pm, Fri-Sat 11am-mid-
night, Sun 5pm-10pm. Credit Cards, Moderate.

41 Elvia's
2727 Fondren (266-9631) Elvia herself often wends through
the crowd, making sure that everyone is having fun. And they
usually are — on more than one occasion, the patrons took it
upon themselves to create a dance floor by getting everyone
to move their tables. A variety of acts, from folk to rock to
zydeco, are transforming this Mexican restaurant (which
serves light dishes from Mexico's interior regions) into a
major music venue. Though some have complained that the
neon lighting makes the room a little too bright, most people
are too busy sampling the impressive beer selection to notice.
Mon 11am-10pm, Tue-Thu 11am-1am, Fri-Sat 11am-2am.
Credit Cards, Inexpensive.

42 Rudi Lechner's
2503 S. Gessner at Westheimer (782-1180) The decor may be a
little dated — it's certainly wacky — but many like the cooking
that practically oozes gemütlich and the cozy darkness of this
Austrian-accented eatery. Popular among a fifty-something
crowd. Mon-Thu 11am-10pm, Fri-Sat 11am-11:15pm, Sun
11:30am-10pm. Credit Cards, Moderate.

Refer to map on pages 162-163

43　Cyclone Anaya's

1015 Durham near Washington (862-3209) and 9347-1/2 Richmond. Outstanding nachos and margaritas, along with blaring ballgames on the TV, crying babies and a rather bizarre birthday ritual (let's just say celebrants usually wind up drenched), make this a great place to meet friends to kick off an evening of partying. The Tex-Mex food is actually pretty humdrum—though enchiladas can be very good—but it's great fun, if you can handle it. Mon-Thu 11am-11pm, Fri-Sat 11am-midnight, Sun noon-10pm. Credit Cards, Inexpensive.

44　Sherlock's Baker St. Pub

10001 Westheimer (977-1857) It used to be a pub; now it's a club — they just keep adding on. And the crowd has expanded to fill the space available. But if you never knew the smaller, more intimate Sherlock's, chances are you'll have a good time. The far-west locale draws an interesting mix of clean-cut professionals, from singles in their early twenties to forty-something (divorced?) revelers. The mostly local cover bands can sound mighty similar after a while, but they're all good to dance to. No cover. Mon-Fri noon-2am, Sat-Sun 5pm-2am.

44　Spellbinder's Comedy Club

10001 Westheimer in the Carilion Center(266-2525) and 4617 Montrose in Chelsea Market. HBO, Showtime and Comic Strip Live alumni put on a show at Spellbinder's; the club features professional, nationally recognized acts, mostly from Hollywood, L.A., or San Francisco. Lounge opens at 6:30pm. Shows Tue-Thu 8pm, Fri-Sat 8pm and 10:30pm, Sun 7:30pm.

45　The Marker Adams Mark Hotel

2900 Briar Park (978-7400) This hotel kitchen has earned a reputation in recent years for its "American Western cuisine." Plenty of wild game, seafood and a respectable wine list make this a good west-side choice for a business dinner. Dinner Mon-Sat 6pm-10pm, Brunch Sun 10:30am-2:30pm. Reservations. Credit Cards, Moderate.

46　Goode Company Barbecue

5109 Kirby (522-2530) and 8911 Katy Freeway, near Wirt Road. Jim Goode looks the way Yankees think a good ol' boy Texan should look, but he cooks better than your mother. Out-of-towners looking to eat real Texas food should try one of his two barbecue outposts for irresistible chicken, brisket, duck and pork. Don't pass on the jalapeno cheese bread or pecan pie, either. Daily 11am-10pm. Credit Cards, Inexpensive.

47　Pappy's Bar & Grill

9041 Katy Freeway, near Campbell (827-1811) and 2651 Richmond. Chili's-like food at modest prices make this pair of ferny burger joints popular for families and young couples. Easy to drop in, watch the ballgame at the bar and munch on nachos. Sun-Thu 11am-10:30pm, Fri-Sat 11am-midnight. Credit Cards, Inexpensive.

48　Taste of Texas

10505 Katy Freeway (932-6901) This is the busiest restaurant in west Houston, where you can expect to wait one to two hours before finally ordering up one of the locally famous tagged and numbered Black Angus steaks. The place is huge, the noise level exhausting, the steaks perfection (and they come with all the extras). Mon-Thu 11am-10pm, Fri 11am-11pm, Sat 4pm-11pm, Sun 4pm-10pm. Credit Cards, Moderate.

49　Guadalajara Mexican Grille

210 Town and Country Village at West Belt (461-5300) Loud, gregarious cantina setting where suburbanites feast on generous portions of Tex-Mex. With good nachos, fajitas and fresh-made tortillas, it's one of the best of the Pappasito's knock-offs. Sun-Thu 11am-10pm, Fri-Sat 11am-11pm. Credit Cards, Moderate.

Refer to map on pages 162-163

50   Dons Records

4900 Bissonnet (667-5701) Oldies addicts from across the nation clamor to enlist owner Don Janicek's services in unearthing classics by the likes of Al Jolson, Glenn Miller and even lesser known pleasers like Yma Sumac. Contemporary artists as well. Mon-Sat 9:30am-5:30pm.

51   Queen of Sheba

5710 Bellaire (665-3009) Exotic and sometimes searing Ethiopian cuisine is served in this little strip-center eatery humming with East African melodies. The national dish of Ethiopia is the stew-like wote. Eat it with the millet bread called injera. Tue-Thu 11am-10pm, Fri-Sat 11am-midnight, Sun 11am-10pm. Credits Cards, Inexpensive.

52   Pico's

5941 Bellaire, east of Hillcroft (662-8383) Many Houstonians would argue that the underrated Pico's serves the city's best Mexican (not Tex-Mex) food. The setting is modest but cheerful. Come for the fruity drinks known as aguas and authentic dishes from the Mexican coast, such as snapper baked in banana leaves. Mexican breakfasts, too. Mon-Thu 9am-10pm, Fri-Sat 9am-11pm. Credit Cards, Inexpensive.

53   Harwin Drive Wholesale District

Harwin between Hillcroft and Sam Houston Tollway. This loose arrangement of warehouse-based shops might easily qualify as our largest outdoor shopping mall. Pass under the Southwest Freeway's Shepherd curve heading west on Harwin, and you'll see wholesalers, discounters, family-owned import stores and factory outlets filling row after row of the inexpensive strip center space here. Have no illusions: this is not a glamour shopper's turf. Come armed with a thick hide and an eye for a bargain (and for occasional fakes) and you might meet success rooting out a new set of tires for your BMW, a new Sony stereo, gold jewelry, K-Swiss tennis shoes or Hartmann Luggage.

The Luggage and Leather Outlet

9880 Harwin (266-0237) Name brands like Samsonite, London Fog and Perry Ellis at deep discounts.

Hosiery Outlets of America

9844 Harwin (266-4535) This outlet offers repackaged and remarked leg wear by Donna Karan, Hanes and Round the Clock at half of department store prices. Also on the agenda: · lingerie by Christian Dior, Olga and Wacoal, plus workout and aerobics garb for men, women and kids, too.

Discount Perfume

9822 Harwin (784-8011) One sees perfume so rarely on sale, so thank the lucky stars for this spot. Many men's and women's designer fragrances will lure your senses, especially at the one-half to two-thirds discounts. If particular brands or labels don't seem to appear, ask if this outlet can order it.

Wholesale Shoe Warehouse

3934 Dunvale (781-8511) Row upon row of shelves stacked with open shoe boxes await customers here: locate the aisle marker advertising your size and try on footwear to your heart's content; no salesperson will interrupt you. Brands include Perry Ellis, Bandolino, Nina and Liz Claiborne.

The Victorian home,
such as the one at 180
Harvard, is symbolic of
the Houston Heights.

THE HEIGHTS

I n 1891 Oscar Martin Carter and Daniel Denton Cooley, calling their new land venture the Omaha and South Texas Land Co., bought 1750 acres of wooded land north of Houston. The Heights, so named because of its 23-foot elevation edge on Houston, was Carter's vision of a middle class, blue collar, master-planned community. Eighty-five miles of streets were laid connecting 10,000 lots. Not a single lot was sold until all the utility connections had been accomplished. And in a mass-transit coup d' etat, The Land Co. finagled a direct trolley connection to downtown Houston.

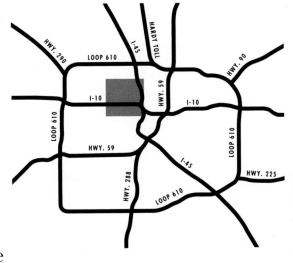

The Heights was then a separate city, with its own town hall, fire station, police station, and jail (admittedly all in one building). The Heights possessed a peculiar quietude, a quaint Victorian charm. In 1918 the Heights relented and came under Houston's wing, but to this day residents insist there's something special about it, something "separate and unique."

Refer to map on pages 174-175

Historical Heights Homes
Listed below are six of the many homes that the Heights is known for, a mini-tour along Heights Boulevard.

The Durham House Bed & Breakfast.

1   Durham House
921 Heights Boulevard (868-4654) Jay L. Durham, the first Fire Chief of the Heights Fire Department, commissioned Heights developer William Wilson in 1903, to build this delicate Queen Anne style home which now serves as a quaint Bed & Breakfast (Double $60-$75). A hexagonal turret topped with a weathervane graces the two-story home, which still retains its original trim work, moldings and white pine floors.

2   Webber House
1011 Heights Boulevard. This brusque Queen Anne structure was executed in blood-red brick by Samuel H. Webber, a brick mason and builder, in the year 1907. Chosen as a setting for the production of the film *Final Verdict*, the massive building still harbors its pre-automobile-age hitching posts, an original iron fence and a Victorian porte-cochere shaded by a graceful rounded turret.

3   1102 Heights Boulevard
1102 Heights Boulevard. Builder Henry MacGregor extracted the plans for this 1896 home from Design No. 30 in the Cottage Souvenir No. 2, one of Knoxville architect George F. Barber's many pattern books. The completed structure was sold to John A. Milroy, an executive with The Omaha and South Texas Land Co. The speculatively built home was one of the Heights' earliest large houses; its owner went on to serve as an eight-term mayor of the Heights, then a separate municipality from Houston. The design of the house is similar to the more ornate structure at 1802 Harvard, listed below.

4   1233 Yale
1233 Yale. This small Queen Anne cottage, built in 1909, sits perched on five-foot-high brick piers. Its five-bay, wrap-around porch, supported by Ionic columns, helped win it a spot in the National Register of Historic Places for architectural significance. The owners cling proudly to its early twentieth-century appearance, maintaining original Victorian colors and molding treatments.

5   1802 Harvard
1802 Harvard. This 1894 home (see page 172) was built from Tennessee architect George Barber's widely used Cottage Souvenir No. 2 plans, as was the more latticed home at 1102 Heights Boulevard. The beautifully restored, towered villa is surely the most photographed home in the Heights. Beginning in 1974, the present owner completely rejuvenated the entire structure, including the five bedrooms, library and greenhouse areas. 1802 Harvard is listed in the American Society of Interior Designers "Significant Interiors" survey.

6   Zagst House
347 W. 20th Avenue. A two-story curved veranda fronted by Ionic columns encircles this plantation-style home, completed shortly after the turn of the century in 1907. No other structure in the Heights communicates the feel and aura of the South as successfully as this seeming migrant from a Mississippi town, once owned by Houston builder and carpenter Stephen R. Zagst.

Refer to map on pages 174-175

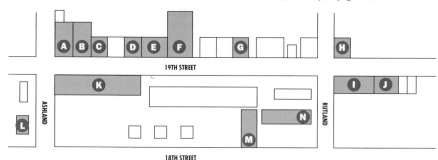

7   Heights Historical "Main Street" Area

A   Carter & Cooley Co. Deli
375 W. 19th Street (864-3354) Deli in historical setting known for great sandwiches and homemade soups. Excellent desserts and salads. Mon-Fri 9am-6pm, Sat 9am-5pm.

B   John's Flowers & Antiques
373 W. 19th Street (862-8717) Combination florist and antique shop. Country primitive antiques. Mon-Fri 9am-5:30pm, Sat 9am-4:30pm.

C   Ashland Attic
365 W. 19th Street (880-1840) Fine new gifts including linen, wedding, jewelry, etc. and some antiques. Tue-Fri 10am-5:30pm, Sat 10am-6pm.

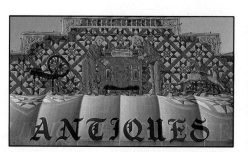

D   Charm of Yesteryear & Ragtime Antiques
355 W. 19th Street (868-1141) Antique furniture, out of the ordinary collectibles. Daily 10:30am-6pm.

E   Antiques on Nineteenth
345 W. 19th Street (869-5030) Co-op of 12-13 dealers. A variety of things. No specialty. Mon-Sat 10am-6pm, Sun 1pm-5pm.

F   Heights Theater
341 W. 19th Street Built in the early '20s, this theater was severely burned in the '60s and roofless for 20 years. Rescued by locals Sharon and Gus Kopriva, it is renovated and now used for a variety of purposes including photo and art exhibits, plays and live musical entertainment. Drop by for more information.

G   Heights Antique Co-op
321 W. 19th Street (864-7237) Co-op of five dealers. Glassware, antiques, collectibles and modern furniture. A variety to choose from. Tue-Sat 10am-5pm.

H   Historic Heights Antiques & Interiors
249 W. 19th Street (868-2600) Fine American furniture and accessories. Everything for the home. Mon-Sat 10am-6pm, Sun noon-5pm.

I   Chippendale Eastlake Louis & Phyfe
250 W. 19th Street (869-8633) Co-op of 20 dealers. Everyone has different antiques and collectibles from Victorian to early American to Oriental. Mon-Sat 10am-6pm, Sun noon-5pm.

Heights Theater.

J   Heights Pavilion
244 W. 19th Street (861-7475) Market place for unique and handmade furnishings and artwork. One of a kind. Mon-Sat 10am-6:30pm, Sun noon-5:30pm.

K   Harold's Men's Wear
350 W. 19th Street (864-2647) Specializing in fine men and ladies wear since 1950. Harold's has clothed everyone from Oiler coach Bum Phillips to *Dallas'* "J.R. Ewing" and a host of celebrities from around the country. Mon-Wed and Fri-Sat 9:30am-6pm, Thu 9:30am-8pm.

L   Ashland House Tea Room
1801 Ashland (863-7613) This charmingly restored 1907 Victorian house had several restaurant incarnations before it finally became this much-admired sleeper. Today it serves

traditional home-cooking, such as pork chops, mashed potatoes, chicken salad and pot roast, as well as English scones and finger sandwiches. The refined setting makes it the perfect spot for lunching with your great-aunt. Mon-Sat 11am-3pm. Credit Cards, Moderate.

M HITS Unicorn Theater
311 W. 18th Street (861-7408) Performing arts school for children in kindergarten to senior high school. Teaches basic acting, singing, dance and auditioning skills. Supplies children's course for the Houston Grand Opera. Shows held each semester for each age group and monthly in the summer. Call for performance information.

8 Yale Pharmacy & Fountain
4100 Yale (861-3113) The oldest pharmacy in the Heights and still serving sandwiches, hamburgers, malts and shakes at lunch. Also has a gift department. Lunch hours: Mon-Fri 8am-3pm, Sat 8am-1pm. Pharmacy hours: Mon-Fri 8am-6pm, Sat 8am-1pm.

9 Kaiser Pavilion in Marmion Park
Heights Boulevard at 18th Street (John Martin Associates, 1986) A charming public meeting space in the park named after James Marmion Sr., the last mayor of the Heights when it was a separate municipality.

10 Yale Ole Tyme Antique Shoppe
1525 Yale (880-1166) Country classics to Victorian, mostly American. Very quaint Ma and Pa down-home shop with down-home prices (and a lot of everything). Tue-Sat 10am-6pm, Sun 1pm-5pm.

Kaiser Pavilion in Marmion Park.

11 Houston Public Library-Heights Branch
1302 Heights Boulevard (861-4149) (J.M. Glover, 1925) Large scale was architect J.M. Glover's style in imparting an aura of permanence and scholarliness to this Italian Renaissance building, erected in 1925. An elongated, tile-roofed main hall recedes from the cast stone entrance bay, whose arch echoes the famous sally port of Rice University's Lovett Hall. Mon and Thu noon-9pm, Tue-Wed and Fri-Sat 10am-6pm.

12 KHW Antiques
718 W. 11th Street (869-8431) Reconditioned furniture. Thu-Fri noon-6pm, Sat 10am-6pm, Sun 1pm-5pm.

12 Charlie Brown's
720 W. 11th Street (868-1166) Specializes in antique restoration and repairs. Also sells a variety of antiques, furniture, glass, silver, rugs, etc. Daily 11am-6pm.

Refer to map on pages 174-175

13 Bébé & tiques
1106 Ashland (861-1519) Specializing in the buying and selling of fine antique dolls. Handmade christening gowns and antique furniture. Thu-Sun noon-5pm.

14 The Black Swan
515 W. 11th Street (880-0539) Furniture, decorative accessories, vintage clothing and jewelry.Tue-Sat 10am-5:30pm, Sun noon-5:30pm.

14 V.S.O.P. Antiques
519 W. 11th Street (880-0539) "Eclectic look," carries mostly furniture. Tue-Sat 10am-5:30pm, Sun noon-5:30pm.

14 A-Byé Antiques
521 W. 11th Street (863-8828) Restoration and sales of antique furniture. Tue-Sat 10am-6pm, Sun 1pm-5pm.

15 Cherie's Collectibles
1102 Tulane at corner of W. 11th Street (861-3734) Furniture and glass. Tue-Sat 10am-5:30pm, Sun noon-5:30pm.

16 R&F Antiques
912 Yale (861-7750) American oak, variety of glass. Mon-Sat 10am-6pm, Sun by appt.

17 Sara's Bed & Breakfast Inn
941 Heights Boulevard (868-1130 or 800-593-1130) 11 rooms. Double $50-$75. Reservations as far in advance as you can. Open all year. Has a balcony suite that sleeps six.

Above, Sara's Bed & Breakfast.

18 Farmers' Market
2520 Airline (862-8866) An association of 30 produce dealers with seemingly endless bins of fresh produce from California to Florida and Mexico. Open daily 6am-5:30pm.

19 Dan Electro's Guitar Bar
1031 E. 24th Street (862-8707) A friendly Heights hole-in-the-wall featuring blues and alternative rock-and-roll. Amateurs are invited to bring their own instruments and jam every Thursday, which is billed as "Songwriters & Old Folkies Nite." There's also a good blues jam session on Wednesday nights. Cover range from $4-$5. Wed-Sat 7pm-2am.

20 11th Street Cafe
748 E. 11th Street at Studewood (862-0089) A thinking person's road food—solid, comfy dishes such as biscuits, meatloaf, fried pork chops and pizza. An intellectual bent sets this place above the ordinary, so come prepared for arty conversation with your breakfast. Tues-Fri 7am-3pm, Sat-Sun 8am-3pm. Open nightly Tues-Sun 5pm-10pm for pizza, burgers and salads. Inexpensive.

Refer to map on pages 174-175

21 Stardust Antique Co-op

1129 E. 11th Street (868-1600) Co-op of five dealers. Antiques and collectibles, western and primitive antiques, Victorian pop-up books, etc. Sat 10am-5pm, Sun noon-6pm.

22 Andy's Home Cafe

1115 E. 11th at Studewood (861-9423) As much a cultural experience as a culinary one, this is a funky after-hours spot for the rock 'n' roll crowd. Breakfast, lunch or late-late-night Tex-Mex in the Heights, all provide plenty of local color. Open 24 hours. Inexpensive.

23 Booked Up

711 Studewood (868-3910) Owned by author Larry McMurtry. Wall-to-wall and floor-to-ceiling books. Mostly humanities related. Daily 10am-6pm.

24 Jimmie's Place

2803 White Oak (861-9707) This 40-year-old-plus ice house is a Heights institution and home to the "White Oak Athletic Association." A favorite watering hole for white collars, blue collars and dingy collars. Bring the parents, kids and pets (preferably leashed). Weekend nights see the regulars mingling with a younger crowd waiting for showtime at Fitzgerald's, located across the street. Mon-Sat 7am-midnight, Sun noon-10pm.

25 Fitzgerald's

2706 White Oak (862-7625) Many bands on the verge of nationwide fame rock the second floor of this old house. Named "Best Live Music Venue" in the 1992 *Public News* Music Poll. Acts include everything from folk rock to reggae/rock, with an emphasis on the rock. The downstairs bar, called Zelda's, is a good place to see new local bands. Daily 8pm-2am.

26 Reddi Room

2626 White Oak (868-6188) If you've got the blues, fire that overpaid therapist and get yourself on down to the Reddi Room. Night after night in this tiny, seedy club (decorated all in red, hence the name), Milton Hopkins and pals belt out the best blues in town. Mon-Sat 11am-2am, Sun noon-2am.

27 Toucans

1606 White Oak (861-8544) Caribbean is the theme here. Eat inside in the cozy dining room or outside under the palapas or on the deck. Shrimp and crawfish specials are great when in season or have a burger. Sun-Fri 11am-11pm, Sat noon-11pm. Credit Cards, Inexpensive.

THE BINZ AREA

The Binz has an interesting heritage. Newly founded Rice Institute sat on the edge of town in the '30s, and the Binz— or the South End—was Houston's *most* fashionable residential district. "It was a very fine part of town," according to one of Houston's "old settlers." But activity concentrated elsewhere in the '50s, most notably in Bellaire and River Oaks, and the South End deviated (successfuly) into suburban retailing, but this was to falter as well. Happily, vestiges of Binz's role in Houston's past survive. Some historical churches stand here, most notably the Holy Rosary Church (3601 Milam), The South Main Baptist Church (4000 Main) and Trinity Church (3415 Main). The Binz has decayed,

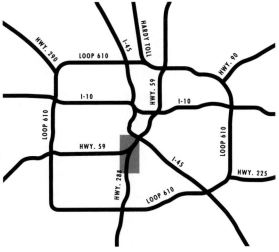

admittedly, but its mix of proud southern homes and randomly disbursed commercial establishments creates its own particular charm.

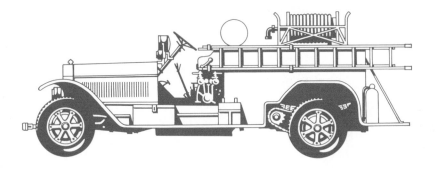

1 Houston Fire Museum

2403 Milam (524-2526) Houston's old Fire Station No. 7, built
in 1899 to shelter firefighting's latest equipment—a horse-
drawn hose wagon and a new American LaFrance steamer—
now opens its doors as The Houston Fire Museum, where "the
story of firefighting lives." The Romanesque building, renovated in 1982, is itself noteworthy and is listed in the National
Register of Historic Places. Within the doors, justifiably proud
Fire Department guides recount their profession's history to
youngsters and grown-up fire buffs alike, their narrations com-
plemented by photos of Houston's famous 1912 Fifth Ward
fire. In the museum's varied fire equipment collection is an
1884 hand-drawn-and-operated pumper, antique bells, an 1893
American LaFrance Water Tower, sirens and fire extinguish-
ers. Helmets are displayed from around the world. An elegant
V-12 powered 1937 fire truck is the museum's showpiece. Free
admission (donations accepted). Tue-Sat 10am-4pm.

2 Spec's Warehouse

2410 Smith (526-8787) Spec Jackson made a name for himself
by whirring through this giant warehouse on roller skates at
warp speed, trying to help customers in the cavernous store.
Spec's Warehouse sells any version of your choice alcoholic
beverage. Whether you're drinking Grand Marnier, unblended
scotch, or just Lone Star—Spec's has it and sells it for a price
that's likely to be below most others. Mon-Sat 10am-9pm.

3 Damian's Cucina Italiana

3011 Smith (522-0439) Damian Mandola's Italian menu
remains the star it's always been and one of Houston's
favorites. Calamari, Parmesan-dusted trout and heaven-sent
pastas all please a finicky downtown crowd. The dining room
is elegant but comfortable, the staff pampering. Mon-Fri
Lunch 11am-2pm, Mon-Thu Dinner 5pm-10pm, Fri-Sat 5pm-
11:30pm, Sun 5pm-10pm. Reservations. Credit Cards,
Expensive.

4 Van Loc

3010 Milam (528-6441) Fresh spring rolls and fragrant soups
are the way to go at this pleasant storefront in Little Saigon.
The restaurant also does well with deep-fried foods, such as
frog legs and eggrolls. Daily 10am-midnight. Credit Cards,
Inexpensive.

5 Alex Patout's

3219 Smith (520-5081) Professional Cajun Alex Patout
(of TV, cookbook fame) brought this handsome dining room
to Houston in 1988. Despite the upscale surroundings, the
kitchen is squarely focused on down-home cooking, such as
plump boudin, fried catfish, white bean soup with tasso and
grilled beef topped with creamed crawfish tails. Mon-Thu,
7am-10pm, Sat 9am-10pm, Sun 9am-8pm. Reservations. Credit
Cards, Moderate.

Refer to map on page 182

6 Dong Ting

611 Stuart at Louisiana (527-0005) Downtown's Chinese restaurant of choice is famous for its clay-pot-baked specialties and outstanding wine list. Carefully chosen details in both the decor and the food make dining here reliable for both business or romance. Mon-Thu 11:30am-10pm, Fri 11:30am-11:30pm, Sat 5:30pm-11:30pm. Reservations. Credit Cards, Expensive.

7 Brennan's Houston

3300 Smith (522-9711) The Brennan family calls it Texas Creole: old-style New Orleans recipes crossed with Texas ingredients and leavened by nineties thinking. Seafood is always fresh, and game can be delicious. This is a charming setting for weekend brunch, especially the Vieux Carre patio. Dinner Sun-Sat 5:45pm-10pm; Brunch Sat 11am-1:30pm, Sun 10am-2pm. Reservations. Credit Cards, Expensive.

The patio at Brennan's.

8 Adkins Architectural Antiques

3515 Fannin (522-6547) An antique hunter's dream come true. Anything from street lamps to pedestal sinks for your bathroom. Hunt on your own or ask for help. It's probably here if you have time to look. Mon-Sat 9am-5pm.

9 Houston Community College Central Campus

1300 Holman (630-7205) Houston Community College, begun in 1971 with 5771 students, has blossomed into a major six-college institution, enrolling almost 70,000 men and women. The college recently shed ties with Houston Independent School District, claimed its share of the tax base, and began expanding into roles more typical of traditional colleges. Still emphasized at HCC are the technology and vocation-based courses.

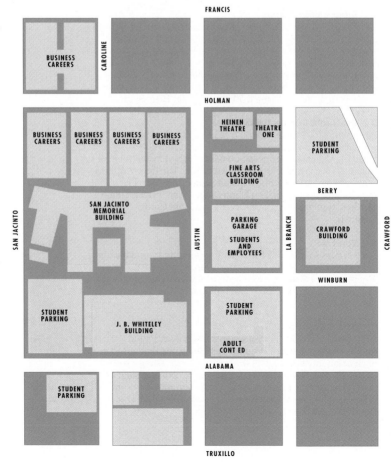

Houston Community College Central Campus

Refer to map on page 182

10 PABA Boxing and Community Center
3212 Dowling (520-1420) A boxing center for children through teens, this nonprofit organization has been training Golden Glove boxers since being founded by the Rev. Ray Martin in 1970. The public is invited to stop by and watch the kids work out. School day hours: 3:30pm-7:30pm. Summer hours: 8am-8pm.

11 Guy's Newsstand
3700 Main (528-5731) They claim to be the city's biggest and best. Large collection of magazines and daily papers. Daily 8am-10pm.

12 Original New Orleans Po-Boys
3902 Main (524-5778) Cajun po-boys wrapped and ready to go or sit awhile in this spartan diner and chew on some of the Louisiana-influenced fast food. Mon-Sat 4:30am-6:30pm.

13 Wadler-Kaplan Sheet Music
3907 Main (529-2676) Here's a warehouse chock-full of sheet music. The specialty of the store is keyboard and string composition, but you'll find Broadway show books and pop collections as well. Students from around the state journey to Walder-Kaplan to dig up hard-to-find pieces, like Corelli's recorder sonatas and J.S. Bach's early works for harpsichord. Mon-Sat 9am-5pm.

14 Pig House
4208 Crawford What the Orange Show has done for the orange, Victoria Herberta would like her Pig House to do for the pig. Although the city no longer allows Ms. Herberta to house her pet swine Jerome here, she still keeps up appearances by decorating her home in honor of the pig. Worth a drive by.

15 Flower District
On Fannin between Palm and Blodgett. Like weeds on the side of the road, shop after shop of flower sellers has sprouted along Fannin from Blodgett to Palm. The small shops sell bouquets and fresh flower arrangements well into the night.

16 Capitol Flag
4822 Fannin (522-7760) The only flag maker in Houston, this little company has been making standard flags and banners as well as custom designs in Houston since 1954. Walk-in traffic accepted. Mon-Fri 8am-5pm; Sat 10am-1pm.

17 Southern Importers & Exporters
4825 San Jacinto (524-8336) Southern Importers is the Halloween costume capital of Houston, where rubber masks (for every occasion) are uncovered, in addition to make-up, costume fabric, party favors, ribbon, gift wrap and decorations of all sorts. You'll encounter a spooky spectrum at the huge stoe, everything from Teenage Mutant Nija Turtles to the tame Donald Duck, plus great party theme and costume ideas. Mon-Sat 9am-6pm.

18 Spanish Village
4720 Almeda near Wentworth (523-1727 or 528-8788) Famous for its margaritas and year-round Christmas lights, this Tex-Mex cantina (never mind the name) is a Houston institution that has nourished generations of students, musicians, hipsters and budget-minded professionals from the Medical Center. Mon-Thu 11am- 9:30pm, Fri-Sat 11am-10pm. Credit Cards, Inexpensive.

On the campus of the
University of Houston
with Philip Johnson's
Architecture Building in
the background.

UNIVERSITY OF HOUSTON/ TSU

O n Houston's near south side, two institutions have grown up over the years, reflecting the growth and change of the city around them. The University of Houston and Texas Southern University began in the early part of this century as minor junior colleges but have steadily grown into major universities, educating genera-tions of young Houstonians. Both schools have been exercises in civic pride, as the peo-ple of Houston have consistently put money and effort into the two campuses, and both have become part of the larger State of Texas sys-tem of public universities.

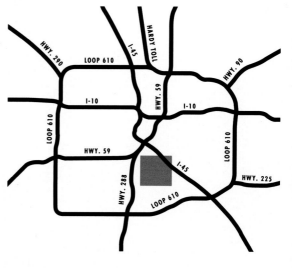

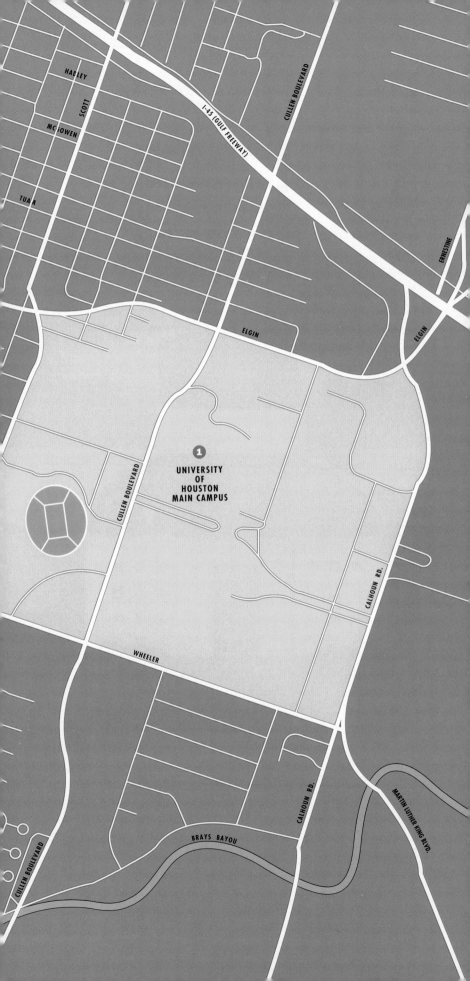

HADLEY

SCOTT

MCGOWEN

CULLEN BOULEVARD

I-45 (GULF FREEWAY)

TUAM

ERNESTINE

ELGIN

ELGIN

CULLEN BOULEVARD

1
UNIVERSITY
OF
HOUSTON
MAIN CAMPUS

CALHOUN RD.

WHEELER

CALHOUN RD.

MARTIN LUTHER KING BLVD.

CULLEN BOULEVARD

BRAYS BAYOU

The Ezekiel Cullen Building, the center of the University of Houston Main Campus since its construction 1950.

Refer to map on pages 188-189

University of Houston-Central Campus

Entrance 1, 4800 Calhoun (743-1000) The University of Houston keeps on growing. It is an institution defined in large part by its size; the original school, founded in 1927 as a junior college with 400 students, now buzzes with over 33,000 students and 2400 faculty members. Generously supported in its early years by Hugh Roy Cullen, the school grew from its humble beginnings to a state-supported university, comprising 13 colleges and schools. The main campus offers 272 degree programs in areas such as architecture, law, optometry, hotel and restaurant management, social sciences, etc. An indication of the campus' present-day scope is the 1.6 million-volume central library. Since the mid '80s, UH has emerged as a major education and research institution. The Texas Center for Superconductivity, the Space Vacuum Epitaxy Center and the Houston Petroleum Research Center all attract large research grants. Because UH is a state-supported institution, tuition averages only about $1000 per year, and admission is guaranteed to those finishing in the top 10% of their high school class. Except for the tuition, everything else at UH seems to be on a grand scale. The Conrad N. Hilton College of Hotel and Restaurant Management is housed in a $28.8 million complex, replete with full-service restaurants, banquet halls and computer and engineering laboratories while the College of Architecture's home is a new structure designed by internationally acclaimed architect Philip Johnson. The Sasakawa International Center for Space Architecture and the Institute for Space Systems Operations help promote joint ventures between NASA and UH. The Law Center's environmental law program, the College of Education, the Program in Creative Writing and the College of Business Administrations' Small Business Development Center all draw special attention. Even the UH continuing education center operates on a large scale. Over 700 courses are offered in real estate brokerage, computer software, foreign languages, advanced English for foreign professionals, etc. Finally, no mention of the University of Houston would be complete without Cougar athletics. University of Houston football teams have been a dominating force in the Southwest Conference (all homes games are played at the Astrodome). Men's basketball has played in historic games (UH-UCLA before 52,693 in the Astrodome, January 20, 1968) and memorable ones (Hakeem Olajuwon and *Phi Slamma Jamma* in the 1983 and 1984 NCAA national championships). Carl Lewis in track and Fred Couples in golf have brought international acclaim to the university.

Blaffer Gallery-University of Houston

Fine Arts Building, Entrance 16 off of Cullen Blvd. (743-9530) Of all Houston's campus-affiliated galleries, Blaffer comes closest to being a serious art space. Along with student/faculty shows, it brings major exhibitions and retrospectives to town and mounts them with professional flair. Free admission. Tue-Fri 10am-5pm, Sat-Sun 1pm-5pm.

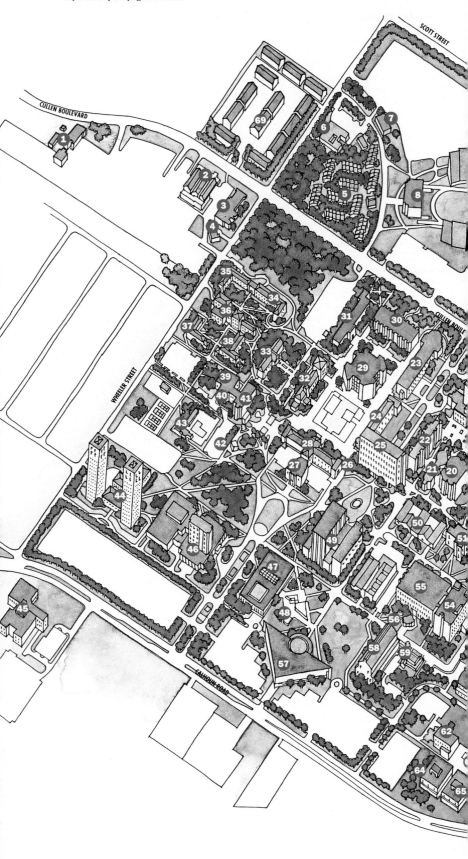

Refer to map on pages 188-189

University of Houston Central Campus

Numbers listed refer to this map only

1 KUHT-TV
2 South Office Annex
3 Cameron Building
4 Consumer Sciences Center
5 Cougar Place (Residence Halls)
6 Child Care Center
7 Police Department
8 Field House
9 Robertson Stadium
10 Hofheinz Pavilion
11 Fouke Athletic Building
12 Melcher Gymnasium
13 Garrison Gymnasium
14 Tennis Courts
15 Baseball Diamond
16 Wortham Theater Complex
17 Communications Building
18 Science and Research 2 Building
19 Science and Research Building
20 Social Work Building
21 Agnes Arnold Auditorium
22 Agnes Arnold Hall
23 Fleming Building
24 Science Building
25 Hoffman Hall
26 Cullen Underground Annex
27 Cullen Performance Hall
28 Ezekiel W. Cullen Building
29 Farish Hall
30 McElhinney Hall
31 Heyne Building
32 Roy G. Cullen Building
33 A.D. Bruce Religion Center
34 Bates (Residence) Hall
35 Law (Residence) Hall
36 Oberholtzer (Residence) Hall
37 Settegast (Residence) Hall
38 Taub (Residence) Hall
39 Alumni Organization
40 Health Center
41 Student Service Center
42 Cougar Cage
43 Swimming Pool
44 Moody Towers Residence Halls
45 Optometry Building
46 Hilton College of Hotel and Restaurant Management
47 University Center
48 University Center Underground
49 M.D. Anderson Memorial Library
50 Technology Annex
51 Technology College Building
52 Fine Arts Building
53 Architecture College Building
54 Cullen College of Engineering Building, North Wing
55 Cullen College of Engineering Building
56 Engineering Lecture Hall
57 Melcher Hall
58 Engineering Laboratory
59 Allied Geophysical Laboratories
60 Band Annex
61 Art and Engineering Annex
62 Krost Hall
63 Law Library (underground facility)
64 Bates Law Building
65 Teaching Unit 2
66 Computing Center
67 General Services Building
68 Science and Research 3 Building
69 Cambridge Oaks Apts.

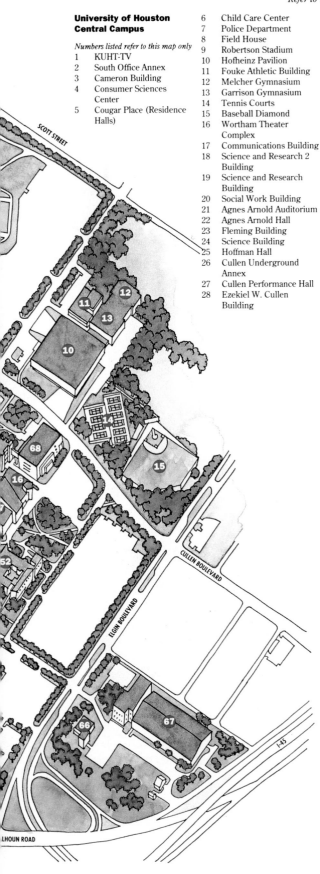

Refer to map on pages 188-189

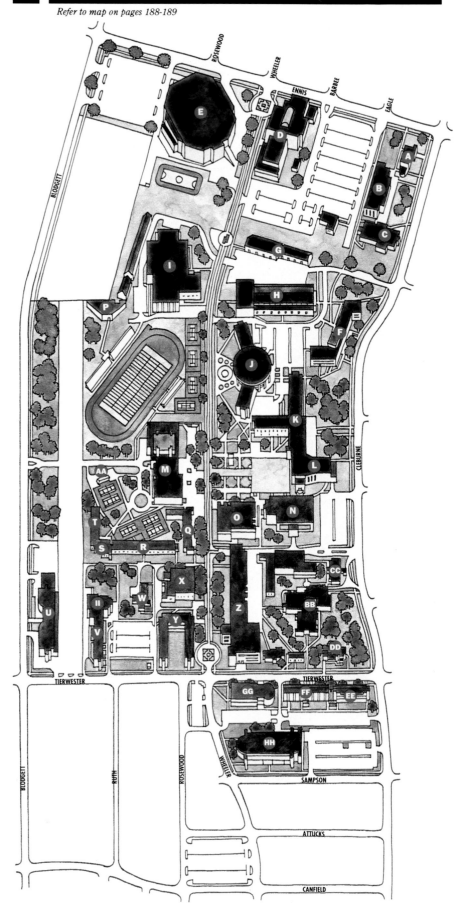

Refer to map on pages 188-189

Texas Southern University

3100 Cleburne (527-7011) Texas Southern University is a state-supported, four-year institution boasting an enrollment of over 10,000 students. TSU's history began in the early part of the century, but it emerged in its present form in the early '50s. The school began as a junior college for Houston's black population, and to this day the university's student body remains primarily African-American. Undergraduate and graduate degrees are offered by TSU in business, law, transportation planning and management, and airway science and technology. Texas Southern's main strengths are the Graduate School of Pharmacy, the Thurgood Marshall School of Law and its renowned debate team. The pharmacy program is quite strong; scholarships are maintained by firms like Pfizer, Smith Kline and Mylan Labs. The Thurgood Marshall School of Law educates the majority—80% —of the state's practicing black lawyers. Under coach Thomas Freeman, the 11-member TSU debate team consistently places in the top ranks of international competitions (former debate team members include U.S. Representative Barbara Jordan and State Representative Rodney Ellis).

A Tradition of Music
(Carroll Harris Simms, 1986)
The bronz scupture by Carroll Simms graces the main courtyard in front of the Ernest S. Sterling Student Center on the campus of Texas Southern University.

Texas Southern University Campus

A	Charles P. Rhinehart Music Auditorium	R	Junior/Senior Men's Hall
B	Rollins-Stewart Music Building	S	Commons
		T	Jones Hall
C	Art Building	U	General Service Building
D	School of Technology	V	I.A. Bolton Hall
E	Health and Physical Education Building	W	Student Health Center
		X	Everett O. Bell Hall
F	Spurgeon E. Gray Hall-School of Pharmacy	Y	R.O. Lanier Hall West
		Z	S.M. Nabrit Science Center
G	Industrial Education Building	AA	Tennis Facility
H	Thornton M. Fairchild Building	BB	C.S. Lane Home Economics Building
I	Edward H. Adams Hall	CC	W.R. Banks Child Development Lab
J	Martin Luther King Humanities Building	DD	Faculty Conference Center
K	Mack H. Hannah Hall	EE	University Hall
L	University Auditorium	FF	H.D. Bruce Hall
M	Ernest S. Sterling Center	GG	George I. Allen Building-School of Business
N	University Library		
O	School of Education and Behavioral Sciences	HH	Thurgood Marshall School of Law
P	Athletic Field House	II	Allee J. Mitchell Annex
Q	E.G. Lanier Hall West		

SHIP CHANNEL AREA

"I christen thee Port Houston; hither the boats of all nations may come and receive hearty welcome," pronounced the daughter of Houston's Mayor Ben Campbell one November afternoon in 1914 from the top deck of the *Windom* on Buffalo Bayou. A 21-gun salute rang out, and via remote control, President Woodrow Wilson personally fired a cannon from Washington, D.C., to open the Houston Ship Channel. Today the Port of Houston ranks second in trade with foreign lands, third in the nation in total tonnage and eighth largest in the world.

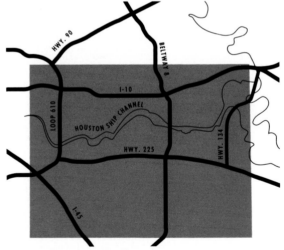

Nearly 5000 ships visit Houston in a year, traveling up the 50-mile man-made channel that transformed Houston from an inland city to an international seaport.

MAXEY RD.

BELTWAY 8

INTERSTATE 10

LOOP 610 — EAST LOOP

FEDERAL RD.

JESSE JONES
TOLL BRIDGE

WASHBURN
TUNNEL

HIGHWAY 225 — LA PORTE FREEWAY

SHAVER

INTERSTATE 45 — GULF FREEWAY

Houston Ship Channel

When the Allen brothers first promoted Houston in 1837, they
touted the raw, cluttered Buffalo Bayou as a commercial waterway. Over the years various groups cleared and dredged sections of the channel so that boats could maneuver its narrow
passages, some even charging a toll to pass through their
improvements. But it wasn't until much later, when trade in
the Galveston harbor became too restrictive, that the bayou
was taken seriously as a port. In 1870 the Buffalo Bayou Ship
Channel Company was formed, and the United States government added money to the cause, established a customhouse
and declared Houston a port of entry. The bayou was dredged
to a depth of 12 feet, and larger vessels began using the channel, but it was still a very secondary port to Galveston. In 1908,
with the backing of William Marsh Rice, Thomas Ball and
Jesse H. Jones, a Harris County Houston Ship Channel
Navigation District was formed, bonds were sold and the
work began to dredge the channel to 25 feet to accommodate
serious shipping. After the offical opening in 1914, a Port
Commission was formed in 1922, and the dream of a Houston
Ship Channel was finally realized. The growth of the petrochemical industry has paralleled the growth of the channel.
Today the channel is not only home to the Port of Houston and

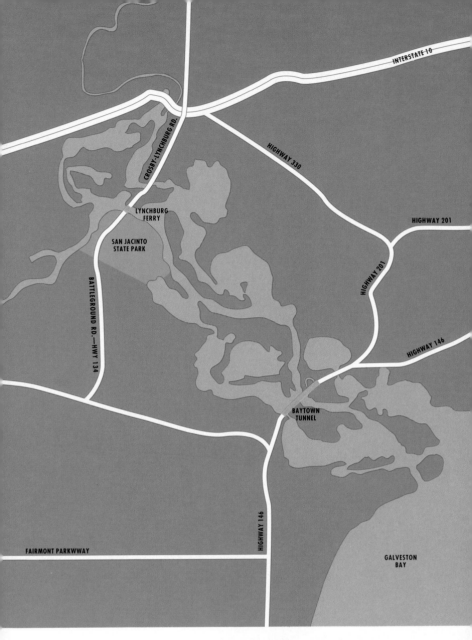

INTERSTATE 10

HIGHWAY 330

HIGHWAY 201

HIGHWAY 201

HIGHWAY 146

CROSBY-LYNCHBURG RD.

LYNCHBURG
FERRY

SAN JACINTO
STATE PARK

BATTLEGROUND RD.—HWY 134

BAYTOWN
TUNNEL

HIGHWAY 146

FAIRMONT PARKWWAY

GALVESTON
BAY

its international trade, it is also home to the world's largest network of oil and gas refineries. The docks and terminals, plants and tank farms of the petrochemical industry line the Ship Channel. All the "majors" are here such as Exxon, Mobil, Shell, Arco, turning crude into finished products such as gasoline and lubricants or into the many derivatives that make up end-products like rubber or plastic. The oil and gas industry—some 150 companies have facilities along the channel—has been a large part of the success of the Ship Channel, importing and exporting not only crude and refined products but drilling and construction equipment the world over. But while petroleum and petroleum products lead the Port's import commodities, containerized cargo has a strong presence. Calling Houston home are OmniPort, the Port Authority's automatic cargo unloading facility, and the Fentress Bracewell Barbours Cut Container Terminal, the largest container terminal on the Gulf of Mexico.

Common along the Ship Channel is the sight of miles upon miles of the pipe and tubing that make up the facilities of the giant petrochemical industry. The towers shown here are used to separate the crude into different components. These materials go on to become fuel, rubber, plastics and the components of an ever-expanding number of products.

Refer to map on page 200

1   Turning Basin Viewing
Off Cypress at the Port of Houston Gate 8. Take in what's probably the most fascinating body of water in the Houston area
from atop this 30-foot-high viewing platform. The Turning
Basin is where some ships have come to be turned around,
with the aid of several tugboats, to exit the Channel. At times
there is very little traffic here; other times you may see mammoth tankers crawl by, pushing out wakes so large you could
surf on them, minute shrimpers stray up the Channel for
repairs or tugboats push chains of barges hundreds of
yards long.

2   M/V Sam Houston Tour Boat
Gate 12 off Avenue R East (670-2416) The Port of Houston
Authority operates the *M/V Sam Houston*, giving free tours of
the Ship Channel on a regular basis. You must call ahead for
reservations to take the 90-minute tour. Almost 45,000 people
a year view the huge ships and facilities along the Channel
every year aboard this vessel. Free. Reservations taken:
Mon-Fri 8:30am-12:30pm. Rides: Tue-Wed and Fri-Sat 10am
and 2:30pm, Thu and Sun 2:30pm.

3   Athens Bar & Grill
8037 Clinton at McCarthy (675-1644) You can ab-Zorba some
Greek fun at this interesting dive down on the Ship Channel.
Greek sailors crowd the place when their ships are in port, and
bellydancers and a little ouzo-oiled Greek dancing is usually
par for the evening. A couple of glasses of retsina, and you'll
forget the mediocre moussaka, pastitso and stuffed grape
leaves. Opa! Mon-Sat 11am-2am. Credit Cards, Inexpensive.

4   Shanghai Red's
8501 Cypress (926-6666) Although you might not think of the
Ship Channel as a romantic body of water, from the window
seats of Shanghai Red's it actually takes on a certain poetic air,
especially at twilight. Cocktails on the outside porch overlook-
ing the Channel are enjoyable, even festive, at happy hour, and
the view of the large ships passing by is a real bonus.
Designed to resemble a ramshackle mining shed, the
Shanghai has passable food; just don't expect culinary fireworks. Lunch Mon-Fri 11am-2pm, Brunch Sat-Sun 10:30am-
2:30pm, Dinner Sun-Thu 5pm-10pm, Sat-Sun 5pm-midnight.
Moderate.

The San Jacinto
Monument towering
over the San Jacinto
Battlegrounds and the
USS Texas.

SAN JACINTO MONUMENT

Drive a few miles out "refinery row"–Texas Highway 225–and you'll no doubt be struck by the sight of a giant, star-capped tower looming over the highway, almost brooding, as if it had some story to tell. That tower is the memorial to the battle of San Jacinto, and its story is of a decisive conflict, critical to Texas and to the entire Southwestern region of the United States. Had General Samuel Houston, a former governor of Tennessee and the leader of a band of Texans, not attacked the unsuspecting Mexican General Santa Anna, the entire region of the Southwest might now be witnessing a very different history indeed. There are very few truly decisive battles in history–battles which had

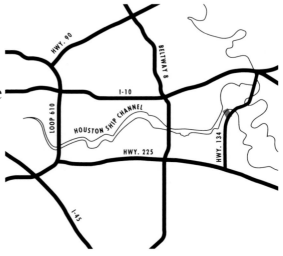

to emerge exactly as they did or an entire chain of events leading up to our present-day world would not have occurred. But the battle of San Jacinto, which took place right here, right in our own back yard, was one of them. It was only a 20-minute battle on the afternoon of April 21, 1836, but it determined the fate of Texas and its destiny forever.

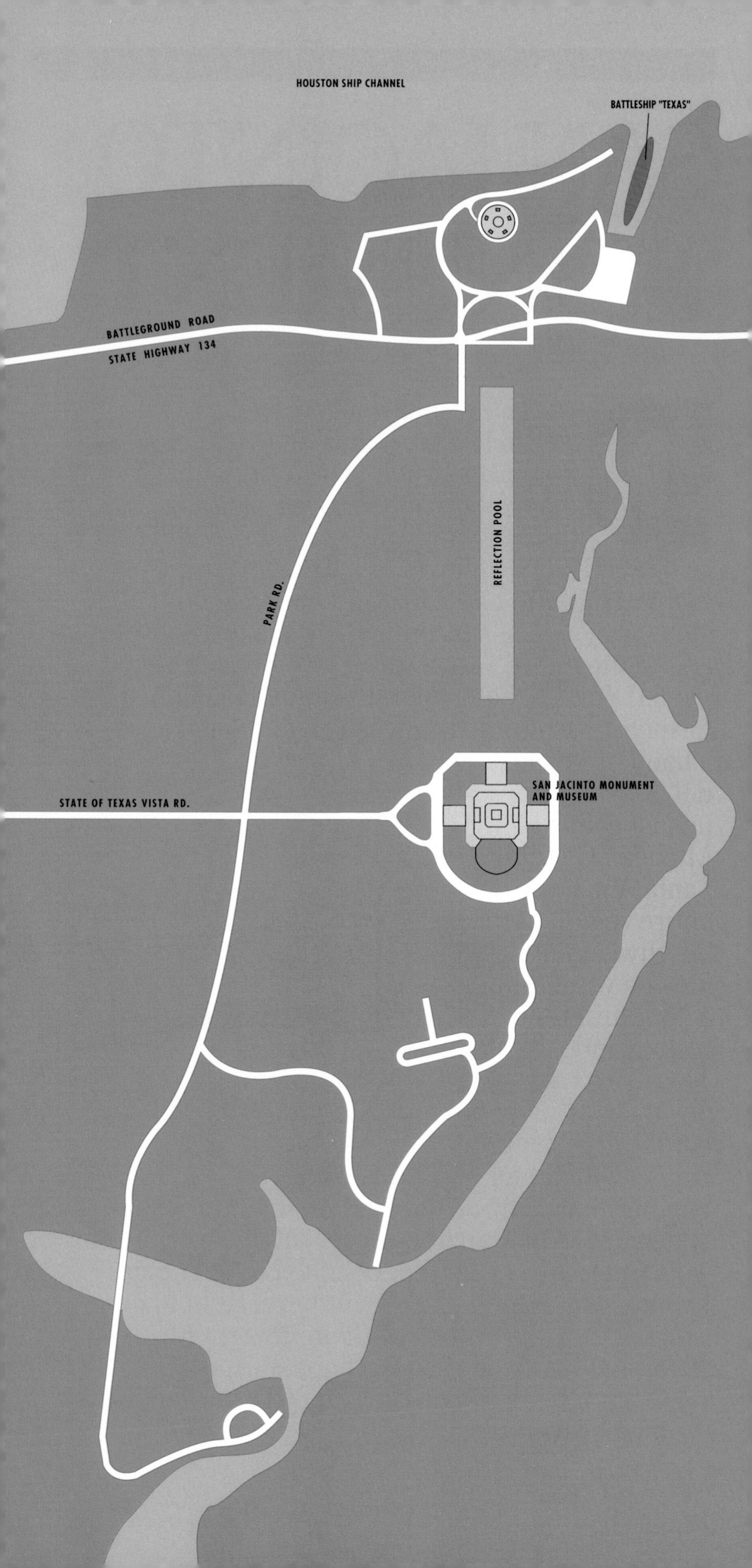

HOUSTON SHIP CHANNEL

BATTLESHIP "TEXAS"

BATTLEGROUND ROAD

STATE HIGHWAY 134

PARK RD.

REFLECTION POOL

STATE OF TEXAS VISTA RD.

SAN JACINTO MONUMENT
AND MUSEUM

For location on Houston Ship Channel, refer to map on pages 198-199   *Refer to map on page 204*

San Jacinto Battleground State Historical Park

21 miles from downtown Houston off State Highway 225, located on the Houston Ship Channel. (Park Superintendent, 479-2431) Here, at the convergence of Buffalo Bayou and the San Jacinto River, on what is now the Houston Ship Channel, lies a 1000-acre park commemorating the battle of San Jacinto, which led to independence for Texas. This is the actual site of the battle, and the grounds are marked so you can follow the movement of the Texan and Mexican forces. The San Jacinto Monument dominates the park, a towering concrete and limestone structure. The Monument's massive base houses the Jesse H. Jones Theater for Texas Studies and the San Jacinto Museum of History; an elevator ride can carry you to the observation floor just below the massive Texas star, where you can look out all four sides of the Monument. The refurbished Battleship Texas is docked in the waters of Buffalo Bayou on the park's northern edge. Free admission. Daily 8am-9pm March 1-October 31, 8am-9pm November 1-February 29 8am-7pm.

San Jacinto Monument

San Jacinto Battleground State Historical Park (off Highway 225) (479-2421) (Alfred C. Finn, 1938) In April 1936, the centennial of the battle of San Jacinto, excavation began for the San Jacinto Monument. Spearheaded by Jesse H. Jones, the monument, which commemorates the Texas soldiers who fought in the battle of San Jacinto, would become the tallest masonry structure in the world. The 570-foot tall obelisk is made of reinforced concrete and covered with Texas Cordova shell stone, cut from quarries near Austin, Texas. At the base of the monument is a 15,000-square-foot, 45-foot high exhibition and theater area. The building steps back to a tapered shaft that rises to meet a 35-foot high, 220-ton, three-dimensional Lone Star. The shaft houses an elevator that carries visitors to the observation floor, where one can view the Texas landscape in all directions, including the Houston Ship Channel and the refineries that line it, the Battleship Texas and the city of Houston in the distance. Free admission, but the elevator to the observation floor is $2 for adults and 50¢ for children. Theater, $3.50 for adults, $2 for children. Daily 9:30am-5:30pm.

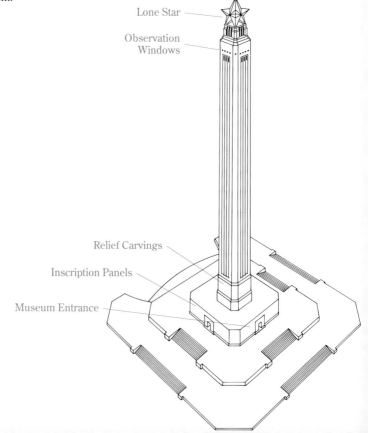

Lone Star

Observation
Windows

Relief Carvings

Inscription Panels

Museum Entrance

Refer to map on page 204

General Sam Houston artifacts abound at the San Jacinto Museum. Above, Houston's signature. Below, a painting entitled "Equestrian Portrait of Sam Houston."

San Jacinto Museum of History

In the San Jacinto Monument (479-2421) On the first floor of the San Jacinto Monument is the San Jacinto Museum of History, which houses a curious amalgam of artifacts ranging from an effigy of a frightful Zapotec tiger god to Santa Anna's pearl white leather gloves. Seymour Stephens' celebrated painting of General Samuel Houston on his horse hangs high above the gallery (left), the most famous piece in the monument. Other notable artifacts hark back to Spanish colonial life, to the Texans' declaration of independence and to the contentious colonial rivalry between Spain and France. Daily 9:30am-5:30pm. Free admission, but the elevator to the observation floor is $2 for adults and 50¢ for children. Theater, $3.50 for adults, $2 for children.

Jesse H. Jones Theater for Texas Studies

In the San Jacinto Monument (479-2421) (Ray Bailey Architects, 1990) This beautifully designed, 160-seat theater is the venue for the 35-minute slide presentation "Texas Forever!! The Battle of San Jacinto." But to just call it a "slide show" is to understate this marvelous production. A battery of 42 projectors whirrs through 3200 transparencies, depicting scenes and conditions in the "Tejas" of the 1820s and 1830s. Charlton Heston narrates to the background of war cries and battle sounds, and colorful paintings by Texas artist Charles Shaw dot the screen. Excellent, clear maps portray the movements of both Mexican and Texas armies across the state; these maps are one of the presentation's several strengths, for in a compressed few minutes one gains an understanding of cause and effect in the events of the Texas revolution, an insight not readily available from written sources. The film has been praised for its accuracy and thoroughness. Daily 9:30am-5:30pm. $3.50 for adults, $2 for children.

Refer to map on page 204

The early policies of Mexico toward her Texas colonists had been extremely liberal. Large grants of land were made to them, and no taxes or duties imposed. The relationship between the Anglo-Americans and Mexicans was cordial. But, following a series of revolutions begun in 1829, unscrupulous rulers successively seized power in Mexico. Their unjust acts and despotic decrees led to the revolution in Texas.

In June 1832, the colonists forced the Mexican authorities at Anahuac to release Wm. B. Travis and others from unjust imprisonment. The battle of Velasco, June 26, and the battle of Nacogdoches, August 2, followed; in both the Texans were victorious. Stephen Fuller Austin, "Father of Texas," was arrested January 3, 1834, and held in Mexico without trial until July, 1835. The Texans formed an army, and on November 12, 1835, established a provisional government.

The first shot of the revolution of 1835-1836 was fired by the Texans at Gonzales, October 2, 1835, in resistance to a demand by Mexican soldiers for a small cannon held by the colonists. The Mexican garrison at Goliad fell October 9. The battle of Concepcion was won by the Texans, October 28. San Antonio was captured December 10, 1835, after five days of fighting in which the indomitable Benjamin R. Milam died a hero, and the Mexican army evacuated Texas.

Texas declared her independence at Washington-on-the-Brazos, March 2. For nearly two months her armies met disaster and defeat; Dr. James Grant's men were killed on the Agua Dulce, March 2, William Barret Travis and his men sacrificed their lives at the Alamo, March 6, William Ward was defeated at Refugio, March 14, and James Walker Fannin and his army were put to death near Goliad, March 27, 1836.

On this field on April 21, 1836, the army of Texas commanded by General Sam Houston, and accompanied by the Secretary of War, Thomas J. Rusk, attacked the superior invading army of Mexicans under General Santa Anna. The battle line from left to right was formed by Sidney Sherman's regiment, Edward Burleson's regiment, the artillery commanded by George W. Hockley, Henry Millard's infantry and the cavalry under Mirabeau B. Lamar. Sam Houston led the infantry charge.

With the battle cry, "Remember the Alamo! Remember Goliad!" the Texans charged. The enemy, taken by surprise, rallied for a few minutes, then fled in disorder. The Texans had asked no quarter and gave none. The slaughter was appalling, victory complete, and Texas free! On the following day General Antonio Lopez de Santa Anna, self-styled "Napoleon of the West," received from a generous foe the mercy he had denied Travis at the Alamo and Fannin at Goliad.

Citizens of Texas and immigrant soldiers in the army of Texas at San Jacinto were natives of Alabama, Arkansas, Connecticut, Georgia, Illinois, Indiana, Kentucky, Louisiana, Maine, Maryland, Massachusetts, Michigan, Mississippi, Missouri, New Hampshire, New York, North Carolina, Ohio, Pennsylvania, Rhode Island, South Carolina, Tennessee, Texas, Vermont, Virginia, Austria, Canada, England, France, Germany, Ireland, Italy, Mexico, Poland, Portugal and Scotland.

Measured by its results, San Jacinto was one of the decisive battles of the world. The freedom of Texas from Mexico won here led to annexation and to the Mexican War, resulting in the acquisition by the United States of the States of Texas, New Mexico, Arizona, Nevada, California, Utah, and parts of Colorado, Wyoming, Kansas and Oklahoma. Almost one-third of the present area of the American nation, nearly a million square miles of territory, changed sovereignty.

Carved into the limestone at the base of the San Jacinto Monument are eight panels that detail the facts of the Texas Revolution. Beginning at the southeast corner and moving to the right, the eight panels read as shown here.

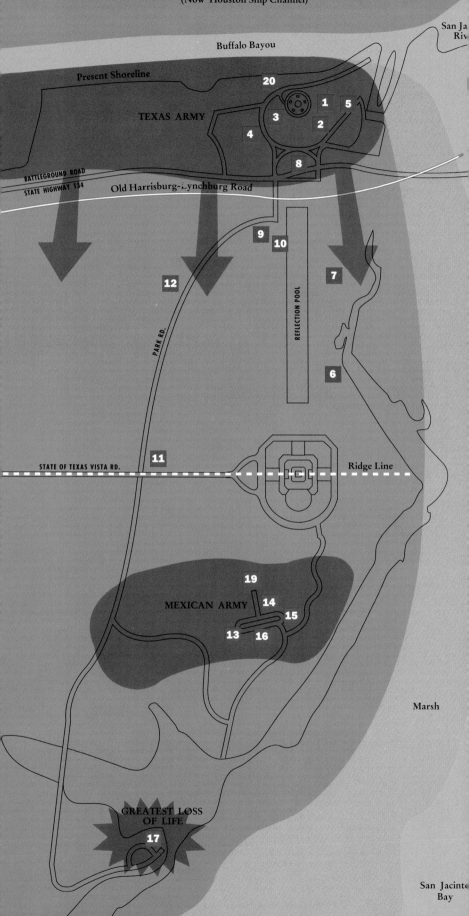

Refer to map on page 208

The San Jacinto Battlefield

San Jacinto Battleground State Historical Park On this site, on the afternoon of April 21, 1836, 950 soldiers of the Texas Army led by General Samuel Houston attacked and soundly defeated a contingient of 1500 Mexican soldiers led by Mexico's president and dictator, General Antonio Lopez de Santa Anna. The Texans had caught the Mexican forces unaware, and when the 20-minute battle was over, some 630 Mexican soldiers had died, another 208 were injured and the remainder were taken prisoner. Nine Texans lost their lives. The capture of General Santa Anna, who had earlier routed the Alamo, secured independence for Texas from Mexico. Laid out on the grounds of the San Jacinto Battleground State Historical Park are 20 granite boulders marking key events or sites of the San Jacinto battle. The markers were placed here by the San Jacinto Chapter, Daughters of the Republic of Texas.

1 **Twin Sisters, April 20, 1836** Replicas of the cannons presented by the citizens of Cincinnati to the Texas Army are placed here.

2 **Burleson's Camp** Campsite of Burleson's troops the night of April 20, 1836.

3 **Millard's Camp** Campsite of Millard's troops the night of April 20, 1836.

4 **Lamar's Camp** Campsite of Lamar's troops the night of April 20, 1836.

5 **Sherman's Camp** Campsite of Sherman's troops the night of April 20, 1836.

6 **Sherman's advance; left wing of infantry, April 21** Sherman's 2nd Regiment attacks first, moving along marsh's border.

7 **Burleson's advance; infantry, April 21** Burleson's 1st Infantry moves on Sherman's right.

8 **Advance under General Rusk, April 21**

9 **Millard's advance; infantry, April 21** Millard's Regulars advance on Mexican breastworks (near markers 13 and 15).

10 **Hockley's advance; artillery, April 21** "Twin Sisters" come into battle.

11 **Mexican position, April 20** Santa Anna relocates headquarters from here to site near marsh on April 20.

12 **Cavalry skirmish under Sherman day before battle** Brief fighting over possession of a cannon on April 20.

13 **Mexican breastworks; cavalry engagement under Lamar, April 21** Millard's Regulars assist Lamar's cavalry.

14 **Mexican cannon**

15 **Mexican breastworks**

16 **Santa Anna's camp**

17 **Almonte captured and greatest carnage of battle occurred** Survivors surrender.

18 *(Not on battleground)* **Site of Vince's Bridge in nearby Pasadena, Texas**

19 **Houston wounded and horse killed under him in battle**

20 Under an oak tree on this spot, General Santa Anna surrendered to General Sam Houston.

Both Sam Houston's brilliant battlefield leadership and the physical geography of the plain of San Jacinto helped make this contest a great military victory for Texas. The Texans heard the order to attack the afternoon of April 21 at around 3:30pm, with the bright afternoon sun at their backs. As they crept towards Santa Anna's breastworks, they hid themselves behind a rise of land, emerging to within a few hundred feet of the unwary Mexican Army. Santa Anna's forces expected no attack. Not in the daytime, at least. The Mexican forces were unprepared for battle, their guns not close at hand; guards had not been posted, and according to legend, the General himself was with a young woman at the time. When the battle was joined, with the element of surprise squarely behind General Houston, the Texans were able to route the much larger Mexican forces and achieve a stunning, total victory.

The large granite markers placed on the battlefield are easy to find.

Refer to map on page 204

USS Texas

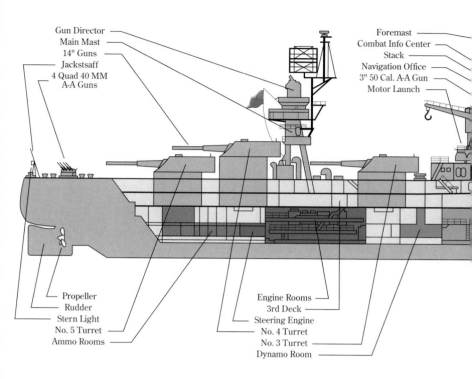

Gun Director
Main Mast
14" Guns
Jackstsaff
4 Quad 40 MM
A-A Guns

Foremast
Combat Info Center
Stack
Navigation Office
3" 50 Cal. A-A Gun
Motor Launch

Propeller
Rudder
Stern Light
No. 5 Turret
Ammo Rooms

Engine Rooms
3rd Deck
Steering Engine
No. 4 Turret
No. 3 Turret
Dynamo Room

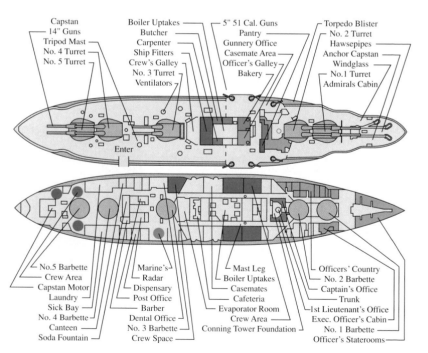

Capstan
14" Guns
Tripod Mast
No. 4 Turret
No. 5 Turret

Boiler Uptakes
Butcher
Carpenter
Ship Fitters
Crew's Galley
No. 3 Turret
Ventilators

5" 51 Cal. Guns
Pantry
Gunnery Office
Casemate Area
Officer's Galley
Bakery

Torpedo Blister
No. 2 Turret
Hawsepipes
Anchor Capstan
Windglass
No.1 Turret
Admirals Cabin

Enter

No.5 Barbette
Crew Area
Capstan Motor
Laundry
Sick Bay
No. 4 Barbette
Canteen
Soda Fountain

Marine's
Radar
Dispensary
Post Office
Barber
Dental Office
No. 3 Barbette
Crew Space

Mast Leg
Boiler Uptakes
Casemates
Cafeteria
Evaporator Room
Crew Area
Conning Tower Foundation

Officers' Country
No. 2 Barbette
Captain's Office
Trunk
1st Lieutenant's Office
Exec. Officer's Cabin
No. 1 Barbette
Officer's Staterooms

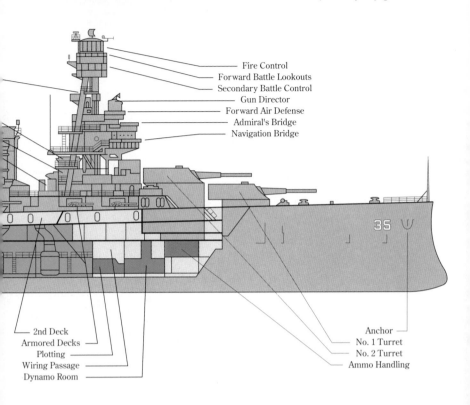

Fire Control
Forward Battle Lookouts
Secondary Battle Control
Gun Director
Forward Air Defense
Admiral's Bridge
Navigation Bridge

35

2nd Deck
Armored Decks
Plotting
Wiring Passage
Dynamo Room

Anchor
No. 1 Turret
No. 2 Turret
Ammo Handling

Battleship Texas

3527 Battleground Road north of Highway 225 (479-2411) Built in 1914, the *U.S.S. Texas* fought in two World Wars before being decommissioned and given to the State of Texas in 1948. She may not be the biggest—573 feet long and sporting a crew of 1625 men in peacetime—and she may not be the most awe-inspiring of battleships, but she saw her share of intense action. The *Texas*, hull number BB 35, saw the dark days of the Kaiser's navy, the U-boat terror, the silent peril of D-Day and the swift island-hopping campaign of General MacArthur. She was commissioned March 12, 1914, just as Europe began to implode, and went on to serve in the North Sea during World War I. This dreadnought class battleship was originally fitted with ten 14-inch guns mounted in five turrets, each with a range of twelve miles. Several major modifications were made to the ship in 1925: she was converted from coal to oil-fired boilers, her twin stacks were replaced with a single one, and she was fitted with a tripod foremast and mainmast. She then took part in the African invasion, setting the stage for the campaign against Mussolini. In 1944 she guarded the

troops at Normandy, going on to serve at Iwo Jima and Okinawa in 1945. In 1988, she left San Jacinto State Park for Todd Shipyards in Galveston for a multimillion dollar refurbishing before returning to her newly spruced-up berth months later amid a cheering, flag-waving crowd. Although all of the ship is not open to the public, you can still roam through enough of the ship to get an idea of what it must have been like to live on this vessel. You are free to walk through the cramped quarters and engine rooms below, stroll the deck, climb up on the small caliber guns located there and negotiate the steep steps of the foremast, taking you to the Navigation Bridge and the Admiral's Bridge. Adults $2, children 5 and under free, children 6-12 $1. Wed-Sun 10am-5pm.

Sailing out of South Shore Harbor on Clear Lake.

CLEAR LAKE AREA

The "city" of Clear Lake grew up around the NASA's Johnson Space Center when the nation was totally focused on an expanding space program and Houston was doing its best to become "Space City." Clear Lake was a "new town" development by the Exxon Company and its subsidiary Friendswood Development Company. When NASA was looking for a site Exxon made a land gift to Rice University, which in turn donated it to NASA to establish the space center.

When the development did mature, the city of Houston annexed the entire area, much to the chagrin of many of the residents. Today the area still revolves around NASA and the many related space enterprises, as well as the ever expand-

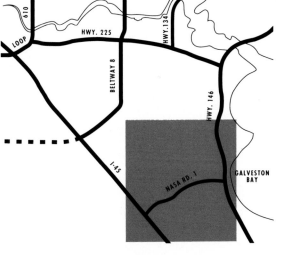

ing sport and recreational complex that has grown up around the waters of Clear Lake and Galveston Bay. The area has become one of Houston's major playgrounds, where over 2500 sailboats are docked and where clubs, restaurants and antique stores lure city dwellers on weekends.

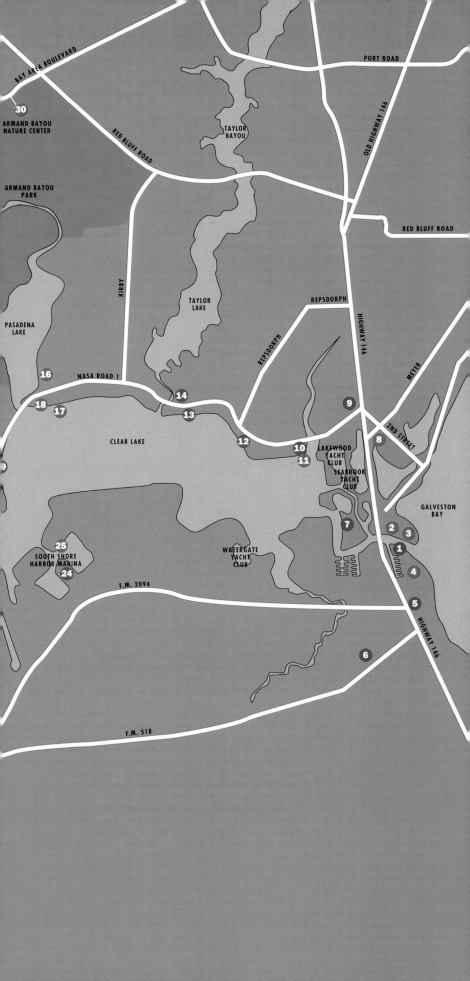

Refer to map on pages 214-215

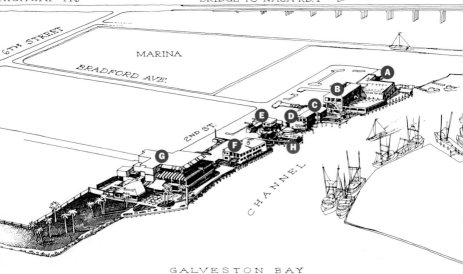

HIGHWAY 146   BRIDGE TO NASA RD. 1 ─▷

GALVESTON BAY

1 Kemah Channel Restaurant Row
2nd Street, Kemah A lively enclave of waterfront restaurants
and bars and an ideal spot for idling away an afternoon or
evening watching the boat traffic. Sailboats and powerboats
crawl through this narrow channel on their way to or from
Galveston Bay. Shrimp and fishing boats are moored along
both sides of the channel as well. The food varies in these
spots, but all offer porches or decks to sip drinks from while
boat- and people-watching.

A The Flying Dutchman Restaurant and Oyster Bar
505 2nd Street, Kemah (334-7575) One of the original Kemah
fishhouses, it is still one of the area's most popular spots for
yacht-watching. Ask to be seated outside downstairs to be
right in the middle of the action. As is traditional in the area,
upstairs dining on the waterfront is more formal and more
expensive. Downstairs Oyster Bar: Sun-Thu 11:30am-10:30pm,
Fri-Sat 11:30am-11:30pm. Upstairs Restaurant: Sun-Thu 5pm-
10pm, Fri 5pm-11pm, Sat 4pm-11pm.

B Brass Parrot *100 Bradford, Kemah (334-1099)* Sun-Thu
11:30am-10:30pm, Fri-Sat 11:30am-11:30pm.

C Pier 6 Fresh Seafood *601 2nd Street, Kemah (334-
4616)* Daily 7am-6pm.

D Fishbones *101 1/2 North Bradford, Kemah (334-6200)*
Mon-Fri 11am-10pm, Sat-Sun 11am-11pm.

E Dexter's Boiling Pot

F Joe Lee's *104 Kipp Avenue, Kemah (334-3711)* Mon-Sat
11am-10pm, Sun 11am-9pm.

G Landry's/Jimmie Walker's *201 Kipp Avenue, Kemah
(334-2513 or 334-4778)* This rambling spot is two restaurants
(and five bars) in one. Downstairs it's funky, noisy, full of off-
the-water sailors refreshing themselves at the bar. Upstairs,
the discreet Jimmie Walker Room, named after the former
longtime restaurant tenant, is a dressier spot, known for its
seafood. Sun-Thu 11am-10pm, Fri-Sat 11am-11pm.

H The *Judy Beth* Charter Fishing Boat
601 2nd Street, Kemah (334-3760) Reservations can be made
individually or in groups to fish aboard *Judy Beth,* a 55-foot
charter boat. Up to 79 people can fish at a time. Call ahead,
because the days and hours change with the seasons.

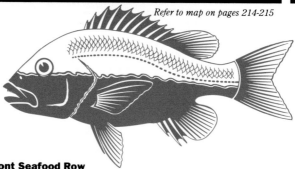

Refer to map on pages 214-215

2   Seabrook Waterfront Seafood Row
Waterfront Drive, also known as 11th Street, Seabrook Fresh crab, shrimp and crawfish, as well as trout, flounder and red-fish, are available at your pick of a variety of small shops, where you know it's right off the boat from the Texas and Louisiana Gulf Coast. Look for **My's Seafood** *(474-4833)*, **Golden Seafood** *(474-2516)* and **Rose's Seafood** *(474-3536)*. Daily approximately 9am-6pm.

3   High Tide Bed & Breakfast
114 Waterfront Drive, Seabrook (861-9492) A little cottagey house right on the bay; the owners come by to cook breakfast, but the guest can buy and cook fresh seafood themselves or go to the many area restaurants. Information hours: Mon-Fri 8am-5pm.

4   Eagle's Nest, Kemah Ketch and Carol & Co.
511 Bradford at 6th Street, Kemah (538-1606) These three shops are adjoining, and you must enter the Eagle's Nest to go to the Kemah Ketch. Eagle's Nest has nature paintings and prints. Kemah Ketch has nautical theme items, including some very nice sea creature sculptural serving pieces; they also have double- and triple-weave cotton afghans that are fantastically complex art. Carol & Co., located behind these two, is a lovely gift gallery featuring custom floral designs, candles, South-western pieces and French country items. Daily noon-9pm.

High Tide Bed & Breakfast.

5   T-Bone Tom's
707 Highway 146, Kemah (334-2133) The locals say the best barbecue, burgers and charbroiled steaks in the area are pre-pared here by hands-on owner Tom Fitzmorris. He's noted for his ribs, chicken and brisket, but it just may be the pecan-smoked sausage that wins most fans. The Polish-style beef-and-pork sausage, redolent of garlic, makes an easy supper...provided you can wait that long to eat it. Mon-Sat 10am-9pm.

6   What's Cookin'?
930 Highway FM 518, Kemah (334-3610) Excellent po-boys, German dishes and wonderful Chicken Cordon Bleu. Slow ser-vice and very crowded on the weekend evenings. Over 150 brands of beer from around the world and a club that you can join if you drink 80 different beers, after which you receive your own stein with your name on it that hangs above the bar from then on. Open daily 11am-2am.

7   Regatta Inn
425 Highway 146 in the Seabrook Shipyard (474-5546) This old-timer has a great view of Clear Creek and Clear Lake but is best known for its extraordinary list of wines by the glass. At last count, the management offered 50 and counting. Daily Lunch 11am-2pm, Mon-Fri Dinner 5:30pm-10pm, Sat-Sun Dinner 5:30pm-11pm.

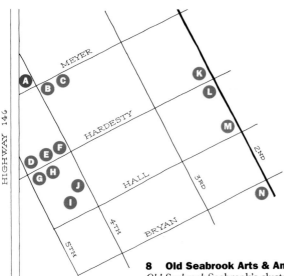

8   Old Seabrook Arts & Antique Colony
Old Seabrook Seabrook's clustered antique shops are within walking distance of one another, if the weather permits. The area has a comfortable, small town ambiance but be aware the shops change names quite often and the quality of items varies.

A   Old Victorian Tea Room
913 Meyer (474-7274) Tearoom in what was once an old library. Handmade crafts and gifts are available. Tue-Fri 11am-2pm.

B   Old Seabrook Antiques Mall
1006 Meyer at 4th Street (474-4451) Ten dealers with items such as antiques and collectibles. Tue-Sat 11am-5pm.

C   Carousel Antiques
1006 Meyer at 4th Street (474-5955) Features antiques, glassware, collectibles, etc. Wed-Sat 11am-5pm.

D   Faulkner Studio & Gallery
1402 5th Street (474-3249) Jewelry and exquisite, high-priced objets d'art. Tue-Sat 11am-5pm, Sun 1pm-5pm.

E   Another Era
909 Hardesty (474-7208) Primitives and collectibles. Tue-Sat 10:30am-5pm, Sun 1pm-5pm, Mon by appointment only.

F   Sentimental Traveler and Sentimental Sleeper
913 Hardesty (474-5259) Specializing in vintage beds and antiques. Tue-Sat 10am-5pm, Sun 1pm-5pm.

G   Gateway
1320 5th Street at Hardesty (474-4455) Metaphysical books and crystals, activities too numerous to list. Tue-Fri noon-5pm, Sat 10am-6pm, Sun noon-5pm.

H   Memories Yesterday & Today
902 Hardesty (474-7112) Antiques, collectibles and gifts. Tue-Sat 11am-5pm, Sun 1pm-5pm.

I   Country Attic
4th Street and Hall in Hall Square (474-9253) Boutique items and gifts. Tue-Sat 10am-5pm, Sun noon-5pm.

J   Mint Condition Herb Farm & Emporium
909 Hall (474-3640) Herb plants, dry herb mixes, teas, books and classes. Tue-Sat 10am-5pm, Sun noon-5pm.

K   Marilyn's Antiques
1401 2nd Street (474-4359) Antiques, something for everyone, glass, china and furniture. Tue-Sat 10am-5pm.

L   Brown's Browse In Antiques
1114 Hardesty (474-2778) Fine antique furniture. Tue-Sat 11am-5pm.

M   Oak Grove Antiques
1305 2nd Street (474-7268) Refinished oak antique furniture and collectibles. Tue-Sat 11am-5pm, Sun 1pm-5pm.

N   Ruth Burke's Seaside Gallery
1105 2nd Street (474-4016) Bay area art, nautical gifts and jewelry. Tue-Sat 10:30am-5:30pm, appointments only Sun and Mon.

Refer to map on pages 214-215

9   Frank's Shrimp Hut

1818 NASA Road 1, Seabrook (474-5701) If boat-watchers go to one of the waterfront restaurants on the Clear Creek channel, people-watchers drop in here for the basic fresh seafood menu. Dine al fresco and watch sunburned Houstonians staggering home from a day on the bay. Also serves breakfast. Tue-Thu 6am-9pm, Fri-Sun 6am-10pm.

10   Seabrook Classic Cafe

2511-A NASA Road 1, Seabrook (326-1512) "The Classic," as it is affectionately referred to by residents, serves decent home-style pork chops and other standards; on weekend mornings, sailing enthusiasts eat hearty breakfasts. Mon-Thu 11am-10pm, Fri 11am-11pm, Sat 8am-11pm, Sun 8am-9:30pm.

11   Rick's Turtle Club

2613½ NASA Road 1, Seabrook (326-7613) This floating bar is a great place to watch the yearly Boat Parade, if you get there early enough. Mon-Sat 11am-2am, Sun noon-2am.

12   Crazy Cajun Food Factory

2825 NASA Road 1, Seabrook (326-6055) The name is a pretty good clue to this rowdy Cajun spot where the motto is "gonna make you hurt yo-self." Big platters of peppery seafood and icy longnecks served at picnic tables are as fancy as it gets. When you've had enough of the water, this is a good spot to drop in on your way back to the city. Sun-Thu 11am-11pm, Fri-Sat 11am-midnight.

13   Louie's on the Lake

3813 NASA Road 1, Seabrook (326-0551) This restaurant and its neighbors along NASA Road 1 have survived for years because of the veiw of the lake. Nice place to unwind after a day on the lake. The food is usually a second thought. Daily 11am-11pm.

14   Toucan's

4106 NASA Road 1, Seabrook (326-3768) Owned by the same group that has Toucan's and the Hobbit Hole up in Houston, the setting has palm trees and plenty of tropical ambiance. Although the kitchen playfully tags the menu with lots of Caribbeanisms, burgers and grilled chicken are more like it. Fun for drinks. Mon-Fri 4pm-2am, Sat-Sun noon-2am.

15 University of Houston-Clear Lake

2700 Bay Area Boulevard (283-7600) Founded in 1974, UH-Clear Lake is an "upper-level" university, enrolling students at the junior, senior and post-graduate levels. The school's 7500 students are almost evenly split between the undergraduate and post-graduate programs. The University is composed of schools for Education, Business and Public Administration, Natural and Applied Sciences, and Human Sciences and Humanities. UHCL has taken a leadership role in the environmental arena, establishing the Environmental Institute which coordinates cooperative private industry/academic projects.

16 Bay Area Museum

Clear Lake Park, NASA Road 1, Seabrook (532-1254) Supported by the Lunar Rendezvous Festival, this little museum is a curious mix of nineteenth-century Americana and lunar missions. The building itself was built in 1901 as a church for Presbyterians in Webster, added on to in 1936 and finally moved to its present site in 1981. It consists of a sanctuary on one side, which is preserved as such, and a meeting hall on the other, which is now used to display lunar landing memorabilia. Tue-Fri 2pm-6pm, Sat 10am-4pm, Sun 1pm-5pm.

17 Clear Lake Queen

Clear Lake Park, NASA Road 1, Webster (333-3334) Enjoy a sunset dinner cruise or afternoon excursion on this paddle-wheeler. Reservations are a must. Weekend daytime excursions may vary; call for information. Dinner cruises $30 for singles, $50 per couple. Fri-Sat 7:30pm-10pm.

18 Water Sports Center of Clear Lake

5001 NASA Road 1, Seabrook (326-2724) Situated at the Harris County Public Boat Landing, a popular point for putting in sailboats and powerboats, this shop rents (and, in some cases, sells) sailboats, jet skis, waverunners, parasails, windsurf boards, paddle boats, canoes and water ski equipment. Lessons are available. Daily from late February to October/November 10am-7pm.

Sailboats at the Water Sports Center.

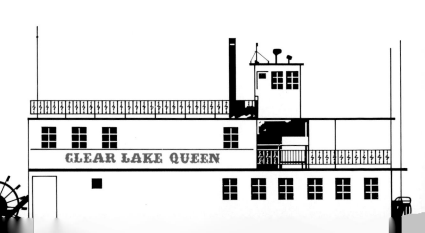

Refer to map on pages 214-215

19 Flamingo Cafe
3002 NASA Road 1, Seabrook (335-7465) Floating barge
restaurant serving seafood po-boys, burgers and chicken
dishes. Live entertainment on Friday and Saturday. Jam ses-
sions on Sunday. Tue-Thu 11am-10pm, Fri-Sat 11am-midnight,
Sun noon-10pm.

20 Nassau Bay Hilton
3000 NASA Road 1, Seabrook (333-9300) The hotel has a very
nice, reasonably priced Sunday brunch buffet. Sun 10am-2pm,
Dinner daily 4pm-11pm.

21 Johnson Space Center-NASA
See NASA section on page 000.

22 Lone Star Steaks
18023 Upper Bay Road off NASA Road 1 (333-9475) Just what
you would think they serve. Unexpectedly good meat loaf.
Mon-Fri 11am-10pm, Sat-Sun 4pm-10pm.

23 Frenchie's
1041 NASA Road 1 (486-7144) What may be the Clear Lake
area's best-liked restaurant serves up homestyle Italian cooking, despite its misleading name. Expect a lengthy wait for a
table, especially on weekend nights. Mon-Thu 11am-10pm,
Fri-Sat 11am-10:30pm.

24 Paradise Reef
*2500 S. Shore Blvd., League City (in the South Shore Harbor
Hotel) (334-1000)* The prettiest hotel and dining room in the
area is an elegant choice for traditional Sunday brunch. Great
view of the marina makes it romantic by night.

25 Bay Area Rowing Club
*Fuel Dock, South Shore Harbor, League City (326-2784 or
333-2060)* Not a boat club as you would think by the name.
It's a health and fitness center located in a floating gymnasium. Open 24 hours every day with personal trainers and
masseuses on staff. Memberships are offered and guests are
invited, but make reservations after 6pm.

26 English Tea Room & Bake Shoppe
2339 Bay Area Blvd., Clear Lake (488-3542) The tea-and-
crumpets spirit of this unassuming cafe is unquenchable.
Come for the finger sandwiches, shepherd's pie, homemade
soup, quiche and freshly made desserts. Mon-Fri Lunch 11am-
3pm, Dinner 6pm-9pm, Sat Breakfast and Lunch 8:30am-3pm,
Dinner 6pm-9pm.

27 Jalapeno Tree
316 W. NASA Road 1, Webster (332-5502) If the jammed parking lot is any indication, the Clear Lake area is perpetually
starved for a good party. Weekend acts at the barn-like restaurant range from country to folk to '50s and '60s rock-and-roll.
Veteran Houston folk-rocker Shake Russell plays to packed
houses here regularly. Mon-Thu 11am-10pm, Fri-Sat 11am-
1pm, Sun noon-10pm.

Jalapeño Tree.

28 Mario's Flying Pizza
618 W. NASA Road 1, Webster (332-2404 or 338-6672) Pizza.
Sun-Thu 11am-11pm, Fri-Sat 11am-midnight.

29 Enzo's Pasta e Vino
720 W. NASA Road 1, Webster (332-6955) Among locals, this
is a favorite Italian eatery, but less-known to day visitors. The
decor isn't much, but the service and food more than make up
for any aesthetic shortcomings. Mon-Thu Lunch 11am-3pm,
Dinner 5pm-10pm, Fri Lunch 11am-3pm, Dinner 5pm-11pm,
Sat 4pm-11pm, Sun noon-9pm.

Refer to map on pages 214-215

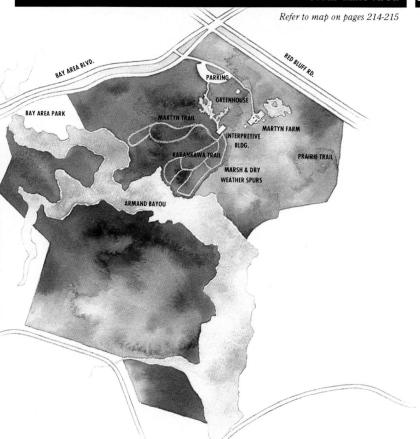

30 Armand Bayou Nature Center and Park

8500 Bay Area Blvd. (474-3074 or 474-2551)
Armand Bayou Nature Center's 2100-acre parcel of urban wilderness provides healthy inspiration for Houston conservationists who protect this refuge's six hiking trails and myriad open prairies as if they owned them. And indeed, they do. Spurred by the untimely death of a local naturalist Armand Yramategui, his companions bought this untouched Houston-area bayou and coastal prairie over several years, beginning in 1970. Middle bayou, now renamed Armand Bayou, provided refuge to ducks, blue herons, even an occasional bald eagle; thanks to conservationists' efforts, the situation today remains the same.

The Martyn Farm at Armand Bayou.

The center's "Hanson farmhouse" came to Armand years ago as the centerpiece in an effort to duplicate life on a turn of the century gulf coast farm; now the tiny tract gives substance to teachers' remarks when they lead schoolchildren and to Armand Center volunteers' "enrichment" classes. Late Saturday mornings, guided nature tours leave the Armand interpretive building; on Saturday afternoons and Sundays tours are offered again—hikers stroll through wooded flats along Martyn Trail near the bayou—then turn northward onto Prairie Trail, edging a salt marsh area. Thus educated, the 70,000 annual sanctuary visitors appreciate the pleasures of keeping the Nature Center ecosystem in its near pristine condition. Wed 9am-dusk, Thu-Fri 9am-4pm, Sat dawn-4pm, Sun noon- dusk. Call for information. Members free, children (4 and under) free, children (5-17) $1, adults (18-61) $2.50, seniors (62+) $1.

Over 700,000 tourists a year look over the rockets on display at the Johnson Space

NASA

"**H**ouston, Tranquility base here. The Eagle has landed." Could any American forget those words, beamed to Mission Control from Apollo 11's lunar landing site in the Sea of Tranquility, some 250,000 miles in space? Indeed, every byte of communication delivered by American astronauts heads to the Mission Control Room, building 35, at Johnson Space Center. JSC remains the most important communications center for the manned space program. The com-plex began life during the Kennedy years as the nerve center for the effort to reach the moon, serving as com-mand headquar-ters for Mercury, Gemini and Apollo. With the Space Shuttle program, the Space Station "Freedom" and the proposed mission to Mars, Johnson Space Center will continue as the heart of NASA's manned space flight communications through the twenty-first century.

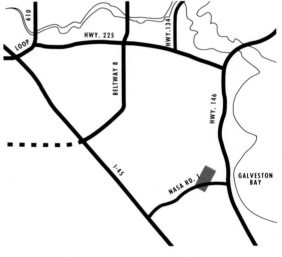

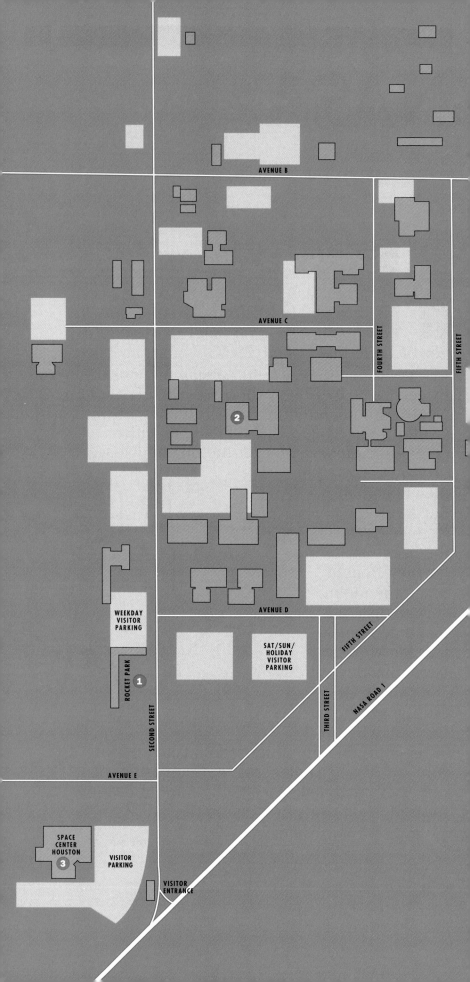

AVENUE B

AVENUE C

FOURTH STREET

FIFTH STREET

AVENUE D

2

WEEKDAY
VISITOR
PARKING

ROCKET PARK **1**

SAT/SUN/
HOLIDAY
VISITOR
PARKING

FIFTH STREET

THIRD STREET

NASA ROAD 1

SECOND STREET

AVENUE E

SPACE
CENTER
HOUSTON **3**

VISITOR
PARKING

VISITOR
ENTRANCE

Refer to map on page 226

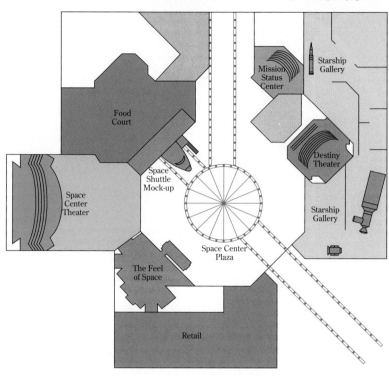

Johnson Space Center

2101 NASA Road 1 (483-4321 or 483-4273) The National Aeronautics and Space Administration's (NASA) Johnson Space Center has been the hub for the United States space program since it opened in September 1963 as the Manned Spacecraft Center. With the backing of Representative Albert Thomas, the site for the space center was established on land donated by Rice University (after having been donated to Rice by Humble Oil & Refining). The center was renamed the Lyndon B. Johnson Space Center in 1973, in honor of LBJ who was the Vice-President when the center was established. The center is made up of 100-plus buildings, most of which are closed to the public. The grounds, including the Rocket Park, are open to the public. Free. Daily 9am-4pm.

1   Rocket Park

Lyndon B. Johnson Space Center. A full-scale mock-up of the huge Saturn V rocket, the type used in the Apollo and Skylab missions. Free. Daily 9am-4pm.

2   Mission Control

Building 30, Lyndon B. Johnson Space Center. Tours of the Mission Control Center—the most famous site at the center—are available. Tickets required, free. Daily 9am-4pm.

3   Space Center Houston

1601 NASA Road 1 (480-7778) A private educational organization operates Space Center Houston, opened in 1992. **Space Center Plaza** is a spectacular multi-use arena, with "reality based" experiences; you'll see a full-scale mock-up of the space shuttle cargo bay, lectures and demonstrations by JSC scientists, training simulators for audience use and one of the world's most complete assemblages of space suits. **Mission Status Center** updates visitors on the workings of NASA as they are taking place at the moment. **The Feel of Space** allows visitors to grapple with flying a Manned Maneuvering Unit, even so far as attempting to repair a simulator satellite; experience a day in the life of a space station astronaut in the "Living in Space" exhibit. **Starship Gallery** and **The Space Center Theater** round out the experience.

Space Center Houston Tram guides visitors on an "insider's" tour of the JSC. Briefing officers narrate as the tram makes stops at Mission Control, the shuttle mock-up facility or the building where the underwater Zero-G simulations take place. The tram's stops vary to adapt to differing work being done at JSC facilities, so one tram tour is likely to be quite different from another.

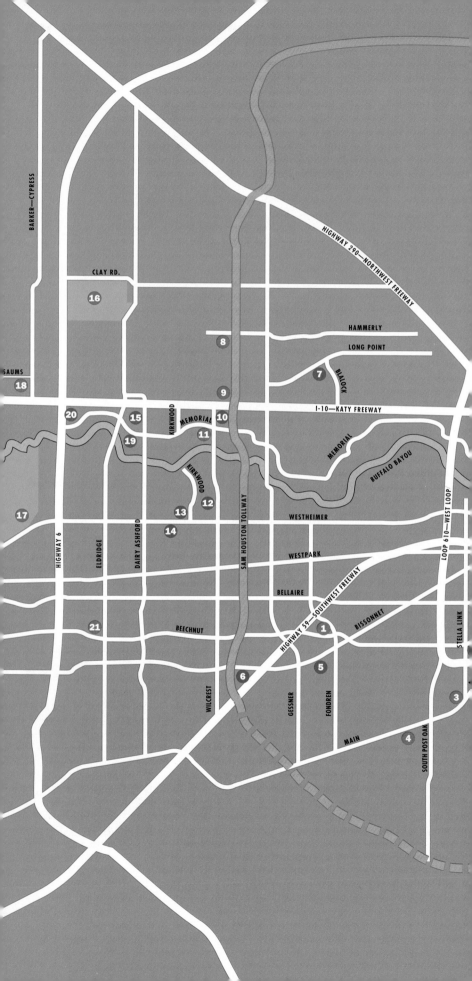

Refer to map on page 228

OUTER HOUSTON

West Houston

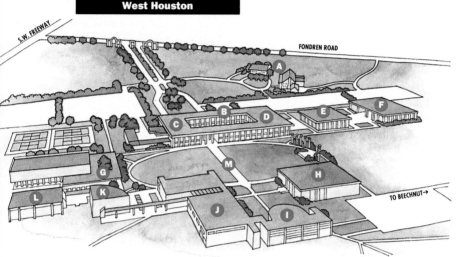

1 Houston Baptist University

Houston Baptist University, founded in 1960, enjoys a reputation locally as a small (2300 students), personal school with
strong programs in the undergraduate area. The College of
Science and Health Professions, including the school of nursing, is recognized as a very good program; the education program, especially in early childhood and elementary levels, is
also esteemed. Business undergraduates must specialize in
two areas for their Bachelor of Business Administration
degrees. Double majors are required of all students except
those in nursing. HBU students laud the Christian principles
and individual values emphasized at their school.

2 Alfred's of Houston

9123 Stella Link Road (667-6541) Most transplanted New
Yorkers wind up here eventually in their search for a bagel or
borscht fix. Houston's closest approximation to a classic
Jewish deli also offers hot pastrami, lox, blintzes and baked
goods. Homesick Yankees find the staff even does a fair
impression of the New York City deli bark. Good people-
watching, especially at breakfast. Sun 8am-5pm, Mon-Wed
8am-3pm, Thu-Sat 8am-8pm. Inexpensive.

3 Wheeler Boot Company

4118 Willowbend near Stella Link Road (665-0224) Wheeler
has crafted the finest handmade cowboy boots for over 30
years. Dave Wheeler uses any leather available on the market
to match customer's specifications. Those in the know say one
can see the difference between Wheeler and other custom-
made boots. Mon-Fri 8:30am-5:30pm, Sat 8:30am-3pm.

4 Softball Country Club

12631 South Main (728-3270) Over 300 local softball teams
compete on this park's seven fields nightly and all day on the
weekends. Air-conditioned clubhouse, covered stands and
electronic scoreboards support the "country club" claims.
Mon-Fri 4pm-11pm, Sat-Sun 9am-11pm.

**Houston Baptist
University Campus**

A President's Home
B Brown Administrative
   Complex
C M.D. Anderson Student
   Center
D Denham Hall
E Atwood I
F Atwood II
G Sharp Gymnasium
H Moody Library
I Cullen Nursing Center
J Cullen Science Center
K Mabee Teaching Theater
L Glasscock Gymnastic
   Center
M Holcombe Mall

Refer to map on page 228

5   Caribbean Cuisine

7433 Bissonnet between Fondren and S. Gessner (774-7428)
Lip-blistering jerk chicken, curried goat and other less-common Caribbean bites make up the short though soulful menu served in this Jamaican luncheonette. Mon-Thu 10am-9pm, Fri-Sat 10am-10pm. Inexpensive.

6   Churrascos

9788 Bissonnet, between US 59 and Beltway 8 (541-2100) and 2055 Westheimer at Shepherd. Here at their original Bissonnet location, Nicaraguan brothers Michael and Glenn Cordua introduced a new wrinkle in Houston's love affair with Latin food, proving there is life beyond Tex-Mex. Even if beef doesn't ordinarily move you, order the namesake churrascos, a simple centercut tenderloin sauced with the robust chimichurri sauce of olive oil, parsley and garlic. Equally remarkable is the wine list, which will appeal to pennypinchers with sophisticated tastes. Lunch Mon-Fri 11:30am-2pm, Dinner Mon-Thu 6pm-9:30pm, Fri- Sat 6pm-10pm, Sun 6pm-8:30pm. Reservations. Credit Cards, Moderate.

7   Korea Garden

9501 Long Point (468-2800) Those interested in a little Seoul food can find several possibilities in the Spring Branch area. Siwon Moon's tidy little restaurant is particularly user-friendly. Come here for the Korean barbecue, which you cook on a small gas-fueled hibachi fitted neatly into the center of the table. Fun for a small party and infinitely entertaining to kids. Daily 10am-10pm. Moderate.

8   Trade Mart

2121 Sam Houston Tollway North at Hammerly (467-2506) Seventy-five booths of antiques—high-quality furniture to collectibles—under one roof. Fri-Sun 10am-6pm.

9   The Market Place

10910 Old Katy Road (464-8023) Some 250 shops, give or take a few, selling antiques to quilts, valuable collectibles to assorted forgettables. Many hidden values here, but you have to look for them. Fri-Sun 10am-6pm.

10   Brenner's

10911 Katy Freeway (465-2901) There is no printed menu at this resolutely untrendy steakhouse on the west side, but you'll never miss it. Set in a 1950s Memorial ranch-style house, this is a Houston tradition for excellent steaks served with salty pan juices and a short list of scrumptious side dishes. Mrs. Brenner is justifiably famous for her Roquefort salad dressing, German fried potatoes and apple strudel. Lunch Tue-Fri 11:30am-2pm, Dinner Tue-Sat 5:30pm-11pm, Sun noon-10pm. Reservations. Credit Cards, Expensive.

11   Edith L. Moore Nature Sanctuary

440 Wilchester (464-4900) The 18-acre Edith L. Moore Nature Sanctuary provides quiet respite from mechanized pressures of Houston streets. Tiny Rummel Creek cuts through this green oasis, where Edith Moore built the cabin that still stands here, now being used as a base of operations for visitors (and for the occasional natural history class). For those craving a less manicured, wilder refuge than the Houston parks offer, this isolated, untouched sanctuary might fully reinvigorate one's senses. Open dawn to dusk.

12   Rotisserie for Beef & Bird

220 Wilcrest (977-9524) Coming here is like a visit to a country inn without ever passing the city limits. Joe Mannke's warmly appealing dining room is an excellent choice for wild-game-lovers and wine aficionados—the wine list is nationally acclaimed. Lunch Mon-Fri 11:30am-2:30pm, Dinner Mon-Sat 6pm-10:30pm. Reservations. Credit Cards, Expensive.

Refer to map on page 228

13 Chez Georges

11920-J Westheimer at Kirkwood (497-1122) Owner/chef Georges Guy and his family give suburbanites credit for excellent taste. The exciting haute French menu runs to soulful soups, glossy fish and long-cooked regional classics, all served in an intimate little bistro next to a half-price bookstore. The six-course prix fixe dinner requires a whole evening to be fully savored. Lunch Mon- Fri 11am-2pm, Dinner Tue-Thu 6pm-10pm, Fri-Sat 6pm-11pm. Reservations. Credit Cards, Expensive.

14 Denis' Seafood

12109 Westheimer near Kirkwood (497-1110) A large, noisy New Orleans-style oyster bar with black-and-white tiled floors, exposed kitchen and lazy arrangement of booths and tables feeds west-side suburbanites with a hunger for Cajun-accented seafood. Tue-Fri 11am-10pm, Sat 5pm-11pm, Sun 5pm-10pm. Credit Cards, Moderate.

15 Lynn's Steakhouse

955-1/2 Dairy Ashford (870-0807) Low-key and glad to stay that way, this west-side steakhouse has legions of suburban fans. Generous meat servings and heavenly bread. Lunch Mon-Fri 10am-2pm, Dinner Mon-Thu 5pm-10pm, Fri-Sat 5pm-11pm. Reservations. Credit Cards, Expensive.

16 Bear Creek Park

Bear Creek Park sits adjacent to a dam used for flood control, so things can be juicy out here. But despite it all, this park has been swamped only a few times. Its mammoth playground seems one vast, uninterrupted slab of grass, but Bear Creek's got a healthy sampling of amenities: 570 picnic tables, 349 grills, 30 soccer fields, 20 horseshoe courts, plus nature trails, horse trails, jogging trails, car trails and more. It's a favorite spot for a weekend foray into green pastures. A Wildlife Habitat and Aviary brings exotic animals into close range; bison, fallow deer, antelope, wild turkeys and even Australian emus range free, when the water's down.

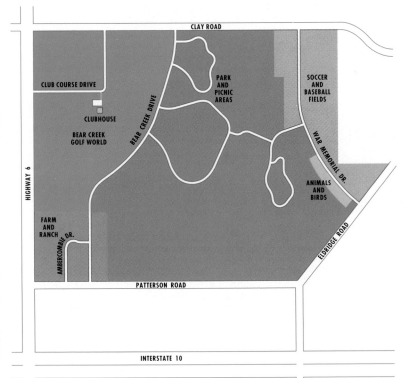

Refer to map on page 228

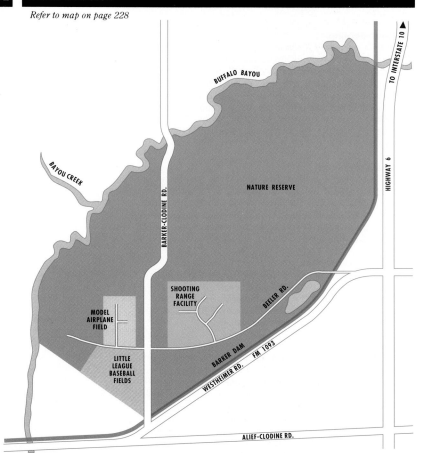

Hot Air Balloon Rides
Above It All Ballooning (341-5550) and
Rainbows End Balloon Port (466-1927)
offer hot air balloon rides, launching from
the West Oaks Mall or near a base at
Jones Road and Highway 290. The rides
last approximately one hour and cost
around $100-$125 per person. Up to four
people can ride. The launches are usually
early in the morning and are dependent
on the weather, especially the winds.

20 Cullen-Barker Park
16756 Westheimer Parkway Cullen-Barker Park
lies just west of State Highway 6 within the bounds
of Addicks reservoir. The 7500-acre park owes its
existence to the realities of Buffalo Bayou flood
control and as such spends part of the year underwater, so periods after extended heavy rains are
best avoided. The park has long been a favorite of
duck hunters, who make the trek to train their
retrievers in the ponds; long-distance cyclists
enjoy its lack of traffic and proximity to roads leading into Clodine and beyond, and sportsmen are
now enjoying a world-class shooting range facility,
with trap, skeet and pistol ranges. Just down the
road from the shooting center is The Dick Scobee
Model Airplane Field, named for the late comman-
der of the space shuttle Challenger, where enthusiasts are seen directing their remote control
planes seven days a week. From time to time there
are competitions and the public is welcome to
watch. In addition to these specialized facilities,
there are Three picnic pavilions, nine soccer fields
and four baseball fields. Park open daily 7am-10pm.
American Shooting Center
In Cullen-Barker Park (496-2177) Sporting clays,
skeet and trap, and pistol and rifle ranges are here,
with instruction available. Call for specific information and requirements. Hours are variable.

Refer to map on page 228

18 Alkek Velodrome
18203 Groeschke at Saums Road in Cullen Park (578-0858)
Alkek Velodrome is one of only a few cycling tracks in the
United States. Regular Friday night races (usually around
6:30pm) begin in late March and continue through November.
"Development Cycling Classes" present four weeks of instruction on paceline riding, sprinting and general bicycle handling
to those wont to take on the steep curves. (Special track bikes
are available.) And once or twice a year Olympic-level competitions are held. Open times vary. Cullen Park open

19 Carmelo's
14795 Memorial Drive near Dairy-Ashford (531-0696) Solid
but unpretentious, this large west-side Italian restaurant fills a
niche and is arguably the best of its kind in the area. A
neighborhood favorite. Lunch Mon-Fri 11am-2pm, Dinner
Daily 5pm-10pm. Reservations. Credit Cards, Moderate.

20 Pasta Lomonte's
14510 Grisby near I-10 and Highway 6 (496-0030) This small
Italian eatery is just one in an enclave of restaurants out in
Grasshopper Square that also includes Ledbetter's, Lupe's
Tortilla and Charlie's Hamburger Joint. Tony and Barbie
Lomonte's food is tasty, the service surprisingly sophisticated.
Mon-Thu Lunch 10am-2pm, Dinner 5pm-9pm, Fri-Sat 5:30-
10pm. Reservations. Inexpensive.

21 Fame City Waterworks
13602 Beechnut (530-3263) A premier waterpark consisting of
15 acres of waterslides and games, including a new birthday
pavilion. Summer hours are daily 10am-7pm.

Refer to map on page 234

North Houston

1 Continental Lounge Zydeco Ballroom
3103 Collingsworth (229-8624) If you don't know how to
dance to zydeco music, fake it. The dance floor's normally so
crowded here that no one will notice. Regionally famous
bands, many from Louisiana, regularly shake the rafters at this
divey club. The neighborhood is a little scary, but you'll forget
all about it once you step inside. Cover. Thu-Sun 8pm-2am.

2 Antique Car Museum
505 North Loop West at Yale (868-2243) Jerry J. Moore's
fabulous collection of over 800 vintage
cars can be seen in this small show-
room, 50 at a time. The entire
collection won't fit here, so
cars are rotated
every three
months. Cords,
Duesenbergs,
Cadillacs,
Packards and Rolls
Royces are in abundance,
all meticulously restored.
Tue-Fri 10am-6pm, Sat 9:30am-7:30pm, Sun 11am-6pm.
Adults $4, children (under 12) $2.

*Above, an award-winning
1930 12-cylinder Cadillac
Roadster Coupe with a
custom-made body from the
collection of Jerry J. Moore
at The Antique Car
Museum.*

3 R J's Boot Company and Shoe Shop
Ella Boulevard at 34th (682-1650) Rocky and Mike Carroll
make custom boots, shoes and clothing, billing themselves as
"The President's bootmakers." The two also created a tiny pair
of navy blue roach-killers emblazoned with Olympic rings
and the Texas flag for 1992 gold medalist Kristi Yamaguchi.
Only first-class leather work done here. Mon-Fri 6am-5:30,
Sat 6am-2pm.

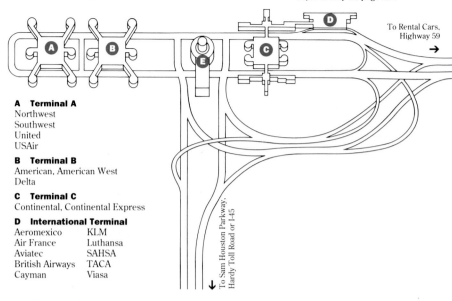

A   Terminal A
Northwest
Southwest
United
USAir

B   Terminal B
American, American West
Delta

C   Terminal C
Continental, Continental Express

D   International Terminal

Aeromexico	KLM
Air France	Luthansa
Aviatec	SAHSA
British Airways	TACA
Cayman	Viasa

To Sam Houston Parkway.
Hardy Toll Road or I-45

To Rental Cars,
Highway 59
→

4   Houston Intercontinental Airport

John F. Kennedy Blvd. (230-3000 for information)
(Original architects Golemon and Rolfe, 1969) Houston's
Intercontinental Airport is located 22 miles north of the downtown business district, and can be accessed by Interstate 45,
US Highway 59 and the Hardy Toll Road. The airport consists
of four terminals, a hotel (Marriott) and parking garages all
connected by an automated underground tram system. There
is covered parking available in garages comnnected to the terminals and remote surface parking with shuttle service. When
opened 1969, the facility was recognized by architects (and
passengers) as a
"conceptual break-
through" in planning.
The airport now han-
dles, on average, over
40,000 passengers
and 800 takeoffs and
landings per day.
Architects Goleman
& Rolfe's mid '60s
master plan envi-
sioned the two origi-
nal terminals (A and
B) being carbon-
copied opposite the
airport hotel, which
bisects the site.
These plans were not
carried through, how-
ever. In the 1980s
Terminal C was
added specifically to
house Continental Airlines, which is based in Houston and
maintains its largest hub here. The Leland International
Airlines Building was added in 1991 to handle the bulk of
Houston's international traffic, including customs and
Immigration.

Light Spikes
(Jay Baker , Llewelyn-Davies Sahni, 1990)
The 24-foot-high lighted sculptures
designed to representing the seven coun-
tries that participated in the Houston
Economic Summit held in Houston in 1990,
now are on permanent display at the
Houston Intercontinental Airport.

11 Atchafalaya River Cafe

14904 North Freeway and other locations (821-1567) Spicy
crawfish, boudin, gumbo and etouffee are the calling cards
at these ersatz Cajun roadhouses, where the loud party
atmosphere rarely lags. Mon-Thu 11am-11pm, Fri- Sat 11am-
midnight, Sun 11am-10pm. Credit Cards, Moderate.

Airport Area Hotels

E   Marriott-Airport
(Refer to map above)
18700 John F. Kennedy Blvd.
(443-2310) 7 stories, 566
rooms. Double $108-$130,
Concierge Level $135, Suite
$175-$250.

5   Sheraton Crown
15700 John F. Kennedy Blvd.
(442-5100) 10 stories, 420
rooms. Double $89,
Concierge Level $95, Suite
$89-$325.

6   Doubletree
15747 John F. Kennedy Blvd.
(442-5100) 7 stories, 315
rooms. Double $108-$118,
Concierge Level $95, Suite
$175-$300.

7   Holiday Inn Express
702 Sam Houston Parkway
(999-9942) 7 stories, 200
rooms. Double $49-$59.

8   L'hotel Sofitel
425 Sam Houston Parkway
(449-9000) 8 stories, 315
rooms. Double $140-$150,
Luxury Level $155-$185,
Suite $220-$600.

9   Marriott-Greenspoint
455 Sam Houston Parkway
(475-4000) 12 stories, 391
rooms. Double $115-$146,
Concierge Level $135, Suite
$200-$300.

10 Wyndham-Greenspoint
12400 Greenspoint
(875-2222) 16 stories, 472
rooms. Double $125-$175,
Suite $175-$500.

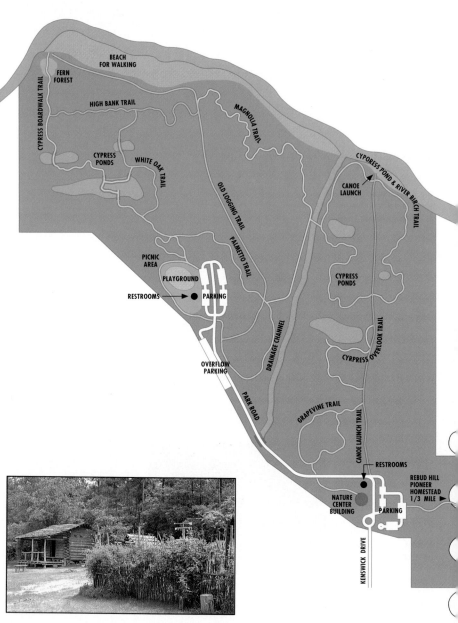

Redbud Hill Pioneer Homestead.

12 Jesse H. Jones Nature Center

20634 Kenswick, Humble (446-8588) Set on the south bank of Spring Creek just north of FM 1960, this 225-acre nature preserve offers a quiet, peaceful retreat to Houstonians hailing from the north end. As a companion park to Mercer Arboretum, Jones offers a canoe launch (call ahead for access by car), five miles of hiking and boardwalk trails over the extensive cypress bogs. The park's Redbud Hill Pioneer Homestead duplicates conditions on an 1820s East Texas settlement; it's open to viewing on selected weekdays. Jones also offers nature appreciation courses for children and adults, like "beginning birdwatching" and "allergenic plants and you."; Park hours: December and January 8am-5pm, November and February 8am-6pm, March-October 8am-7pm. Rosebud Hill Pioneer Homestead hours: Wed & Sat 1pm-4pm.

13 Mercer Arboretum

22306 Aldine-Westfield Road (443-8731) Charles and Thelma
Mercer called this plot of East Texas woods home for years
but had to sell their gardens—for health reasons—back in
1974 to Harris County. Over the years, 200 acres were added
and the parcel was protected from development, in keeping
with the Mercer's wishes. The 214-acre preserve named for
the pair has metamorphosed into a showcase of horticultural
engineering: the original garden has grown into a series of 13
full-fledged botanical gardens covering 43 acres; interpretive
plaques line miles of trails, and even a full-blown reproduction
of the Big Thicket is in the works. There is now even a
library—The Harris County Baldwin Boetcher Library—
holding a variety of children's and nature-related volumes.
Indeed, Mercer contains lots of facilities, perhaps too many,
but the efforts to make nature accessible do not seem to
overwhelm the arboretum. Land west of Aldine-Westfield road,
for example, still remains in a natural state—developed with
trails—but otherwise undisturbed. There, a wildflower-lined
road leads to a picnic area with facilities for (gulp) 70, but the
place usually stays calm enough. Here one picks up the
Hawthorn loop, Post Oak loop and Hickory Bog loop trails, the
prettiest in the park. Near Forest Garden Trail, a canoe launch
drops into Cypress Creek, making an excellent put in for a trip
downstream to Jones Park (or points even further). Be sure
also to catch the Ox-Bow Pond, created when Cypress Creek
meandered off course. Horticulture classes are offered on
weekends at Mercer for adults and children, as are five-day
summer children's programs. Fees are negligible. Group tours
can be arranged, but call a few weeks in advance. The Botanic
Information Center sports a sizeable meeting hall that can be
reserved by interested groups; the picnic pavilion and outdoor
classroom may be reserved as well. Finally, during the last
weekend in March, Mercer holds a giant plant sale, when
native herbs, shrubs, trees, etc.—most grown in the
Arboretum—find new homes. Daily, April-October 8am-7pm,
November-March 8am-5pm.

14 Del Friscos

14641 Gladebrook (893-3339) Popular northside steakhouse.
This homey restaurant can be a little hard to find tucked away
on a side street off the busier W. FM 1960. Mon-Thu 11am-
11pm, Fri- Sat 11am-midnight, Sun 11am-10pm. Credit Cards,
Moderate.

15 Buttarazzi's

5311-A West FM 1960 (537-5396) This Northern Italian spot
reminds many patrons of the elegant neighborhood restaurant
in the film *Moonstruck.* Located in The Champions Village, it is
not well-known outside of the FM 1960 area but should be.
Plan to spend some time here at dinner, for service is
leisurely. Lunch Mon-Fri 11:30am-2pm, Dinner 5:30pm-10pm,
Fri-Sat 5:30pm-11pm. Credit Cards, Moderate.

Refer to map on page 234

15 Empress of China

5419-A West FM 1960 (583-8021) Smug inside-the-Loopers may find it hard to accept, but one of the city's best wine lists, designed by Richard Ho, can be found at this Franco-Chinese restaurant in the Champions area; even more impressive are the prices—they're not much more than retail. But don't overlook Scott Chen's excellent nouvellesque food when you stop in to share a bottle. The steamed salmon with ginger and scallions is sublime. Sun-Thu 11am-3pm, 5pm-10pm, Fri-Sat 11am-3pm, 5pm-10:30pm. Moderate.

16 SRO

6982 West FM 1960 (537-0691) Houston is a town that has its share of sports bars, and the biggest (locals say the best) is the SRO in north Houston. The 3-level bar has enough TVs spread around—67—to make you think you're in a house of mirrors. Batting cages, a 3-on-3 basketball court, golf driving and putting areas round out the club. Besides beer in buckets, food is available. Mon-Sat 11am-2am, Sun 11am-midnight.

17 Cynthia Woods Mitchell Pavilion

2005 Lake Robbins Drive, in The Woodlands (363-3300) Twenty-seven miles north of Houston in The Woodlands, Cynthia and George Mitchell have built an outdoor theater to stage pop and classical performances. The stage and 3000 seats are covered by a dramatic, translucent, tent-like roof soaring 88 feet in the air. Behind the covered seating, on a lawn sloping up a small hill, as many as 7000 more spectators can watch the performance. The concerts featured run from Frank Sinatra to country western stars Alabama, Ray Charles to the Houston Symphony. The Pavilion's season runs from late April until early October.

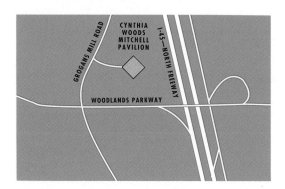

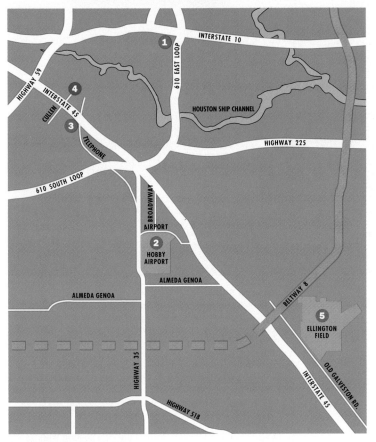

1   Anheuser-Busch Brewery

775 Gelhorn near I-10 at Loop 610 (670-1696) The highlight
of the Anheuser-Busch Brewery may just be the gift shop at
the end of the tour, where you are left to marvel at just how
many items there are that can be adorned with the myriad of
logos that Anheuser-Busch controls. Jackets, caps, key chains
and wastepaper baskets don't begin to scratch the surface.
The actual tour itself is rather short and unspectacular. It is
unguided, so you walk down carpeted halls peering through
glass windows into the processing and bottling areas. A complimentary bar awaits you at the end of the trip, just before you
enter the gift shop. Free admission. Mon-Sat 9am-5pm.

2   Hobby Airport

*7800 Airport Blvd. at Broadway (643-4597)
for information.* Houston's commuter airport, with most departures from this airport
going to points in Texas. Once Houston's
"Municipal Airport," the facility was closed
after Houston Intercontinental Airport
opened, but later reopened when Southwest
Airlines began service in Texas. Native
Houstonian Howard Hughes tinkered his
way to aviation fame beginning here at
Hobby Airport, where he took it upon himself to erect the airport's first control tower
in 1938. Currently Southwest, American,
Delta, Northwest, TWA and United fly from
have gates at Hobby.

*Jim Love's oilwell/airplane hybrid is a whimsical relief
for the Hobby Airport traveler.*

Refer to map on page 228

3   Orange Show

2401 Munger (926-6368) Houston's best example of folk art, this structure was built over a 25 year period by postman Jeff McKissack. The self-taught artist believed in good health and nutrition and would spend his spare hours collecting objects and building his concrete and plaster homage to the orange. Using ceramic tiles set into the plaster walls, McKissack spelled out phrases such as I LOVE ORANGES, ORANGES FOR ENERGY, and LOVE ORANGES AND LIVE. McKissack's thoughts weren't always on the orange: WE ARE GLAD YOU ARE HERE, I LOVE YOU and WHOSE HOUSE IS OF GLASS MUST NOT THROW STONES AT ANOTHER. He also planned the structure to house events, and to that end built a stage with multi-level seating with plenty of large tractor seats. After McKissack's death in 1980, The Orange Show Foundation was created to maintain the facility as a cultural and educational resource. The foundation also presents a wide range of performances and artistic events, and you are encouraged to call the above number for specific information.This is truly a delightful place and well worth a Saturday afternoon. Admission $1 for adults, children free. March-December Sat-Sun 12pm-5pm.

4   Ballatori

4215 Leeland (224-9556 or 224-9588) Once a bank (you may dine in the vault), this University of Houston neighbor now resembles an Italian villa. Expect an old-fashioned, one-red-sauce-fits-all style of cooking and you won't be disappointed. Regulars say it's better at lunch than dinner. Lunch Mon-Sat 11am-2pm; Dinner Mon-Thu 5pm-10pm, Fri-Sat 5pm-midnight.

5   Ellington Field (formerly Elington Airforce Base)

11903 Galveston Road (481-2828) Ellington Field now serves as a facility for NASA, The 147th Fighter Interceptor Group of the Air National Guard and a U.S. Army helilicopter battalion; the one-time World War I aviation training facility hosts the Wings Over Houston Airshow every fall.

Refer to map on page 241

Major Shopping Malls
With listing of anchor tenants.

1 Greenspoint Mall
12300 North Freeway
Approx. 130 Stores
Dillard's
Sear's
Mervyn's
J.C. Penney's
Foley's
Montgomery Ward

2 Memorial City Shopping Center
Katy Freeway at Gessner
Approx. 141 Stores
Mervyn's
Sear's
Foley's
Montgomery Ward

3 Willowbrook Mall
Highway 249 at West FM 1960
Approx. 150 Stores
Macy's
Dillard's
Foley's
Sear's
Montgomery Ward
J.C. Penney's – To open in November '92

4 Sharpstown Center
7500 Bellaire Blvd. at Southwest Freeway
Approx. 180 Stores
Montgomery Ward
J.C. Penney's
Foley's
Craig's
Palais Royal

5 Town & Country Mall
800 W. Sam Houston Parkway North
Approx. 100 Stores
Dillard's
J.C. Penney's
Neiman Marcus
Marshall Field's

6 West Oaks Mall
Highway 6 at Westheimer
Approx. 110 Stores
Dillard's
Foley's
J.C. Penney's
Mervyn's
Sear's Apparel

7 Baybrook Mall
19400 Gulf Freeway I-45 at Bay Area Blvd.
Approx. 182 Stores
Macy's
Mervyn's
Dillard's
Montgomery Ward
Sear's

8 Almeda Mall Shopping Center
1220 Gulf Freeway I-45 at Almeda Genoa
Approx. 60 Stores
Foley's
J.C. Penney's
Palais Royal

9 Northwest Mall
9900 Hempsted 610 Loop at Highway 290
Approx. 80 Stores
Foley's
Palais Royal
J.C. Penney's

10 Westwood Mall
S.W. Freeway at Bissonnet
Approx. 90 Stores
Sear's
Dillard's

Refer to map on page 242

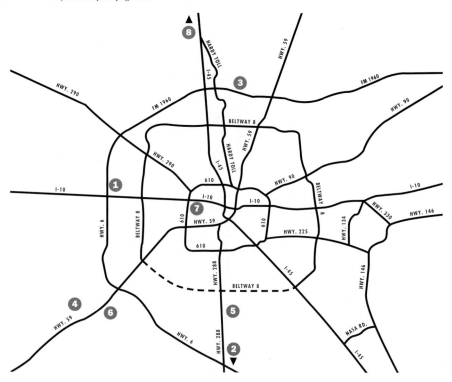

Greater Houston Area Public Golf Courses

There are quite a few good Houston area golf courses available to the general. Memorial Park golf pro Fred Collins looks at some of the better courses, offering a variety of terrains.

1 Bear Creek – Masters

16001 Clay Road (859-8188) Designed by Jay Riviere, Bear Creek is ranked in the top 100 public courses by *Golf Digest.* It hosted the 1984 NCAA Golf Championship won by the University of Houston. Built in the Addicks Reservoir on county land by private investors, the course is surrounded by large trees on the first nine with Bear Creek running through the middle of the course. Has two of the finest finishing holes in the area. Fun to play and normally in real good condition.

2 Columbia Lakes

188 Freeman Blvd., West Columbia (409-345-5151) A resort/membership course open to the public is set close to the Brazos River in a setting of large pecan and oak trees. The course was originally designed by Jack Miller and redesigned in 1981 by Tom Fazio. Very undulating greens require a very straight tee shot. It is designed through a housing development with OB on most every hole but generally not to close. Hosted Southern Texas P.G.A. Sectional and several college tournaments. It has a golf school and convention facilities. Worth a drive to go play.

3 Cypresswood

21602 Cypresswood Drive (821-6300) Cypresswood as two 18-hole golf courses and you cannot go wrong with either one. Built and designed by Carlton Gipson and Rich Forester on a hilly East Texas-type of terrain, it demands a variety of shots not needed on a lot of our flat-land courses. Hosted Texas State Open in 1990 and is ranked as one of the top courses in Texas. Take all the clubs in your bag if you plan to play here.

Refer to map on page 242

4 Old Orchard
13134 FM 1464, Richmond (277-3300) This new course
opened in 1990 on the west side of town. It has 27 holes, 18 of
them set in an old pecan orchard, which makes for a tight
adventure. This is not a housing development course and is
well designed and built by Carlton Gipson, Keith Fergus and
Harry Yewens. It is a very challenging course for all levels of
players because of the placement of tees. This is a course you
will want to play again and again because of the variety of
holes and beauty of the course. The clubhouse is the old farm
house, and the cart barn is just that, the old barn with a party
room on top. Try not to miss playing here.

5 Southwyck
2901 Clubhouse Drive, Pearland (436-9999) This is also a
fairly new course, opened in 1988 on what would have been a
flat piece of property. Ken Cavanaugh who designed it,
though, turned it into a links style course with a lot of mounds
and bunkers. There are not many trees, but you have plenty of
other trouble with the water and rough; also, the wind tends to
blow more on that side of town which makes for a good test of
golf. If you are looking for a little something different, try this
one for a challenge. It has plenty of length, if you want it, with
a variety of teeing areas.

6 Greatwood
6767 Greatwood Parkway, Sugarland (343-9999) Designed by
Carlton Gipson and opened in 1989 in conjunction with a new
housing development south of town near the Brazos River,
Greatwood has a variety of different kinds of holes with a large
number of fairway bunkers as well as green side bunkers. The
large greens are very hilly and fast, so bring your best putting
stroke. Most of the course is not developed yet so there are
not many homes around, which makes for a pleasant atmosphere with the large number of trees and water on the
course. It is pretty tight, but there is not much OB yet on the
course.

7 Memorial Golf Course
1001 East Memorial Loop Drive (862-4033) This inter-city
course hosted the Houston Open in the '50s and was the site
of the Doug Sanders' Invitational in the early and mid '80s.
From the back tees, the course plays 7300 yards and was
designed by John Bredemus who also built the Colonial
Country Club in Fort Worth. The course has been changed
over the years, though, by removing most of the fairway
bunkers and the loss of a large number of trees. The front is
pretty open but the back is very tree-lined. The greens are flat
and round in the old style of design. It is not always in as good
a condition as the other courses, but the green fees are much
lower and it is always a good test of golf. It is also surrounded
by a large park and a jogging and exercise track.

8 TPC Woodlands
1730 South Millbend, The Woodlands (367-2990) This course
has hosted the annual Houston Tour stop for the last few years
(now called The Shell Houston Open), and you won't find
more of a challenge than right here. Designed by Von Hagge-
Devlin, it has a lot of water to carry and avoid, from your tee
shots to your approaches. The greens are fairly flat but you
can use the break. If you play it around tournament time,
watch out for the rough; it can get pretty high. They have built
stadium mounds around a lot of the greens which make for
a nice backstop. Built through a housing development, but
OB does not come into play that much. The last two holes
are real gems.

Young competitor at
the Houston Livestock
Show and Rodeo.

ANNUAL EVENTS

Houstonians like to party, like to get out on weekends and like to go to any celebration that has fireworks. We like to watch people run, look at our neighbor's flowers and go to ethnic festivals. But more than anything else, we like to "Go Western." When the trail riders pull into Houston in late February, the locals pull out their collections of hats, boots and fancy shirts. It's time for the biggest social event of the year, The Houston Livestock Show and Rodeo.

Houston Livestock Show and Rodeo
Astrodome and Astroarena, 8400 Kirby at Loop 610 (791-9000)
The Houston Livestock Show and Rodeo is an event like no other in Houston, because for 17 days in late February and early March, every Houstonian is somehow involved. Children create western art while office workers shed their business attire and don western wear; socialites and union workers alike throw backyard parties and hold chili cookoffs; and every shop in town has some kind of western display. There are fun runs, barbecue cookoffs and contests of every sort, from hay-hauling to photography. And all of this is *before* you get to the actual livestock show or rodeo. The real purpose of the event which began in 1932 is for young farmers to show their stock, to compete and to gain financial support for their continuing education. And every year civic-minded Houstonians show up to bid enormous amounts of money for the winning animals, to contribute to scholarship funds and to generally support the youngsters' efforts.

Trail Riders
Hit the trail! Every February, 12 to 14 groups like the "Magnificent 7" or the "Sommerville Yequa Riders" can be seen riding over back roads and alongside busy freeways, following several horse-drawn, covered wagons on their way to Houston to help kick off the Houston Livestock Show and Rodeo. The trails begin from rural communities as far as 385 miles away, from places like Los Vaqueros and Hildago, with names right out of the old west: The Valley Lodge Trail, The Mission Ride Trail, The Texas Independence Trail, The Texas Cattlemen's Trail. Approximately 6000 trail riders saddle up and make the trip to Houston's Memorial Park and eventually on to the Rodeo Parade.

The Rodeo Parade
The Rodeo Parade takes place on the Saturday morning after the trail riders converge on Memorial Park. The parade a festive western kick-off, the official proclamation to

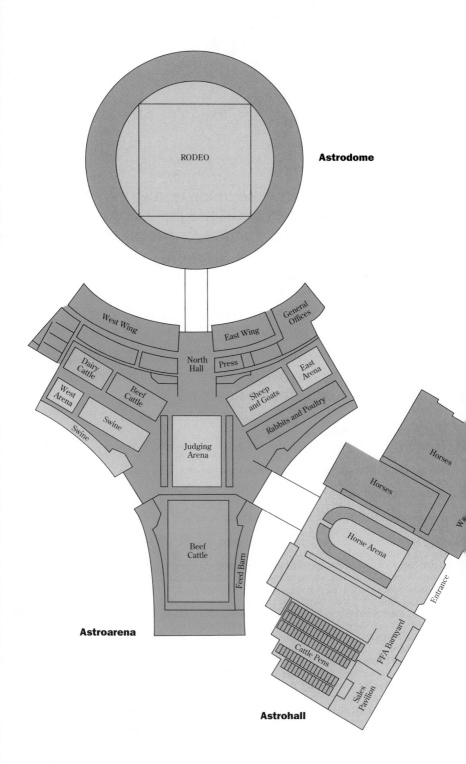

Astrodome

RODEO

West Wing

East Wing

General Offices

North Hall

Press

Dairy Cattle

Beef Cattle

East Arena

West Arena

Swine

Sheep and Goats

Swine

Rabbits and Poultry

Judging Arena

Beef Cattle

Feed Barn

Astroarena

Horses

Horses

Horse Arena

Wa

Entrance

Cattle Pens

FFA Barnyard

Sales Pavilion

Astrohall

Houstonians that rodeo time is here. After 10 to 12 days in the saddle, tired, dusty and weary trail riders line up in Memorial Park and head down Memorial Boulevard to the corner of Texas and Louisiana. They then march through downtown, Texas flags flying to the cheers of young and old alike.

The Rodeo

The Houston Rodeo, though taking place in the comfort of the Astrodome, is a sport of the past and steeped in Texas tradition. The rodeo dates back to days of the old west when ranch hands gathered on the plains in good-natured competition, besting each other in calf roping or bronc riding. Our Houston Rodeo is evidence that the sport retains much of this heritage, but the rodeo is also about fierce competition. These days, riders compete for a purse totaling $450,000, second only to that of Las Vegas' National Finals Rodeo. Rodeo competition consists of six events. Three are the rough stock events, in which the rider must stay on the animal for eight seconds, using only one hand: saddle bronc, bareback and bull riding. The timed events require the cowboy or cowgirl to perform a feat while racing against the clock: steer wrestling, calf roping and barrel racing. The latter is solely a Women's Professional Rodeo Association event. Other crowd-pleasing events include the chuck wagon races and calf-scrambles. Halfway through the each evening's rodeo there is a break for the entertainment. Country and western stars who have performed at the Houston Rodeo read like the Who's Who of the music world. The first performer was Gene Autry, and since then the roster has included regulars like Johnny Cash, Waylon Jennings, Willie Nelson and Hank Williams, Jr. But not all of the acts are western. Elvis, Cher and Earth, Wind and Fire have played to a sold-out Dome.

The Livestock Show

Red Brangus, Brown Swiss, Santa Gertrudis and Texas Longhorn. These breeds and many others are among the 28,000 entries at the Houston Livestock Show. Also on hand are llamas, sheep, horses, goats, mules and donkeys. Under the roof of the Astrohall complex, the best livestock raisers in the country—from 35 different states—compete in show classes for more than 20 beef cattle, 22 poultry, six swine, five rabbit and four dairy-goat breeds. Special breed shows such as the International Brahman Show, the International Brangus Show and the American Hereford Association Regional Show are also part of the show. But the highlight of the Houston Livestock Show is the champion steer auction, in which prominent Houstonians bid hundreds of thousands of dollars for the top steer.

Barbecue Cookoff

The barbecue cookoff at the rodeo began in 1974 and since then has become known as the "World's Championship Bar-B-Q" contest. On the Friday when the trail riders converge on town—and the following Saturday—the northwest corner of the Astrodome parking lot is packed with Houstonians competing neck and neck for the title of "Best All Around Bar-B-Q Crew." Contestants must cook a minimum of ten pounds of beef, lamb, chicken or pork over wood-burning fires while committees and judges supervise the process. Trophies are presented for the best food in each category, as well as for the team with the most unique pit or "most colorful" cooks. General admission tickets are limited to 15,000 per day, so samplers must get in line early.

Rodeo Run

The 10 K (6.2 miles) Rodeo Run kicks off the rodeo parade. About 4500 runners lead the way south to the Dome from downtown. Runners begin around 10am at the corner of Texas Avenue and Smith Street, heading southwest on Main and then south on Greenbriar to the finish at the Dome. The Rodeo Run began in 1988 and has since been something of a fixture both with the rodeo and with the local running crowd.

Saddle Bronc Riding

The rider must, using only one hand, hold on to a six-foot-long, thick leather rein fastened to the horse's halter. After leaving the holding stall, the rider must stay on the bucking horse for eight seconds.

Bareback & Bull Riding

The rider sits only on a thick leather rigging with no saddle. His handhold is a simple leather strap attached to the rigging; he must stay in synch with the horse or bull for eight seconds, just as in saddle bronc riding.

Steer Wrestling

The rider, dubbed the "dogger," times his horse to pass a running steer, guided by another horseman, the "hazer." The dogger slips from his saddle and wrestles the steer to the ground by twisting the horns. This is a timed event.

Calf Roping

Calf roping demands a fast, well-trained horse. The rider must chase a calf and lasso it with a 25-foot lariat rope. The horse stops and backs off, keeping the rope tight, as the rider jumps to the ground, throws the calf down and ties its feet together. This is a timed event.

Houston Tenneco Marathon
(757-2700) This traditional January event has bloomed into an international-class road race. Since its beginning in 1952— when only 117 runners competed—the event has steadily grown to now include over 6000 entrants running for over $150,000 in prize money. Top runners from around the world as well as thousands of local running enthusiasts take on the 26.2-mile course before large crowds of cheering Houstonians. The race begins and ends at the George R. Brown Convention Center. In between it weaves its way from downtown, through a variety of neighborhoods, through the Galleria area and back downtown by way of Memorial Park. Along the way the runners are supported by fans waving signs and yelling encouragements and entertained by DJs, bands, performers and even belly dancers.

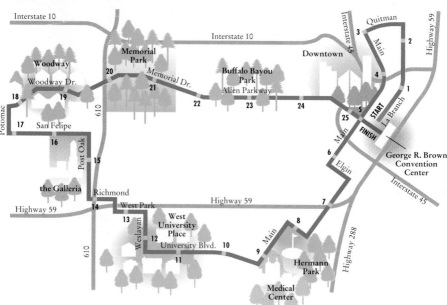

Azalea Trail
The River Oaks Garden Club Forum of Civics, 2503 Westheimer (523-2483) The Azalea Trail, Houston's elegant showcase of Southern culture, winds through beautifully landscaped back yards and gardens in the River Oaks area each March. The headquarters for the event is the The River Oaks Garden Club Forum of Civics at Westheimer and Kirby, where trail-goers can visit the club's gardens and buy tickets to visit a number of different private residences. The Bayou Bend Gardens are always on the tour (see pages 142-143 for more information on Bayou Bend), as well as the stately colonial mansion's priceless American antiques. If the weather cooperates, and it usually does, there is no more pleasant time in Houston than meandering through other people's back yards along elegant streets such as River Oaks Boulevard, Del Monte Drive and Overbrook Lane. The event is held over two weekends and the Garden Club changes the homes every year, so the same tour can never be seen twice.

FotoFest
George R. Brown Convention Center and galleries throughout Houston (840-9711) Fotofest debuted in 1986 as the first international photography festival in the United States. Over 100 exhibitions, photography-related meetings, workshops and social events showcase the work of major photographic artists from over 30 countries every March. The George R. Brown Convention Center houses many of the exhibitions; some 80 more are displayed in museums and galleries throughout the Houston area.

K-9 Fun Run
(433-6421) The Houston Humane Society K-9 Fun Run, a two-mile trek and one-mile walk, trots through Sam Houston Park every March. Dalmatians, golden retrievers, cocker spaniels and multi-media dogs show up at Allen Parkway for the chance to compete in the Doggy Costume Contest, The Cover Dog Contest and the race's official Spokesdog nomination. T-shirts and commemorative Dogdannas are included in the race packet, of course. Registration fees run between $15 and $20.

Leo Touchet's photograph of a New Orleans funeral at FotoFest.

The Great Duck Race
Sam Houston Park (521-DUCK) One of Houston's most spectacular—and funniest—fund-raisers floats by every March. Houstonians pay to adopt more than 30,000 bright yellow rubber ducks that then are dumped into Buffalo Bayou from the Sabine Bridge, floating on to the finish line. The Great Houston Duck Race is a charity event, sponsored by the Delta Gamma Foundation, benefiting the blind and visually impaired of Harris County.

St. Patrick's Day Parade
Downtown. The Saturday before St. Patrick's Day—March 17—has been the climax of the year for many of Houston's Irish and would-be-Irish. Since the late fifties, the St. Patrick's Day Parade has wound through downtown, these days starting around Louisiana and Rusk and finishing in Sam Houston Park. For many the party carries over to a variety of bars and clubs, notably Grif's Inn in the Montrose, where the street is closed to hold the overflow crowd.

River Oaks Tennis Tournament
River Oaks Country Club, 1600 River Oaks Blvd. (529-4321) The River Oaks Tennis Tournament, still serving 'em up after almost 60 years, remains the oldest professional tournament in the country still playing at its original site. Since its inception in 1931, the tournament has hosted the big names of tennis— from Frank Parker and Jack Kramer to three-time winner Ivan Lendl. Tennis players in the know laud the March clay court event as a showcase for emerging talents like Zina Garrison. Be advised, however, that the River Oaks is as much the place to see and be seen as it is athletic event, and as a private production, tickets can be somewhat elusive.

Pin Oak Charity Horse Show
Great Southwest Equestrian Center, 2501 S. Mason Road (578-PONY) Entering its fifth decade, Pin Oak Charity Horse Show remains the premier event in Houston for equestrian enthusiasts. Riders compete in saddlebred, hunter-jumper, walker and other event categories for $200,000 in cash and prizes. All proceeds of this April event benefit Texas Children's Hospital.

Westheimer Arts Festival
Westheimer at Montrose (521-0133) Every April and October, over 300 artists of various media enter this juried show on lower Westheimer, with attendees and festival-goers number-ing as high as 50,000 over a weekend. The festival takes on a carnival atmosphere, with street music, food, drink and a parade of interesting humanity. A portion of the proceeds is donated to The High School for the Performing and Visual Arts.

Houston International Festival

Sam Houston Park and surrounding areas (654-8808) The Houston International Festival is the city's celebration of the performing and visual arts. For ten days each spring the streets of downtown bustle with outdoor music stages, an outdoor juried arts and crafts exhibition, dance performances, street performances, fireworks and exotic international foods. More than 2000 artists participate each year. While choosing a different country to celebrate each year, the emphasis of the event remains promoting Houston's indigenous art community.

WorldFest (Houston International Film Festival)

Various locations (965-9955) The Houston International Film Festival, redubbed WorldFest and rounding out its second decade, has traditionally boasted eclectic combinations of high-brow films and bottom-fishing documentaries. After opening at The Museum of Fine Arts, WorldFest screens about 100 features throughout the area, at the Museum, the Greenway III, the UH Clear Lake Auditorium and other venues. Founder Hunter Todd has helped the film festival attract esteemed entries: 1992 saw 12 Academy award submissions, versus the usual two or three. Passes to this late April festival and individual screening tickets are available.

Shell Houston Open

The Woodlands Tournament Players Course (367-7999) The Houston Open Golf Tournament—now renamed the Shell Houston Open—has attracted nationally prominent players since its inception in 1946. About 150 golf pros hit the links at the Woodland's Tournament Players Course in pursuit of a purse valued at over $1 million. The Open is played each year to crowds upwards of 150,000, usually in late April-early May.

Summer Symphony Festival

The Cynthia Woods Mitchell Pavilion, The Woodlands; Miller Outdoor Theater in Hermann Park; Jones Hall (227-ARTS) The Houston Symphony Orchestra, under music director Christoph Eschenbach, stays busy performing several pops and classical summer programs. The Cynthia Woods Mitchell Pavilion in the Woodlands resonates to the orchestral tones in late spring and summer months; past performances have been in May, June and September, and there is an admission fee. Miller Outdoor Theater is the venue for Houston Symphony shows in June and July, combining pops and light classical fare, and admission is free. Finally, during July, the Symphony stages its true "Summer Festival" in Jones Hall; strictly Bach, Beethoven, Britten and Bizet type stuff here.

Heights Home Tour

(868-0102) The Heights Home Tour weaves through one of Houston's oldest and most historical neighborhoods, passing under gingerbread verandas and along the pecan-shaded streets. Some of Houston's best-preserved cottages of the Victorian style stand door to door in the Heights, where historical preservation has seen its greatest success in Houston. The tour falls on Mother's Day weekend.

Cinco De Mayo

Miller Outdoor Theater in Hermann Park (520-3292) ¡ Fiesta ! On May 5, 1862, General Ignacio Zaragosa led Mexican troops in defeating invading French forces of Napolean III; "Cinco de Mayo" has since been celebrated as Mexican Independence Day. In Houston, the holiday is honored on the weekend nearest May 5 with a parade through downtown. At Miller Outdoor Theater in Hermann Park, Cinco de Mayo is celebrated with mariachi bands, folklorico dancers and, of course, plenty of Mexican food. In Hispanic neighborhoods throughout the city, local groups sponsor dances, food fairs, concerts and beauty pageants.

Juneteenth

Miller Outdoor Theater in Hermann Park (520-3292)
Juneteenth is a holiday unique to Texas. It celebrates June 19,
the day "word" finally reached Texas in 1865 that President
Lincoln had signed the Emancipation Proclamation, legally
freeing all slaves. The National Emancipation Association
supports various community events during the early weeks of
June, each aimed at raising awareness of African-American
heritage and accomplishment. Miller Outdoor Theater hosts
an annual commemoration where blues and jazz performers
entertain the weekend closest to June 19.

Doug Sanders Celebrity Golf Classic

Deerwood Country Club (864-3684) The Doug Sanders
Celebrity Golf Classic tees off early each June with the likes
of Clint Eastwood, Dinah Shore and Charlie Pride. The
tournament moved around for years but finally landed
squarely on the greens of the Deerwood Club in Kingwood,
where it's been since 1966.

Asian Performing Arts Gala

Various locations (526-1709 Ticketmaster) Houston's Asian
population is booming, and this June festival reflects how
eclectic that cultural mix has become. The "Asian Fest," at the
Wortham Center's Cullen Theater, blends the cultures of
China with those of the subcontinent (India, Pakistan and
Bangladesh); southeast Asian cultures like Thailand, Vietnam
and Indonesia are presented next to the Pacific traditions of
Japan, Korea and Polynesia. The fest showcases the classical
arts of these disparate lands as well as their folkloric arts.

Freedom Festival

Freedom Festival is a sort of exaggerated Fourth of July. The
mammoth show literally envelopes downtown for the week
preceding Independence Day; you'll be greeted, however, by
row after row of traditional American food—foot longs, funnel
cones and corn dogs—and by stages of musicians, troupes of
dancers and loads of merrimakers. Big-name bands have been
a part of Freedom Festival in the past, so watch the papers for
listings. Parking can be difficult for this one, due to the large
crowds, so it's advisable to park and walk or take Metro.

Fourth of July

Houstonians have a fetish for fireworks. Take the Fourth of
July, for example. You'll see fireworks at any locale, whether
you're in the Museum District, south Houston, downtown or
west Houston. At Miller Outdoor Theater, The Houston
Symphony plays cheerful renditions of Sousa marches and, of
course, of Tchiakovsky's *1812 Overture* with fireworks
bursting overhead. Admission is free. Firework displays are
also seen at Astroworld, Sam Houston Park downtown (for the
Freedom Festival) and at Lakeside Country Club, off of
Kirkwood.

Beware the Ides of August!

Miller Outdoor Theater, 100 Concert Drive (520-3292) Every
summer you'll hear of University of Houston productions of
the Bard's light, short comedies in Miller Outdoor Theater.
Recent productions included *The Merry Wives of Windsor* and
The Taming of The Shrew, but the company often takes on
major plays like *Richard II* or *Romeo and Juliet,* pulling them
out of their original time frame and setting them in the
twentieth century, making grave tragedies accessible to a
wider audience.

Festiva Italiana

St. Anne's Catholic Church, 2140 Westheimer (524-4222)
Festiva Italiana, put on by the Italian Federation, opens its
doors on the grounds of St. Anne's Church in mid-September
for a full three days of Italian music, wine and food from the
Tuscan and Milanese regions.

Egyptian Festival

St. Mark's Coptic Orthodox Church, 424 Mulberry (669-0311)
The Egyptian festival brings the music, food, dance and culture of the land along the Nile to Houston. The festival is usually held the weekend after Labor Day.

Greek Festival

3511 Yoakum Boulevard (526-5377) On the second weekend of October, the Greek Festival springs to life under the shadow of the Greek Orthodox Cathedral, at 3511 Yoakum Boulevard, adjacent to The University of St. Thomas campus. Aromas of spanakopita, baklava, souvlaki and traditional Greek foods fill the air during this giant three-day event. The festival, supported by the Houston Greek community, centers around dances, religion (tours of the cathedral are conducted) and, of course, Greek food.

The Wings over Houston Airshow

Ellington Field (531-9461) The Wings over Houston Airshow takes off annually at Houston's Ellington Field. This Airshow, usually held over a weekend in late October, has become one of the major Airshows in the country. The U.S. Air Force Thunderbirds or the Navy's Blue Angels awe audiences each year with aerial acrobatics. The show attracts a healthy representation—the F-117 Stealth fighter and the B-1 among them—of aircraft from current Air Force and Navy inventories. Nostalgia buffs are always charmed by the groaning humm of the World War II vintage radial engine planes, compliments of The Confederate Air Force.

Thanksgiving Day Parade

Main Street and others, downtown. Foley's has sponsored this Thanksgiving Day Parade on the streets of downtown for over 60 years. Baton twirlers, majorettes, drummers and tuba players line up at the corner of Main and Travis every Thanksgiving at 9am, usually with the accompaniment of a national television star or celeb. With the floats, marching bands, batons and brass, the Foley's Thanksgiving Day Parade is a favorite for children.

Restaurants

Nightlife

Shopping

Antiques

Museums

Parks

Book Stores

Public Art

Galleries

Sports

Educational Institutions

Hotels

Jerry Herring began Herring Design in Houston in 1973, and has seen the firm become a national force in graphic design. In 1984, Jerry and Sandy Herring formed Herring Press, publishers of *Houston: A Self-Portrait*, the AIA *Houston Architectural Guide, Historic Galveston, Presence: The Transco Tower* and *Santa Fe*, among others.

George Fuermann is a former editor and long-time columnist for the *Houston Post*. George began at the *Post* in 1950 and retired in 1983, but continues to contribute a weekly wine column. He has written numerous books about Houston including *Houston: Land of the Big Rich, Houston Recalled: Six Miniatures* and *Houston: The Once and Future City*. George was editor of a new edition of *The First Texas Cook Book* and also wrote the cookbook *Tony's*. He is a past chairman and member of the Houston Municipal Art Commission and past chairman of the Houston Committee on Foreign Relations.

Teresa Byrne-Dodge has covered the Houston restaurant scene as journalist/critic since 1983. She has contributed to many local and national publications and is the editor of the *1992 Zagat Houston Restaurant Survey*.

Jim Sanders is a Houston free-lance writer and former ad agency creative director. A native of Nacogdoches, Texas, Jim graduated from The University of Texas and Stanford, and has marked time at Harvard and Cambridge. His company, Jim Sanders Creative, provides services to many of the city's major arts organizations.

Fred Collins is the PGA Teaching Professional at Houston's Memorial Park Golf Course. The son of professional golfer Ross Collins, Fred became a professional golfer himself 14 years ago. Fred authored the book *"Constants in the Golf Swing,"* has written instructional articles for *Gulf Coast Golfer* and *Texas Golf,* and appears frequently on KSEV Radio's sports talk shows.

Jan Grafton is a native Houstonian who attended St. John's School and Rice University, where she received a Bachelor of Arts degree in English and Art and Art History. She worked for *Houston Metropolitan Magazine* for more than five years and developed their calendar of events listings, and produced fashion and design features in conjunction with the magazine's Design Editor. She currently holds a retail marketing position and produces freelance writing projects.

Robert Macias is a writer and editor based in Houston. He works regularly for *Houston Metropolitan Magazine* as Managing Editor for Special Issues. He recently completed his first feature film script, titled *"Spin Monkeys."*

Walker Stewart, a native Houstonian, earned a B.A. in Medieval European History—with minors in German and Continental Philosophy—from the University of Texas at Austin in 1989. A follower of the history of the American Southwest—especially of Texas history— Walker writes on modern developments from a "past" perspective. He began his writing career at *Houston Metropolitan Magazine.*

Tom McNeff has been a graphic designer in Houston for 16 years. Tom's illustrations have been displayed in *Communication Arts Magazine, Communication Arts Annual, New York Society of Illustrators Annual*, and most recently, articles in *Southern Accents* and *Step-by-Step Graphics* magazines. Tom has won numerous awards from organizations such as The New York Art Directors Club, New York Society of Illustrators, Art Directors Club of Houston and Dallas Society of Visual Communications.

William Soo, a native of Taiwan, The Republic of China, came to the U.S. in 1974, graduating from The University of Houston in 1988. William, a graphic designer and illustrator, produced the maps for the AIA *Houston Architectural Guide.*

Steve Freeman, a graphic designer, has been recognized by organizations such as The American Institute of Graphic Arts (AIGA), The American Library Association, The New York Art Director's Club, Art Directors Club of Houston, Dallas Society of Visual Communicators and Austin Graphic Arts Society. A native Houstonian, Steve is a past president of AIGA-Texas.

Ellen McCormick Martens has been a typesetter for twelve years. She is also a painter of landscape and still life.